CW00853120

Nearctic Collembola or Springtails,of the Family Isotomidae

J. w. Folsom

BIBLIOLIFE

SMITHSONIAN INSTITUTION

UNITED STATES NATIONAL MUSEUM

BULLETIN 168

NEARCTIC COLLEMBOLA OR SPRINGTAILS, OF THE FAMILY ISOTOMIDAE

BY

J. W. FOLSOM

UNITED STATES

GOVERNMENT PRINTING OFFICE

WASHINGTON : 1937

ADVERTISEMENT

The scientific publications of the National Museum include two series, known, respectively, as *Proceedings* and *Bulletin*.

The *Proceedings* series, begun in 1878, is intended primarily as a medium for the publication of original papers, based on the collections of the National Museum, that set forth newly acquired facts in biology, anthropology, and geology, with descriptions of new forms and revisions of limited groups. Copies of each paper, in pamphlet form, are distributed as published to libraries and scientific organizations and to specialists and others interested in the different subjects. The dates at which these separate papers are published are recorded in the table of contents of each of the volumes.

The series of *Bulletins*, the first of which was issued in 1875, contains separate publications comprising monographs of large zoological groups and other general systematic treatises (occasionally in several volumes), faunal works, reports of expeditions, catalogs of type specimens and special collections, and other material of similar nature. The majority of the volumes are octavo in size, but a quarto size has been adopted in a few instances in which large plates were regarded as indispensable. In the *Bulletin* series appear volumes under the heading *Contributions from the United States National Herbarium*, in octavo form, published by the National Museum since 1902, which contain papers relating to the botanical collections of the Museum.

The present work forms No. 168 of the *Bulletin* series.

ALEXANDER WETMORE,
Assistant Secretary, Smithsonian Institution

WASHINGTON, D. C., *May 15, 1937.*

CONTENTS

NEARCTIC COLLEMBOLA, OR SPRINGTAILS, OF THE FAMILY ISOTOMIDAE

By J. W. Folsom*

INTRODUCTION

Though all the known Nearctic species of Collembola of the family Isotomidae are considered in this paper, our fauna undoubtedly contains many additional ones. Of the 66 species and 16 varieties herein treated, 28 species and 2 varieties are described as new. Of the Nearctic forms, 21 species and 9 varieties are also Palearctic in distribution. Specimens of most of the Nearctic species have been compared with Palearctic specimens, not only by me but also by my European colleagues, with whom I have been exchanging material for more than 30 years.

I have studied nearly all the type specimens of Isotomidae described from North America, notably those of Packard, MacGillivray, and Guthrie.

When living in Cambridge, Mass., I made descriptions and drawings from the Packard collection of Collembola in the Museum of Comparative Zoology, through the courtesy of Samuel Henshaw This collection consisted mostly of the material described by Packard (1873) in his "Essex County" paper. This paper had no illustrations, but in the course of its preparation Dr. Packard made a great many pencil drawings, which he gave to me, and these have been a useful aid to the recognition of the species that Packard described.

*Dr. Justus Watson Folsom, the author of this bulletin, died at Vicksburg, Miss., on September 24, 1936, at the age of 65, shortly after the manuscript was sent to the printer. A native of Massachusetts, Dr. Folsom was an entomologist of wide training and experience. Since 1925 he had been associated with the United States Department of Agriculture as entomologist, prior to which he taught entomology at the University of Illinois for nearly a quarter of a century. At the time of his death he was stationed at the Cotton Insect Laboratory of the Bureau of Entomology and Plant Quarantine at Tallulah, La Though accomplished in many branches of entomological science, including anatomy and ecology as well as taxonomy, Dr. Folsom became a world-famous authority on the orders Thysanura and Collembola and published many papers dealing with these primitive insects. The present monograph, on the Isotomidae, is one of the most exhaustive studies of any group of Collembola ever undertaken and serves as a fitting climax to the author's long career as a biologist.—Editor.

In addition, I collected in eastern Massachusetts, including Essex County, most of the species that Packard described from that region, and compared them with his types

Of the MacGillivray (1896) cotypes and other specimens of *Isotoma*, I have studied three sets: The collection of the Museum of Comparative Zoology; the collection of Cornell University, through the courtesy of Prof. C. R. Crosby; and a set of specimens given to me by Dr. MacGillivray.

Guthrie's (1903) types and other material were kindly loaned to me by Prof. H. F. Nachtrieb, and many additional specimens were received from Dr. Guthrie.

The entire collection of Prof. F L. Harvey, with his notebooks, I bought from Mrs. F L. Harvey

The Apterygota of the California Academy of Sciences described by Schött (1896a) were destroyed by fire, so I was informed by the secretary of that institution.

Important among large collections received for study were those of the Illinois State Natural History Survey, through the courtesy of C. A. Hart and Dr. T. H. Frison; the New York State Museum, through S. C. Bishop and D B Young; the American Museum of Natural History, through Dr. F. E. Lutz, and Stanford University, through Prof. V. L Kellogg.

From California, collembolan material in abundance came from the late Prof. C. F. Baker, Prof. E. O Essig, and A. P Morse. From Oregon, a large collection was received from Dr. H. E. Ewing, and from Florida one from Prof. T. H Hubbell. From Iowa, specimens in abundance were contributed by C. N. Ainslie, and from Tennessee many by G. G. Ainslie. Much Pennsylvania material came from Dr. H. A. Surface, and a great number of New York specimens from Dr M. D. Leonard, Prof. C. R. Crosby, Dr. H Glasgow, Prof. J. D Hood, and E. A. Maynard.

For Canadian species acknowledgments are due to Prof. E. M. Walker, and especially to Charles Macnamara, who has for many years been sending me a wealth of material.

The greater part of the material used, however, I collected, chiefly in Massachusetts, Ohio, Illinois, Wisconsin, and Louisiana The omission of a collector's name in the data concerning specimens means that they were collected by me. Similarly, the omission of references (in parentheses) to the ownership of specimens indicates that they are in my collection.

The illustrations, made by me, were drawn from type specimens when possible

The most important part of the material studied has been given to the United States National Museum.

NOTES ON THE EVOLUTION OF THE MUCRONES

A comparative study of the diverse forms of mucrones found in Isotomidae leads to the inference that some of the forms have been derived from others. The present account by no means exhausts the subject. It consists simply of such conclusions as came to mind during my systematic study of Isotomidae.

A primitive type of mucro is found in *Guthriella*, essentially the same form that occurs in several species of *Achorutes*.[1] In *Guthriella vetusta*, for example (pl. 10, fig. 104), the mucro is like that of *Achorutes socialis* in its apical tooth, anteapical tooth, and outer and inner lamellae extending from the anteapical tooth to the base of the mucro. In *Ballistura* the mucro remains fundamentally as in *Guthriella*.

With this generalized type of mucro as a basis, we may infer, by comparing the various forms of mucrones with one another, that specialization of the mucro has occurred in three main ways, as follows:

1. *Lamellar development* The two primary lamellae may increase in size, and new lamellae may be added. Extreme conditions of lamellar development are shown in *schäfferi* (pl. 17, figs. 173, 174) and *rainieri* (pl. 16, figs. 164–167). In the complex mucrones of these species the apical tooth, anteapical tooth, and outer and inner lamellae are evident, but additional lamellae are present, with additional teeth for their support. The extra lamellar expanse is correlated with a superaquatic habit.

2. *Addition of teeth.* The species *titusi* (pl. 18, figs. 186, 188) shows the primitive pair of lamellae and the two primary teeth, with an added third tooth, supporting a lamella. This third tooth, lateral in position and anterior to the anteapical tooth, occurs in many species of the family.

The fourth tooth, as in *communa* (pl 17, fig. 180) is never lateral but is usually in line with the first and second teeth. In *sepulcralis* the mucro, normally tridentate (pl. 20, fig. 213), is occasionally quadridentate (pl. 20, fig. 214) as an individual variation. Many other species have four teeth normally. The fourth tooth in *palustris* (pl. 26, fig. 287) and in *retardatus* (pl 25, fig. 279) supports a lamella.

A few species, as *rainieri* (pl. 16, fig. 165), show a fifth tooth, near the fourth.

3. *Lamellar reduction.* Lamellate mucrones are characteristic of the more primitive species of Isotomidae, and these species are relatively few. In *Proisotoma* various stages in lamellar reduction are exemplified in different species, but in *Isotoma* the mucrones are typically without lamellae. As lamellae disappear the teeth that supported them tend to remain, however, and in the nonlamellate

---

[1] In the use of *Achorutes* instead of *Hypogastrura*, opinion 65 of the International Commission on Zoological Nomenclature has been followed

species of *Isotoma* the third and fourth teeth are often present as vestiges.

Variations.—Though the mucrones in Isotomidae have assumed many different forms, there are few species in which the two primary teeth—apical and anteapical—are not present. With the reduction of the furcula they still remain, as in *Folsomia* and other genera. Moreover, they persist in most Entomobryidae. Mechanically, these two are the most important teeth in the act of springing.

The teeth of the mucrones vary greatly in size and form. The apical tooth may enlarge and elongate, as in *albella* (pl. 31, fig. 359), *marissa* (pl. 29, fig. 327), and other species. On the other hand, it may become reduced partially as in *arborea* (pl. 28, fig. 312) and in *grandiceps* (pl. 36, fig. 426); or until it is merely a minute tooth at the base of the anteapical tooth, as in *palustris* (pl. 26, fig. 287).

The third, or lateral, tooth in *titusi* (pl. 18, figs. 187, 188) and other of the more generalized species supports a lamella, but it has persisted in many species after the lamella has disappeared. It is strongly developed in *trispinata* (pl. 29, fig. 333) and *marissa* (pl. 29, fig. 327).

The form of the mucro varies not a little among individuals of the same species and even in different instars of the same individual.

PHYLOGENETIC AND TAXONOMIC NOTES

Isotomidae are generally regarded as having originated from forms resembling *Achorutes*,[2] which in turn appear to have come from ancestors like *Podura*, with a well-developed furcula (Willem, 1900).

The much-discussed *Tetracanthella* and genera allied to it are accepted as links between Isotomidae and Achorutidae.[2] Even better links, however, between these two families are found in the species of *Guthriella* that are treated in this paper.

The habitus of *Guthriella* is like that of *Achorutes*. The body, legs, and furcula are stout. The body segments are bulging, with deep intersegmental constrictions, with very narrow intersegmental membranes, and without imbrication (except between the genital and anal segments in one species). The integument is tuberculate throughout but soft, the body sclerites being indicated but not sharply bounded. The prothorax is exposed, tuberculate, and pigmented, and in *muskegis* it bears a pair of setae. The third abdominal segment is a relatively simple ring. The abdomen is without a median ventral groove. The third antennal segment bears a pair of subcylindrical sensory rods, which in *antiqua* are curving, subtended by a chitinous ridge and accompanied by two accessory rodlike setae, the whole organ being almost exactly like that of *Achorutes socialis* (Folsom, 1916, pl. 11, fig. 47). The fourth antennal segment has stout, curving,

---

[2] See footnote 1, p. 3

pointed olfactory setae, as in *Achorutes*. The manubrium is naked ventrally. The dentes are subcylindrical and in *antiqua* apically rounded; dorsally they are tuberculate, but the tubercles are not different from those of the rest of the integument. The mucrones, with an apical tooth, an anteapical tooth, and equal outer and inner lamellae, are essentially like those of some species of *Achorutes*. Those of *antiqua* and *muskegis* are remarkably like those of *Achorutes socialis* Uzel. The pigment is dark blue.

The three species of *Guthriella* belong, however, in the family Isotomidae. The postantennal organ is externally a single tubercle, elliptical in contour, and in *muskegis* with an anterior notch like that in many species of *Proisotoma*. The furcula arises apparently from the fifth abdominal segment. The body has no intersegments. The prothorax and anal segment are relatively shorter than in Achorutinae. Anal spines are absent. The tibiotarsus has a distal subsegment. The claws are isotomid in type. The unguiculus has a pair of inner lamellae. The manubrium is relatively slender. The body setae are more numerous than in Achorutinae.

The species of *Guthriella* have near the base of the furcula a peculiar lateral suboval sclerite, the homolog of which I have not found as yet in Poduridae.

The primitive genus *Guthriella* leads into *Proisotoma* through the subgenus *Ballistura*. Linnaniemi (1912) rejected *Ballistura* as being an unnatural group, but I find it a convenient group to use for a few species in this country and in Europe as well, even though it does intergrade with *Proisotoma*. The species of *Ballistura*, typified by *B. schötti* Dalla Torre, have for the most part the same characters as *Guthriella*, but differ from that genus in having flatter body segments, wide intersegmental membranes, and imbricate tergites, with a smooth integument; while the dentes are dorsally smooth or have a relatively few rounded lobes.

Archisotoma is an aberrant genus, the single species of which resembles *Ballistura*, especially in the form of the third urotergite and in the characters of the manubrium and dentes.

The monotypic genus *Ȧgrenia* has a few of the characters of *Isotoma*, but it is closer to *Proisotoma* on account of its simple third urotergite, stout tuberculate dentes, lamellate mucrones, and short body setae.

Proisotoma schafferi and *P. rainieri* are also related to *Ballistura*.

Most of the species of *Proisotoma* are referable without difficulty to that genus; the few that are not are the species that connect *Proisotoma* with *Isotoma*.

Ankylosis of the genital and anal segments occurs in many species that are in other respects dissimilar. Hence the subgenus *Isotomina*, based solely upon that character, is too unnatural to be used. Its use would logically even separate individuals of the same species (those of *P. sepulcralis*, for example, in which the ankylosis occurs occasionally) into different genera, in some instances.

Ankylosis of the last three abdominal segments, and the subventral position of the anus, are the most important distinguishing characters of the genus *Folsomia*, which in most respects is allied to *Proisotoma*. *Folsomia* has affinities with *Isotomodes* also; in the possession of manubrial hooks, for example.

Isotoma is essentially a natural genus, even though there are intergrades between *Isotoma* and *Proisotoma*. The characters given by Börner (1906) for separating the two genera hold good in all but a few instances.

The presence of bothriotricha need not exclude *Isotomurus* and *Axelsonia* from the family Isotomidae, to which they evidently belong by reason of all their other characters.

Anurophorus, though lacking a furcula, is actually a very specialized form (Willem, 1900).

Attention should be called to the primitive nature of *Folsomides*. In this genus the body segmentation is of the simplest kind, the segments being essentially alike, relatively unmodified. Even the third and fourth abdominal segments are simple rings. The fifth and sixth are also simple and not greatly shortened. The furcula is short. Should it be regarded as reduced or not? If the ancestors of *Folsomides* had a well-developed furcula, we would expect to find remaining in *Folsomides* modifications of the posterior abdominal segments, particularly the furcal segment, which are associated with a strongly functional furcula. These segments, however, are still primitive in form. It is possible, then, that the furcula in *Folsomides*, instead of being reduced, actually represents an early stage in the evolution of the organ.

Folsomides recalls *Tullbergia* in its habitus, but it is placed in Isotomidae chiefly on account of the nature of its postantennal organ.

Isotomodes is in many respects like *Folsomides*, particularly as regards the sensory organ of the third antennal segment, but it is more specialized in having the genital and anal segments ankylosed and the anus ventral in position. The manubrial hooks, strongly developed in *Isotomodes*, reappear moderately developed in *Folsomia*.

The following genera of Isotomidae are not yet known to occur in North America: *Actaletes* Giard (1889), *Uzelia* Absolon (1901), *Cryptopygus* Willem (1902c), *Proctostephanus* Börner (1902b), *Axelsonia* Börner (1906), *Coloburella* Latzel (1917), *Pseudanurophorus* Stach (1922a), *Börnerella* Denis (1924d), *Spinisotoma* Stach (1926), and *Astephanus* Denis (1927).

DEFINITIONS

The expression "Haut gefeldert" I have translated as "integument reticulate." Börner (1901b, 1902a) called attention to this kind of integument, which is smooth externally but with an underlying network dividing the integument into minute polygonal areas (pl. 22, figs. 236, 237). It is characteristic of *Anurophorus*, *Tetracanthella*, and *Uzelia* and occurs also in three of our species of *Proisotoma*, namely, *titusi*, *vesiculata*, and *bulbosa*. In the last-named species the integument is minutely tuberculate, becoming smooth and reticulate on the posterior regions of the body segments and on the intersegmental membranes.

The term "urotergite" refers to the tergite of an abdominal segment, following Packard, who designated the abdominal segments of arthropods as "uromeres."

Frequently the furcula apparently arises from the fifth uromere, but morphologically it always belongs to the fourth, as Willem (1900) showed.

In the descriptions of mucrones the teeth are numbered in the order that happens to be most convenient, without strict regard to their theoretical evolutionary sequence.

The relative lengths of the antennal segments vary in different individuals of the same species and in different instars of the same individual to such an extent that the antennal ratios given in this bulletin are only close approximations.

Family ISOTOMIDAE Börner

Isotominae SCHAFFER, 1896, p. 179 —BORNER, 1903, p 170, 1906, p 160
Isotomini BORNER, 1901a, p 43; 1901b, p. 14
Isotomidae BORNER, 1913a, p 319.

Pronotum membranous and without setae (except in *Guthriella*). Mesonotum not projecting over the head Third and fourth urotergites approximately equal in length, or the fourth longer than the third; one being never more than one and one-half times as long as the other. Last two or last three abdominal segments sometimes ankylosed Postantennal organs almost invariably present, each consisting externally of a simple tubercle. Antennae 4-segmented, relatively short. Trochanteral organ absent. Tarsi with one or two claws. Inner edge of unguis always simple, never basally split or doubled. Furcula present (except in *Anurophorus* and its allies), often appended apparently to the fifth abdominal segment. Manubrium seldom naked ventrally, but with setae. General clothing of simple setae, the largest of which are sometimes serrate or fringed, but never clavate and fringed on all sides. Integument smooth and with sclerites, except in achorutoid species, in which it may be tuberculate and without definite sclerites. Scales absent.

KEY TO GENERA OF ISOTOMIDAE

1. Anal spines present_____Tetracanthella (p. 10)
   Anal spines absent_____2
2. Furcula absent_____Anurophorus (p. 12)
   Furcula present_____3
3. Body cylindrical, greatly elongate, in length as much as six to
   eight times its height. Prothorax unusually long. Fourth
   abdominal segment simple, relatively unmodified. Terga not
   imbricate. Furcula very small, appended to the fourth abdominal segment and not extending beyond the middle of the
   third abdominal segment. Eyes reduced in number or absent.
   Postantennal organs long and narrow. Sense organ of third
   antennal segment with two papillae, each in a deep circular
   pit. Unguiculus present. Tenent hairs absent. Manubrium
   longer than dentes. Dentes smooth dorsally, not tuberculate
   or crenulate. Mucrones bidentate. Clothing of short simple
   setae. Body pigment absent_____4
   Body not remarkably elongate. Prothorax reduced more or
   less. Fourth abdominal segment not a simple ring, but modified by changes in form or by ankylosis. Furcula not very
   small. Eyes various in number, but commonly eight on each
   side. Postantennal organs of various forms. Sense organ of
   third antennal segment with a pair of rods or papillae not situated in deep pits, but naked or covered basally by a single integumentary fold_____5
4. Genital and anal segments simple, or relatively unmodified, without ankylosis. Anus not ventral. Manubrial hooks not
   strongly developed, represented by two pairs of narrow curving
   ridges. Integument smooth_____Folsomides (p. 13)
   Genital and anal segments modified, shortened, ankylosed.
   Anus ventral. Manubrial hooks strongly developed. Integument granulate_____Isotomodes (p. 16)
5. Last three abdominal segments ankylosed, forming a single mass,
   in which sutures are mostly obsolete. Anus ventrocaudal.
   Furcula not attaining the ventral tube. Mucrones bidentate
   (tridentate in *guthriei*), not lamellate. Tenent hairs absent.
   Eyes usually reduced in number or absent. Body pigment
   often weakly developed or absent. Integument smooth__Folsomia (p. 19)
   Last three abdominal segments not ankylosed, though the last
   two may be. Anus caudal. Furcula of various lengths.
   Eyes usually 16, though fewer in some species. Pigmentation
   usually well developed_____6
6. Fourth abdominal tergite almost always longer than the third;
   the two subequal, however, in a few species. Third urotergite
   not ventrolaterally prolonged backward to any significant
   degree (pl. 9, fig. 89). Paratergite of fourth abdominal segment distinct, not united to the tergite of the genital segment.
   Genital and anal segments sometimes ankylosed. Furcula not
   attaining the ventral tube in most of the species. Manubrium
   often longer than the dentes, with ventral setae usually few in
   number and subapical in position; or naked ventrally. Dentes usually stout, and dorsally smooth or with tubercles or
   lobes or a relatively few coarse transverse folds. The dentes
   when slender and tapering are longer than the manubrium and

have many dorsal crenulations—rarely dorsal tubercles. Mucrones lamellate or not, commonly bidentate or tridentate. Tibiotarsus often with a distal subsegment. Unguiculus with a pair of inner lamellae in some species. Tenent hairs present or absent. Clothing of simple setae, usually very short. Integument almost always smooth, but tuberculate or reticulate in a few species_____7

    Fourth abdominal tergite usually shorter than the third, the two sometimes subequal. Third urotergite ventrolaterally prolonged backward (pl. 31, fig. 358; pl. 38, fig. 441). Paratergite of the fourth abdominal segment always united to the tergite of the genital segment, or the two ankylosed without suture (pl. 31, fig. 358; pl. 38, fig. 441). When the furcula is extended, the membrane between the paratergites of the third and fourth abdominal segments is exposed (pl. 38, fig. 441). Genital and anal segments rarely ankylosed. Furcula long, almost always extending to the ventral tube. Manubrium much shorter than dentes, with many ventral setae. Dentes long, slender, tapering, dorsally with very many transverse folds or crenulations. Mucrones lamellate in a few species, tridentate or quadridentate. Tenaculum with many ventral setae. Tibiotarsus without a distal subsegment. Tenent hairs present or absent. Clothing of relatively long setae, the largest of which are not infrequently unilaterally serrate or branched. Integument smooth_____10

7. Body segments bulging, with deep intersegmental constrictions. Sclerites weakly chitinized. Terga (except genital and anal) not imbricate, without well-developed intersegmental membranes. Pronotum not greatly reduced, pigmented and tuberculate. Third urotergite simple. Genital and anal segments not ankylosed. Furcula extending almost or quite to the ventral tube. Manubrium slightly longer or shorter than dentes, naked ventrally. Dentes stout, subcylindrical, tuberculate dorsally. Mucrones bidentate, bilamellate. Tibiotarsus with a distal subsegment. Unguiculus with a pair of inner lamellae. Tenent hairs present or absent. Integument tuberculate Pigment dark blue_____Guthriella (p 33)

    Body segments not bulging, without deep intersegmental constrictions. Sclerites more strongly chitinized. Terga imbricate, with evident intersegmental membranes Pronotum pigmented or not, not tuberculate. Integument rarely tuberculate_____8

8. Outer lamella of unguiculus absent. Hind femur with a thornlike process. Corpus of tenaculum with a large anterior accessory lobe. Fourth antennal segment relatively short; shorter than to slightly longer than the third. Bothriotricha present_Archisotoma (p 66)

    Outer lamella of unguiculus present. Hind femur without a thornlike process Corpus without an accessory lobe. Fourth antennal segment relatively long. Bothriotricha absent_____9

9. Unguis with a pair of strong lateral teeth connected by a basal membrane, or tunica. Dentes tuberculate dorsally, with a strong subapical seta that extends beyond the mucro. Third and fourth urotergites subequal in length. Genital and anal segments ankylosed. Furcula attaining the ventral tube. Manubrium with many ventral setae_____Ågrenia (p. 68)

Unguis without a tunica. Dentes very rarely tuberculate or smooth dorsally; usually stout, though slender in a few species, usually with dorsal transverse folds, few to many in number; with large rounded dorsal lobes in a few species. Third urotergite usually shorter than the fourth, the two rarely subequal. Genital and anal segments ankylosed or not. Furcula not attaining the ventral tube, as a rule. Manubrium often longer than the dentes, rarely with many ventral setae, commonly with one pair of ventral subapical setae; in a few species naked, rarely with two, three, or four pairs of ventral subapical setae--**Proisotoma** (p. 38)

10. Abdominal fringed bothriotricha present. Mucrones lamellate, quadridentate, with a lateral seta------------------**Isotomurus** (p 70)

Abdominal bothriotricha absent. Mucrones rarely lamellate.**Isotoma** (p 78)

Genus TETRACANTHELLA Schött

Lubbockia HALLER, 1880, p 4

Tetracanthella SCHÖTT, 1891a, p. 191.—BÖRNER, 1902a, p. 106.—LINNANIEMI, 1912, p. 100.

Deuterolubbockia VON DALLA TORRE, 1895, p 14.

Genotype.—Tetracanthella pilosa Schött.

Eyes eight on each side. Postantennal organs of the isotomine type elliptical, simple. Antennae 4-segmented. Fourth antennal segment with terminal tubercle, subapical papilla, and usually olfactory setae. Mouth parts mandibulate. Body elongate. Prothorax much shortened. Genital segment enlarged; anal segment reduced; anus ventral. Anal spines four (two in one species). Unguiculus present (or absent). Tenent hairs present (or absent). Furcula present (or absent), short, not attaining the ventral tube. Mucro ankylosed with dens (or not). Clothing of simple setae. Integument reticulate, not tuberculate.

The parenthetical qualifications given above apply to certain European species of the genus.

Tetracanthella combines achorutine with isotomine characters, with the latter predominant. Its strongest affinities are with *Anurophorus.* (On this subject see Börner, 1902a, 1903, 1906.)

TETRACANTHELLA WAHLGRENI Axelson

PLATE 1, FIGURES 1–9

Tetracanthella pilosa SCHÖTT, 1891a, p. 192 (part); 1894, p. 77 (part); 1902, p. 18 (part)—LIE-PETTERSEN, 1896, p 19—WAHLGREN, 1899b, p 336; 1900b, p. 5; 1906b, p 248.—AXELSON, 1900, p. 111.

Tetracanthella coerulea SCHAFFER, 1900a, p 245; 1900b, p. 251.

Tetracanthella wahlgreni LINNANIEMI (AXELSON), 1907, p. 80; 1912, p. 103.—BAGNALL, 1914, p. 7.—FOLSOM, 1919a, p 7; 1919b, p 275.—WAHLGREN, 1919, p. 750.—REMY, 1928, p 64.—HANDSCHIN, 1929, p 56.

*Description.—*Dark blue. Body elongate, narrowing posteriorly (pl 1, fig. 1). Eyes (pl. 1, fig. 2) eight on each side, on black patches; the two inner posterior eyes of each side smaller than the others; the three posterior eyes in a group apart from the five anterior. Post-antennal organ (pl. 1, fig. 2) narrowly elliptical, four times as long as the diameter of an adjacent eye, often with a constriction near the middle. Antennae shorter than the head (as 10·13); segments in relative lengths about as 9:13:10.19 or 17:24:23:38. Sense organ of third antennal segment (pl. 1, fig. 3) in an oblique groove, with a pair of oblique, basally bent sense rods, subtended by a thick chitinous ridge, and covered with an integumentary fold. Fourth antennal segment with curving slender olfactory setae. Unguis (pl. 1, fig. 4) stout, untoothed. Unguiculus extending one-half to three-fifths as far as the unguis, lanceolate, acuminate. Clavate tenent hairs two, extending as far as, or farther than, the unguis. Femur with a single long clavate hair (pl. 1, fig 1) Second, third, and fourth abdominal segments subequal in length dorsally. Anus ventral. Genital and anal segments ankylosed, the former bearing two pairs of spines (pl 1, figs 5, 6). Posterior spines a little longer than hind ungues, feebly curving, on stout papillae almost half as long as the spines Anterior spines similar to the posterior, but a little shorter. Ano-genital segment with many long stiff hairs, many of which extend backward beyond the end of the abdomen and are often apically bent and minutely clavate Furcula quite short, appended to the fourth abdominal segment and extending to the posterior margin of the third abdominal segment. Manubrium stout, two to two and one-half times as long as the mucrodentes, with several pairs of dorsal setae (pl. 1, fig. 7). Mucro and dens confluent. Mucrodentes convergent, in form as in plate 1, figure 8, each with three setae. Rami of tenaculum bidentate; corpus with a single stout curving seta. General clothing (pl. 1, fig 9) of short equal curving simple setae across the middle of the segment, with a transverse row of long erect simple sensory setae. Cuticula not tuberculate, but reticulate Length, 2 mm.

Remarks.—According to Linnaniemi (1912) the rami of the tenaculum are tridentate, sometimes bidentate; and the corpus bears at times two setae He says that in Finland *T. wahlgreni* lives under moss and lichens, as well as under stones, on the rocky summits of the mountains, where it may almost always be found, not infrequently in considerable numbers. Sometimes it can be taken also on pools of water It has made its appearance early in summer, before the snows have melted on the mountaintops Common as the species is on the summits of the mountains, it is seldom found in the timber region, but oftener, however, in the subalpine zone.

Distribution.—*T. wahlgreni*, which has been reported from Norway, Sweden, Finland (north of the Arctic Circle), Spitsbergen, Bear Island, Greenland, and Northwest Territories, is essentially arctic or subarctic in distribution.

Northwest Territories: Bernard Harbour, June 18, on a pond in a swamp, F. Johansen (National Collection, Ottawa).

Greenland: Umanak, July 22, in moss, W. E. Ekblaw (American Museum of Natural History, University of Illinois).

Genus ANUROPHORUS Nicolet

Anurophorus NICOLET, 1841, p. 52 (part); 1847, p. 384 (part).—TULLBERG, 1869, p 12; 1871, p. 154; 1872, p. 53.—ABSOLON, 1901, p. 212.—BORNER, 1906, p. 161.—LINNANIEMI (AXELSON), 1912, p 105.
Adicranus BOURLET, 1841–42, p. 126.
Lipura GERVAIS, 1844, p. 440 (part).
Bourletia MACGILLIVRAY, 1893, p. 313.

Genotype.—*Anurophorus laricis* Nicolet.

Furcula and anal spines absent. Body subcylindrical, rounded posteriorly, with segments mostly subequal in length. Anus ventral. Pronotum membranous. Abdominal segments without ankylosis. Eyes eight on each side. Postantennal organs present, of the isotomine type. Antennae cylindrical, 4-segmented. Unguiculus present but rudimentary. Body setae simple. Integument smooth, reticulate.

ANUROPHORUS LARICIS Nicolet

PLATE 2, FIGURES 10–15

Anurophorus laricis NICOLET, 1841, p. 53; 1847, p. 385.—TULLBERG, 1869, p. 13; 1871, p. 154; 1872, p. 53.—REUTER, L. and O. M., 1880, p. 208.— VON DALLA TORRE, 1888, p. 158; 1895, p. 14.—UZEL, 1890, p 74.—SCHOTT, 1894, p. 86; 1902, p. 18.—REUTER, 1895, p 33.—LIE-PETTERSEN, 1896, p. 20; 1907, p. 60.—SCHÄFFER, 1896, p. 164; 1900a, p. 240.—POPPE and SCHAFFER, 1897, p 266.—CARL, 1899, p. 283; 1901, p. 246.—CARPENTER and EVANS, 1899, p. 257.—WAHLGREN, 1899a, p 185; 1906a, p. 222; 1906b, p. 251; 1919, p 745.—ABSOLON, 1900a, p. 25; 1900b, p. 414; 1901, p. 213.— WILLEM, 1900, p. 28; 1902a, p. 21.—BORNER, 1901a, p. 43; 1901b, p. 9; 1901c, p. 341; 1902a, p. 105; 1903, p. 171.—EVANS, 1901a, p. 156; 1901b, p 153; 1908, p. 197.—BECKER, 1902, p. 26.—KRAUSBAUER, 1902, p 69.— ÅGREN, 1903, p. 131; 1904, p. 14.—GUTHRIE, 1903, p. 98.—AXELSON, 1904, p. 68; 1905b, p. 29; 1906, p 11.—LINNANIEMI (AXELSON), 1907, p. 45; 1911, p. 12; 1912, p. 105.—CARPENTER, 1907, p. 54.—COLLINGE, 1910, p. 10.—COLLINGE and SHOEBOTHAM, 1910, p 110.—BARTHOLIN, 1916, p 168.—STACH, 1921, p. 158.—BROWN, 1923, p. 262.—DENIS, 1924a, p. 259; 1924d, p. 210.—HANDSCHIN, 1924a, p. 109; 1924b, p. 85; 1928c, p. 126; 1929, p. 55.—WOMERSLEY, 1924a, p. 31; 1925, p 219; 1927, p. 376.
Adicranus corticinus BOURLET, 1841–42, p. 127.
Lipura laricis GERVAIS, 1844, p. 442
Lipura corticina GERVAIS, 1844, p. 442.—LUBBOCK, 1873, p. 191.—PARONA, 1879, p 608.—TOMÖSVÁRY, 1882, p. 125.—PARFITT, 1891, p. 349.
Bourletia laricis MACGILLIVRAY, 1893, p 313.

Description.—Dark blue with irregular whitish spots (pl. 2, fig. 10). Antennae blue; legs pale blue. Eyes (pl. 2, fig. 11) eight on each side, unequal. Postantennal organ (pl. 2, fig. 12) elliptical, from two to three times as long as the diameter of an adjacent eye, situated in a narrow groove (pl. 2, fig. 11) between the eyes and the base of the antenna. Antennae a little shorter than the head; second and third segments subequal in length; fourth almost twice as long as the third. Sense organ of third antennal segment (pl. 2, fig. 13) with a pair of linear, slightly curving rods subtended by a chitinous ridge. Third antennal segment with a few olfactory setae; fourth with many (Ågren). Latter with two terminal sensory papillae: an upper, stout globose or cordate; and a lower, elongate, curving, apically rounded; subapical papilla also present. Abdomen rounded posteriorly. First four abdominal segments subequal in length. Unguis (pl. 2, fig. 14) stout, untoothed. Unguiculus rudimentary, spinelike. Tenent hairs 3 or 4, feebly knobbed (4 or 5, Stach). Clothing (pl. 2, fig. 15) of sparse short rather stiff setae, with long stiff sensory setae on the posterior part of the abdomen. Integument reticulate, not tuberculate. Maximum length, 1.5 mm.

Remarks.—From Dr. Schäffer I received European examples of this species, with which the North American specimens that I have seen (including those of Guthrie) agree.

The largest tenent hairs are commonly three in number in specimens from the United States.

As Stach (1921) notes, the long sensory setae of the body are knobbed, and there is one of these on each side of the mesothorax and the metathorax.

The unguiculus when rudimentary is variable in length, and in the variety *cuspidata* Stach (1921) it is well developed.

Variety *pallida* Absolon (1901), which is whitish but intergrades with the typical form, was taken in Bohemia, usually in caves though sometimes under stones and in moss.

Though its typical habitat is under loose bark, *A. laricis* occurs also in such diverse situations as on the ground under wood, stones, or dung; on fungi; on the surface of fresh water; and on snow. Absolon found the species in small dry caves in Bohemia.

Distribution.—This species, known from all parts of Europe and from Siberia, is without doubt more widely distributed in North America than the following few records indicate:

New York: New York City, July, F. Silvestri. Lakeville, October 23, E. A Maynard.

Minnesota: Lake Pepin, August 23, J. E. Guthrie (University of Minnesota).

Colorado: Eastern slope of Pikes Peak (8,300 feet), June, July, August, G. W. Goldsmith.

Genus FOLSOMIDES Stach

Folsomides STACH, 1922a, p. 17.

Genotype.—*Folsomides parvulus* Stach.

Body cylindrical, greatly elongate, segments not strongly imbricate Prothorax unusually long. The abdominal segments are simple rings, subequal in length (except the anal segment) and without ankylosis; fourth segment slightly longer than the third; genital and anal segments relatively unmodified. Anus caudal. Head prognathous, mandibulate; mandibles with well-developed molar surface. Eyes reduced in number (either one or two on each side, in the known species) Postantennal organs present, relatively large, elongate, narrow, straight to feebly curving, with thick wall. Antennae arising relatively far forward, 4-segmented. Sense organ of third antennal segment consisting of a pair of papillae, each situated in a pit Fourth antennal segment with slender curving olfactory setae. Unguiculus present Tenent hairs absent. Ventral tube emitting a pair of short rounded vesicles. Furcula present, small, appended to the fourth abdominal segment. Manubrium much longer than dens plus mucro; manubrial hooks undeveloped Dentes smooth dorsally, not crenulate or tuberculate Mucro bidentate, either separated from dens by a suture or confluent with dens. Anal spines absent Clothing of short simple setae. Body pigment absent.

Hitherto only a single specimen of this peculiar genus has been known—the genotype, *F. parvulus*, found in Hungary and described by Stach, to whose generic description I have added a little.

Folsomides is evidently next to *Isotomodes*, in which, however, the genital and anal segments are ankylosed, the anus is ventral, and the manubrial hooks are strongly developed. *Folsomides* is unique among Collembola in the primitive nature of the segmentation of the body. The abdomen, with its simple, ringlike, equal segments is almost vermiform; even the genital and anal segments are relatively unmodified, as compared with those segments in other Collembola. Both *Folsomides* and *Isotomodes* show affinities with *Folsomia* and *Proisotoma*.

KEY TO SPECIES OF FOLSOMIDES

1. Two eyes on each side. Mucrodentes about one-half as long as
   manubrium_____**parvus** (p. 14)
   One eye on each side. Mucrodentes about two-thirds as long as
   manubrium_____**stachi** (p. 16)

FOLSOMIDES PARVUS, new species

PLATE 2, FIGURES 16–20

Description.—White. Greatly elongate (pl. 2, fig. 16); body subcylindrical, six times as long as broad. Eyes (pl. 2, fig. 17) two on each side; equal, one in front of the other, separated, each on a small irregular black pigment spot. Postantennal organ (pl. 2, fig. 17) close to the anterior eye, narrowly elliptical or subelliptical, thick-walled, varying in length from a little shorter to a little longer than the width of the first antennal segment, with four guard setae. Antennae inserted forward on the head, two-thirds as long as the latter, with segments in relative lengths about as 2 : 3 : 3 : 5; fourth segment stout, elliptical, with slender curving olfactory setae. Sense organ of third antennal segment with a pair of papillae, each in a shallow pit. Thorax long, three-fifths as long as abdomen, with tergites in relative lengths about as 10 · 18 15. Abdominal segments without ankylosis, in relative lengths about as 13· 14· 13: 15: 13: 9; fourth segment thus a little longer than the third. Anal segment simple, unmodified. Anus caudal. Unguis (pl. 2, fig. 18) feebly curving, simple, untoothed. Unguiculus minute, lanceolate, acuminate, untoothed, extending about one-third as far as unguis. Tenent hairs absent. Ventral tube (pl. 2, fig. 19) simple, with a pair of hemispherical vesicles, side by side. Furcula (pl 2, fig 20) small, appended to the fourth abdominal segment and extending slightly beyond it. Manubrium stout, not tapering, rounded apically, about twice as long as dens plus mucro, with several short stiff dorsal setae. Dens and mucro confluent. Mucrodens gradually narrowing from the base, smooth dorsally, with three short stiff dorsal setae; mesally with a pair of narrow chitinous basal ridges. Mucro subequally bidentate; apical tooth hooked; anteapical feebly hooked. Clothing of sparse minute equal stiff simple setae, longer and more numerous posteriorly; sensory setae longer, stiff, outstanding, simple, in a row across the middle of the body segment; longest and most numerous on the anal segment. Integument smooth. Length, 0.75 mm.

Remarks.—*Folsomides parvus* differs from *F. parvulus* Stach chiefly as indicated in table 1.

TABLE 1.—*Comparison of* Folsomides parvulus *and* F. parvus

Species	Antennal joints I.II	Postantennal organ	Unguiculus	Mucro	Long tibio-tarsal hair
F *parvulus*	1 2	Bent	Stout, subovate	Demarcated from dens	Present
F *parvus*	2 3	Straight	Slender, lanceolate	Confluent with dens	Absent.

F. parvulus was taken in Hungary under a large stone on moist soil in a farmyard near a cow barn The five cotypes of *parvus* were found in Douglas fir soil, at an elevation of 8,500 feet

In Homer, Ill., May 13, 1924, under a log on damp bottomland, I found a single specimen of a species of *Folsomides* that is extremely close to Stach's *parvulus*. Additional material is necessary, however, for definite determination

Cotypes.—U.S N.M. no. 42993.

Distribution—Recorded as follows:

Colorado Eastern slope of Pikes Peak, July 1, Engelman Canyon, G. W. Goldsmith.

FOLSOMIDES STACHI, new species

PLATE 2, FIGURES 21–23; PLATE 3, FIGURES 24–26

Description.—White. Greatly elongate; body cylindrical, in length six times the height of the abdomen Eyes (pl. 2, fig. 21) one on each side, each on a small round black spot. Postantennal organ (pl. 2, fig. 21) close to the eye, narrowly elliptical, straight or feebly curving, in length about four times the diameter of the eye, with four guard setae. Antennae about two-thirds as long as the head, with segments in relative lengths about as 5:6:7:8. Body segments in relative lengths about as 14:27:25:21:23:24:27:20:15. Fourth abdominal segment thus a little longer than the third. Genital and anal segments not ankylosed. Anus caudal. Unguis (pl. 2, figs. 22, 23) stout, curving, untoothed. Unguiculus extending one-half as far as unguis on hind feet, one-third as far on the remaining feet, lanceolate, acuminate, untoothed. Tibiotarsus with a distal subsegment indicated. Tenent hairs absent. Furcula small, appended to the posterior part of the fourth abdominal segment, and extending not quite to the middle of the third. Manubrium (pl. 3, figs. 24, 25) longer than mucrodens (about as 3:2), gradually narrowing, with five pairs of setae in dorsal aspect (pl. 2, fig. 25). Dens and mucro confluent. Mucrodens (pl. 2, figs. 24, 25) stout, gradually tapering from the base, with three small dorsal setae, mesally with a pair of narrow chitinous basal ridges. Mucro minutely bidentate (pl. 2, fig. 26); apical tooth hooked; anteapical retrorse Rami of tenaculum tridentate; corpus with an anterior median basal lobe. Clothing of minute, stiff, simple setae, limited to a few transverse rows across the middle of each body segment, with a few longer erect sensory setae; genital and anal segments with a few long setae. Integument smooth. Length, 0 6 mm

Remarks —This new species, which is dedicated with pleasure to my colleague Dr Jan Stach, was taken by me at Tallulah, La., April 7, in humus in a cypress forest.

Cotypes.—U.S.N.M. no. 42992.

Genus ISOTOMODES Linnaniemi

Isotoma Axelson, 1903a, p 6; 1906, p 11
Isotomodes Linnaniemi (Axelson), 1907, p. 34; 1912, p 106 —Shoebotham, 1911, p. 34.—Handschin,[1] 1925b, p. 164.

Genotype.—*Isotomodes productus* Linnaniemi.

Body greatly elongate. Prothorax unusually long. Genital and anal segments shortened and not distinctly separated from each other. Anus ventral. Integument granulate. Clothing of simple setae. Antennae 4-segmented, arising relatively far forward. Head narrow and low. Mouth parts mandibulate, projecting a little. Sense organ of third antennal segment present, consisting of two sense rods, each seated in a deep pit almost surrounded by a thick chitinous border. Fourth antennal segment with several olfactory setae. Postantennal organ large, elongate, elliptical to parallel-sided, with relatively weak chitinous wall and with several guard setae. Unguiculus present. Furcula present. Manubrium conspicuously broad basally; dentes not crenulate; between the dentes two pairs of remarkably strong basal hooks. Ventral tube short. Anal spines absent. Eyes absent in the known species.

The genus *Isotomodes* was founded on a single species, *I. productus* Axelson, found in Finland, Russia, and England under stones on damp humus and in Morocco under stones as a myrmecophile.

In the species *tenuis*, described here from Massachusetts, some of the generic characters are less pronounced than in the genotype. The prothorax, for example, is not so long as in *productus;* the anus is not quite ventral in position; the sensory pits of the third antennal segment are more open; the olfactory setae of the fourth antennal segment are not so strongly differentiated from ordinary setae; and the ventral tube is not especially short. Like *productus*, *tenuis* has bidentate mucrones, elongate postantennal organs, and no eyes. *I. productus* is unpigmented, but *tenuis*, though white to the naked eye, shows scattered specks of black pigment under the microscope. In specific characters, the two species differ considerably,

Linnaniemi notes that in certain respects *Isotomodes* occupies a place between *Folsomia* and *Cryptopygus*.

In his figures of *productus*, Linnaniemi (1912) shows a trace of a dorsal suture between the anal and genital segments; but in *tenuis* I have found no trace of such a suture. The terminal structure of the abdomen is much like that of *Cryptopygus* Willem (1902c), which is described as having the anal segment completely concealed in a depression of the genital segment. I believe that in *Isotomodes*, however, the anal segment is not concealed, but is simply ankylosed with the genital segment, this opinion being supported by the existence of the suture shown by Linnaniemi.

Isotomodes agrees with certain species of *Folsomia* in respect to its weak pigmentation, eye reduction, ankylosis of the last two abdominal segments (last three in *Folsomia*), reduced furcula, bidentate mucrones, and the presence of manubrial hooks. As in some species of *Proisotoma*, the body setae are short and simple, the furcula is short, and the dentes are dorsally without crenulations or tubercles.

ISOTOMODES TENUIS, new species

PLATE 3, FIGURES 27–34

Description.—Greatly elongate (slenderer than in pl 3, fig. 27, which is from a flattened specimen); length about nine times the height of the body. White, with a few scattered black specks, largest and most numerous on the posterior part of the abdomen.

Eyes absent. Postantennal organ (pl. 3, fig. 28) elongate, a little shorter than the width of the first antennal segment, straight or slightly curving, with almost parallel sides, usually emarginate at the middle of the anterior margin, six to eight times as long as broad, with a posterior row of strong guard setae seated on a cuticular thickening Antennae shorter than the head (as 5:7), with segments in relative lengths about as 4 : 7 · 6 : 10. Sense organ of third antennal segment (pl 3, fig. 29) with a pair of rods immersed in a deep pit. Fourth antennal segment with olfactory setae Body subcylindrical, abdomen slightly dilating posteriorly. Prothorax not unusually long (one-fifth to one-half as long as mesothorax); fourth abdominal segment longer than the third (as 6:5); anal segment not evident Anus ventral Claws largest on third pair of feet. Unguis (pl 3, fig. 30) slender, curving, untoothed. Unguiculus extending less than half as far as unguis, lanceolate, pointed, untoothed. Tenent hairs absent. Furcula appended to the fourth abdominal segment, short (pl. 3, fig 27), extending scarcely to the middle of the third abdominal segment. Manubrium (pl. 3, fig. 31) stout, longer than dentes (as 5 3), with several dorsal setae and two pairs of ventral subapical setae. Dens stout, narrowing but little, with unusually thick ventral wall, without dorsal crenulations, with a few setae dorsally and ventrally, and with the pair of basal hooks exceptionally large. Mucro half as long as dens, subequally bidentate (pl 3, figs. 31, 32); apical tooth feebly hooked; anteapical tooth suberect Rami of tenaculum (pl 3, fig. 33) quadridentate, slender, tapering; corpus with a single long stout curving seta. General clothing (pl. 3, fig. 34) of short, stiff, simple setae, becoming longer and more curving toward the end of the abdomen; erect sensory setae short and simple. Integument minutely granulate Maximum length, 1 mm.

Remarks.—Table 2 gives the relative lengths of the body segments of four individuals. The considerable variation in the length of the prothorax is due to the fact that this segment is normally capable of being lengthened or shortened considerably by muscular action and, furthermore, elongates more or less in preserved specimens under the influence of potassium hydroxide.

TABLE 2.—*Relative lengths of the body segments of four specimens of* Isotomodes tenuis, *new species*

THORACIC SEGMENT—			ABDOMINAL SEGMENT—				
1	2	3	1	2	3	4	5+6
14	45	46	36	40	40	48	44
6	24	20	17	20	20	24	22
9	43	44	32	36	38	46	45
9	18	19	10	16	18	20	19

The only specimens of this species that I have seen are 12 that I found at Arlington, Mass., on March 20, in damp moss on stones in a bog.

Cotypes.—U.S.N M. no 42991.

Genus FOLSOMIA Willem

Isotoma TULLBERG, 1871, p 150 (part)
Folsomia WILLEM, 1902b, p 280.—BORNER, 1903, p 171, 1906, p 164.—AXELSON, 1905b, p. 29.—LINNANIEMI (AXELSON), 1907, p 21; 1912, p 109.

Genotype.—*Isotoma fimetaria* (Linnaeus, Tullberg).

Fourth, fifth, and sixth abdominal segments ankylosed, forming a single mass (pl. 7, fig. 74). Anus ventrocaudal. Furcula short, not attaining the ventral tube, appended to the fourth abdominal segment. Mucrones usually bidentate, rarely tridentate, without lamellae. Manubrial hooks moderately developed. Tenaculum with a single ventral seta. Eyes in most species reduced in number or absent. Postantennal organ narrow, often slightly bent. Sense organ of third antennal segment with two oblique rods and a protecting integumentary fold. Fourth antennal segment with a terminal tubercle, a subapical papilla, and usually with olfactory setae. Unguis simple, without lateral teeth, and seldom with an inner tooth. Unguiculus present, simple, untoothed. Tenent hairs absent. Body setae simple, rarely feebly and unilaterally feathered. Bothriotricha absent. Body pigment commonly weakly developed or absent. Integument smooth.

Species of *Folsomia* exhibit various stages of reduction in the number of eyes, the length of the furcula, size of body, and amount of pigment. The blind species are white, in correlation with their habit of living in darkness

KEY TO SPECIES OF FOLSOMIA

```
1  Eyes absent.  White species.  Manubrium shorter than dentes.
     Dentes with many dorsal crenulations_____2
   Eyes present.  Pigmented species, with one exception_____3
2. Postantennal organs subelliptical or subovate.  Unguis un-
     toothed in the typical form.  Dentes twice as long as manu-
     brium_____fimetaria (p. 28)
   Postantennal organs long and narrow, with parallel sides.
     Unguis strongly unidentate.  Dentes one and one-half times
     as long as manubrium_____nivalis (p. 32)
3  Eyes 16  Manubrium longer than dentes  Dentes with a few
     dorsal crenulations_____4
   Eyes fewer than 16  Tenent hairs absent_____6
4. Mucrones  bidentate_____5
   Mucrones tridentate.  Unguis untoothed.  Tenent hairs absent.
     Grayish blue_____guthriei (p. 22)
5. Unguis untoothed.  Tenent hairs absent.  Manubrium with
     one pair of ventral subapical setae.  Grayish, bluish, or
     brownish_____elongata (p. 21)
```

FOLSOMIA SILVESTRII, new species

PLATE 4, FIGURES 35–39

Description.—White, mottled with blue; anterior borders of body segments white; posterior borders of mesonotum to third urotergite, inclusive, edged narrowly with dark blue. First and second antennal segments mostly white but mottled with blue; third and fourth segments blue. Legs white, with more or less pigment except on tibiotarsi. Manubrium pigmented basally; dentes unpigmented. Eyes (pl. 4, fig. 35) eight on each side, the two inner proximal eyes much smaller than the others. Postantennal organ (pl. 4, figs. 35, 36) elongate subelliptical, from three and one-half to six times as long as wide, and three to five times as long as the diameter of an adjacent eye, with a notch near the middle of the anterior margin. Antennae equal to head in length or a little shorter (as 9:10); third segment slightly longer than the second; fourth about twice as long as the third, stout, elliptical. Sense organ of third antennal segment with a pair of short pegs subtended by a chitinous thickening. Fourth antennal segment without special olfactory setae. Last three abdominal segments ankylosed, forming a single mass, rounded posteriorly; anus ventrocaudal. Tibiotarsi with a distal subsegment, sometimes incomplete. Unguis (pl. 4, fig. 37) stout, with a pair of small lateral teeth and an inner tooth (sometimes absent) two-fifths from the apex. Unguiculus broadly lanceolate, acuminate, with inner lamella strongly rounded basally; extending two-thirds as far as the unguis on the hind feet, and about half as far on the other feet. Tenent hairs 1, 2, 2 or 2, 2, 2; one of the two hairs being stronger than the other. Furcula (pl 4, fig. 38) short, extending only to the second abdominal segment. Manubrium longer than dentes (as 9:7); ventrally with many stiff setae and a subapical pair much longer and stouter than the others. Dentes with a few dorsal crenulations in the middle region that become smaller distally; ventrally with a moderate number of stiff setae. Mucrones (pl. 4, fig. 38) one-fourth longer than hind unguiculi, bidentate; apical tooth smaller than the anteapical and slightly hooked; second tooth erect. Tenaculum quadridentate; corpus with either one or two strong curving anterior setae; an additional seta occurring just in front of the corpus. Clothing (pl. 4, fig. 39) short, slightly curving, longer posteriorly, simple; sensory setae erect, relatively short, simple. Integument smooth. Maximum length, 1.3 mm.

Remarks.—Five individuals out of 18 had two eye spots on each side, a large anterior and a small posterior spot. Other specimens showed transitional stages between one eye spot and two.

Cotypes —U S.N.M. no. 42994.

Distribution.—Recorded as follows:

New York: New York City, July, F. Silvestri, for whom the species is named.

FOLSOMIA ELONGATA (MacGillivray)

PLATE 4, FIGURES 40-46

Isotoma elongata MacGillivray, 1896, p. 49.
Isotoma bidenticula Guthrie, 1903, p. 66.

Description.—Body slender, subcylindrical. General color mottled grayish or greenish gray above, less often bluish or brownish; white beneath; legs and furcula white; antennae white, or mottled with pigment. Most of the body segments are pale anteriorly, giving the effect of whitish bands. Eyes (pl. 4, fig. 40) eight on each side, unequal; ocular areas elongate. Postantennal organ (pl. 4, fig. 40) narrowly elliptical or subelliptical; as wide as, and three or four times as long as, the diameter of the adjacent eye. Antennae varying from a little shorter to a little longer than the head, with segments in relative lengths about as 4:7:6:13 or 5.9.8:15. Sense organ of third antennal segment (pl. 4, fig. 41) with two rods and three setae. Fourth antennal segment with slender sensory setae. Last three abdominal segments ankylosed, forming a smoothly rounded mass. Anus ventrocaudal. Tibiotarsus without a distal subsegment. Hind claws larger than the others. Unguis (pl. 4, fig. 42) stout, curving, without teeth. Unguiculus extending one-third (first pair) to one-half or two-thirds (third pair) as far as the unguis, sublanceolate, acuminate or setaceously produced, untoothed. Tenent hairs absent, represented by a single simple hair. Furcula appended to the fourth abdominal segment, short, extending only to the middle of the third abdominal segment, in lateral aspect rapidly narrowing from a broad base. Manubrium one-third to one-half longer than dentes, stout, with several stiff dorsal setae and two long subapical ventral setae; manubrial hooks well developed. Dens (pl. 4, fig. 43) stout, with five or six dorsal crenulations beyond the middle. Mucrones (pl. 4, figs. 44, 45) bidentate; apical tooth almost straight or slightly hooked; anteapical tooth frequently larger than the first tooth, suberect or feebly curving. Tenaculum with quadridentate rami and a single stout curving ventral seta. General clothing (pl. 4, fig. 46) of short equal slightly curving setae, absent on the anterior and posterior regions of most of the body segments. Long outstanding simple sensory setae are present on the occiput, coxae, and body segments, occurring in a row across the middle of each of the first three abdominal segments. Maximum length, 1.6 mm.

In moderately pigmented specimens the pigment forms a reticulation, marking off the hypodermis cells. In large heavily pigmented individuals there are suggestions of three interrupted stripes above: One median and two subdorsal. Furthermore, the body segments are often margined posteriorly with blackish. Specimens show occasionally a trace, dorsally, of the suture between the fourth and fifth abdominal segments. The apical tooth of the mucro varies in length and may be reduced or even absent (pl. 4, fig. 45).

Remarks.—The preceding description was made from cotypes, supplemented by specimens received from A. D. MacGillivray, C. F. Baker, F. L. Harvey, and A. P. Morse. All this material was collected at Fort Collins, Colo., by C. F. Baker.

Thirteen cotypes of *bidenticula* Guthrie, loaned to me through the courtesy of Prof. H. F. Nachtrieb, proved to be this species.

Folsomia elongata occurs on the ground under wood, dead leaves, and stones; under loose bark; on pools of fresh water; and under flowerpots in greenhouses. In central Illinois I have taken full-grown specimens in abundance late in winter (February 4), and found the species to be active, though sluggish, under logs during cold weather when the ground was frozen.

Distribution.—Recorded as follows:

Maine: Orono, April 15, in moss from swamp, F. L. Harvey.

Illinois: Homer, February 4, 5, 23, 29, March 14, 25, 31, April 2, 5, 6, 7, 8, 11, 13, 16, 18, October 10, 23. Urbana, April 10, 11.

Iowa: Sioux City, January 29, C. N. Ainslie.

Kansas: Manhattan, February 3, D. B. Whelan.

Minnesota: Minneapolis, December 16, J. E. Guthrie (University of Minnesota).

Colorado: Fort Collins, January 10, C. F. Baker (Museum of Comparative Zoology). Pikes Peak, July, August, Douglas-fir-forest soil (8,300 feet), G. W. Goldsmith.

FOLSOMIA GUTHRIEI (Linnaniemi)

PLATE 5, FIGURES 47–49

Isotoma minima Guthrie, 1903, p. 63.
Proisotoma guthriei Linnaniemi, 1912, p 132.

Description—"Light grayish-blue in color, body subcylindrical, elongate, almost naked except on the fifth and sixth abdominal segments, which bear some long scattered hairs. Fourth, fifth and sixth abdominal segments apparently so fused as to form almost a continuous segment. Antennae gray, little longer than the head; Ant. IV longest, very much swollen, III much rounded, shorter than II and slightly longer than I. Ocelli 16. Post-antennal organ [fig. 47] long, narrowly elliptical, slightly emarginate along anterior edge.

"Furcula [fig. 48] short, not reaching to ventral tube; insertion at junction of fourth and fifth abdominal segments. Manubrium stout and thick. Dentes straight, not tapering greatly toward distal end, irregularly serrulate along greater part of lower [dorsal] edge, upper edge with a few stout, scattered hairs. Mucrones and dentes together about as long as the manubrium. Mucrones [fig. 49] long and narrow, tridenticulate, the distal tooth almost straight, the ante-distal tooth close to, and at right angles to it; proximal tooth smaller and set about the middle of the mucrones, pointing slightly distal-wards. Each tibia bears one long simple hair in the position of a tenent hair. The claws are unarmed.

"* * * Length, three-fourths millimetre" (Guthrie).

Remarks.—I have seen two of the cotypes of this species, which were loaned to me by Prof. H. F. Nachtrieb. Owing to the fact that these specimens were mounted in balsam, the unpigmented structures were almost invisible. It could be seen, however, that the last three abdominal segments are ankylosed, putting this species into the genus *Folsomia*. Faint traces of sutures between the united segments were distinguishable.

Though this species is much like *Proisotoma minuta* (Tullberg), as Linnaniemi (1912) observed, it is nevertheless distinct, and forms a link between *Folsomia* and *Proisotoma*.

Guthrie says:

This species probably occurs more abundantly than its numbers in my collection would show, its minute size and light gray color lending a mimicry which shields it from all but the most careful observation. It seldom jumps, seeming averse to that mode of motion, but moves about uneasily when its hiding places are exposed to the sunlight. I have taken it in the greenhouse of the University, under moist boxes and flower pots, where it usually lived among the faeces of a certain small millipede, though possibly this coöccurrence was purely accidental. Out of doors it is sometimes met with under stones and damp boards, usually where there is a slight layer of thin, slimy mud. Not uncommonly it is taken with *I. bidenticula* [*elongata* MacGillivray], the light-colored young of which it greatly resembles until one observes it with a compound lens.

Distribution.—Recorded as follows:

Minnesota: Minneapolis, August, September, J. E. Guthrie (University of Minnesota).

FOLSOMIA SEXOCULATA (Tullberg)

PLATE 5, FIGURES 50, 51

Isotoma sexoculata TULLBERG, 1871, p. 152; 1872, p. 48.—SCHOTT, 1894, p. 74.—LIE-PETTERSEN, 1896, p. 18; 1907, p. 61.—SCHÄFFER, 1896, p. 183.—WAHLGREN, 1900a, p. 367; 1906b, p. 255.—CARPENTER and EVANS, 1904, p. 216.

Isotoma (Folsomia) sexoculata AXELSON, 1905b, p. 29.

Folsomia sexoculata LINNANIEMI (AXELSON), 1911, p. 14; 1912, p. 109.—BARTHOLIN, 1916, p. 168.—CARPENTER and PHILLIPS, 1922, p. 14.—HANDSCHIN, 1924a, p. 110; 1924b, p. 85; 1928c, p. 127; 1929, p. 57.

Description.—Body stout. Gray or blackish gray with unpigmented segment borders and clear rounded spots on the head and the sides of the segments. Young individuals are gray, weakly pigmented. Eyes (pl. 5, fig. 50) three on each side, equal; eye spots two on each side. The two anterior eyes on each side are close together and occupy a single pigment spot; the posterior eye is remote from these. Postantennal organ long, very narrow, bent, sometimes notched. Antennae as long as the head, situated on a well-developed antennal base; segments in relative lengths as 2:4:3.5:7:5. Sense organ of third antennal segment typical. Fourth segment with an apical rounded tubercle, a subapical papilla, and several long olfactory setae. Last three abdominal segments ankylosed, with occasionally a trace of a suture between the fourth and fifth segments. Unguis (pl. 5, fig. 51) rather large, with small lateral teeth but without an inner tooth. Unguiculus broadly lanceolate, with apex setaceously prolonged, untoothed. Tenent hairs absent. Furcula appended to the fourth abdominal segment, extending almost to the anterior margin of the second abdominal segment. Manubrium rather slender, with a strong subapical ventral seta and several fine dorsal setae. Dentes one-fifth longer than manubrium, narrowing distally, dorsally crenulate, the crenulations ceasing rather far from the mucro, with several dorsal and ventral setae. Mucro conspicuously large, about one-sixth as long as dens, bidentate, without subapical seta. Rami of tenaculum quadridentate; corpus with one seta. Clothing of comparatively short dense simple setae; outstanding sensory setae simple. Maximum length, 2.1 mm.

Remarks.—The preceding description is based on that of Linnaniemi (1912) with the aid of specimens received from Dr. C. Schäffer.

In the collembolan fauna there are few species that are so typically littoral as this one. It occurs exclusively on the seashore under seaweed, moist stones, and pieces of wood near the edge of the water (Linnaniemi).

Distribution.—*F. sexoculata* is known from east Greenland, Jan Mayen Island, Spitsbergen, Norway, Sweden, Denmark, Finland, Germany, Switzerland, Great Britain, and Ireland.

FOLSOMIA QUADRIOCULATA (Tullberg)

PLATE 5, FIGURES 52–58

Isotoma quadrioculata TULLBERG, 1871, p. 152; 1872, p. 48; 1876, p. 36.—STUXBERG, 1887, p. 43.—UZEL, 1890, p. 66.—MACGILLIVRAY, 1891, p. 274, 1896, p. 58.—MONIEZ, 1891, p. 70.—SCHOTT, 1894, p. 74; 1902, p. 21.—VON DALLA TORRE, 1895, p. 10.—REUTER, 1895, p. 28.—LIE-PETTERSEN, 1896, p. 18; 1898, p. 13; 1907, p. 60.—MEINERT, 1896, p. 170.—SCHÄFFER, 1896, p. 183; 1900a, p. 248; 1900b, p. 255.—POPPE and SCHAFFER, 1897, p. 268.—LUBBOCK, 1898, p. 619.—SCHERBAKOV, 1898a, p. 58; 1898b, p. 12.—CARL, 1899, p. 310; 1901, p. 261.—WAHLGREN, 1899b, p. 337; 1900a, p. 367;

1900b, p. 5; 1906a, p. 222; 1906b, p. 255.—ABSOLON, 1900a, p 28.—SKORIKOW, 1900, p. 206.—BÖRNER, 1901a, p. 45.—BECKER, 1902, p. 27 —KRAUSBAUER, 1902, p. 42.—ÅGREN, 1903, p. 143; 1904, p. 21 —GUTHRIE, 1903, p. 65 — AXELSON, 1904, p. 69; 1905a, p 791; 1906, p 12 —EVANS, 1908, p 199.
Isotoma (Folsomia) quadrioculata AXELSON, 1905b, p. 29.
Folsomia quadrioculata LINNANIEMI (AXELSON), 1907, p 21; 1909, p. 13; 1911, p 12; 1912, p. 111.—BAGNALL, 1909, p. 500.—COLLINGE and SHOEBOTHAM, 1910, p. 110 —BARTHOLIN, 1916, p. 168.—SHOEBOTHAM, 1917, p. 221.— BROWN, 1918, p. 186; 1919, p. 64 —FOLSOM, 1919a, p. 8.—WAHLGREN, 1919, p. 745.—DENIS, 1921, p. 125; 1927, p 192.—STACH, 1921, p 160 —CARPENTER and PHILLIPS, 1922, p. 14.—SCHÖTT, 1923, p 10.—HANDSCHIN, 1924a, p. 110; 1924b, p. 85; 1926, p. 125; 1928c, p. 127; 1929, p. 58.—WOMERSLEY, 1924a, p. 33; 1924b, p. 169; 1925, p. 219; 1927, p. 377.—REMY, 1928, p. 66.

Description.—Dirty pale gray to grayish black, pigmented with blackish spots, irregular in their form, size, and distribution. Small specimens may be white, or white with scattered spots of grayish blue. Large specimens are often blackish, mottled with white (unpigmented) spots; pale across the intersegmental regions; unpigmented ventrally; with antennae, legs, and manubrium pigmented. In small specimens the appendages are white, or pigmented basally. Eyes (pl. 5, fig. 52) two on each side, one behind the other, each on its own pigment spot, the posterior eye being the smaller. Postantennal organ (pl. 5, fig. 52) long, narrow, with parallel sides, feebly curving, three to four times as long as the diameter of the adjacent eye. Antennae varying from a little shorter to a little longer than the head; first segment about half as long as the second; second a little longer than the third; fourth two to three times as long as the first; antennal formula about 20.38:35 62. Sense organ of third antennal segment as in plate 5, figure 53. Fourth antennal segment with terminal tubercle, subapical papilla, and slender curving olfactory setae. Antennal base well developed. Body stout. Fourth, fifth, and sixth abdominal segments ankylosed; with a trace of a dorsal suture between the fourth and fifth. Anus ventrocaudal. Tibiotarsal subsegment absent. Unguis (pl. 5, fig. 54) curving, simple, without teeth. Unguiculus small, extending about half as far as the unguis on the third pair of feet; one-third as far on the first and second pairs; lanceolate, pointed, untoothed. Tenent hairs absent. Furcula appended to the fourth abdominal segment, short, not quite attaining the posterior margin of the second abdominal segment. Manubrium: dens: mucro about as 5:3:1. Manubrium (pl. 5, fig. 55) with two pairs of ventroapical strong chitinous hooks between the bases of the dentes, and two pairs of ventral subapical setae. Dentes (pl. 5, fig. 56) stout, not tapering greatly, with a few crenulations near the middle of the dorsal region. Mucrones (pl. 5, figs. 56, 57) bidentate; apical tooth more or less hooked; second tooth usually larger than the first, erect or curving slightly forward. Rami of tenaculum quadridentate; corpus with a single stout curving seta. Clothing (pl. 5, fig.

58) of rather long stiff dense simple setae slanting backward, becoming longer toward the posterior part of the abdomen; abdominal segments with long slender simple erect sensory setae. In addition, some of the largest individuals have a moderate number of erect setae considerably shorter than the sensory setae; stout stiff setae occur on the bases of the legs. Maximum length, 1.5 mm.

Remarks.—This species varies in pigmentation, the amount of pigment increasing, as a rule, with the size of the individual. Variety *pallida* Axelson (1905a, 1905b, 1912) is entirely white, except the black eye spots. Variety *anophthalma* Linnaniemi (1912) is white, without any pigment, even the ocular pigment being absent, though the corneae are present. This variety, found originally in Norway and northern Russia, and recorded from Greenland by Remy (1928), occurred among examples of the typical form collected in Canada by Charles Macnamara.

One individual that I examined had the two eye spots on each side, but after treatment with potassium hydroxide they failed to show the posterior corneae.

In some Canadian specimens each femur had a distal subsegment.

Specimens from Illinois had slenderer dentes and mucrones than those from Northwest Territories.

Our examples of the species agree with European material received from Schäffer.

Folsomia quadrioculata occurs on damp ground under stones, wood, or fallen leaves; in humus and in moss; under loose bark, in flower-pots, on pools of fresh water, and on the seashore under driftwood, seaweed, or stones.

The species is easily recognized by its broad body, characteristic dirty-gray color, and slow movements. When disturbed it springs actively in spite of its short furcula. In Finland it winters full grown, and comes to life now and then on mild days; never appearing on the snow, however, but remaining among leaves or in moss in the woods (Linnaniemi, 1912).

Distribution.—This species, one of the commonest collembolans in northern and middle Europe, and known from Italy also, has been reported from the following arctic localities: Nova Zembla, Spitsbergen, King Charles Island, White Island, Bear Island, Jan Mayen Island, and Greenland.

New York: Lakeville, November 13, E. A. Maynard.

Illinois: Homer, May 3, 11, July 5. Urbana, April 13.

Minnesota: Minneapolis, June 1, J. E. Guthrie (University of Minnesota).

Canada: Arnprior, Ontario, June 30, September, October, C. Macnamara. Bernard Harbour, Northwest Territories, June 18, July 9, F. Johansen (National Collection, Ottawa).

FOLSOMIA DIPLOPHTHALMA (Axelson)

PLATE 6. FIGURES 59-67

Isotoma diplophthalma AXELSON, 1902, p 106
Folsomia quadrioculata TULLBERG, var *diplophthalma* AXELSON, 1907, p. 30;
    1909, p 13.—COLLINGE and SHOEBOTHAM, 1910, p 110.
Isotoma binoculata COLLINGE and SHOEBOTHAM, 1909, p 88.
Folsomia diplophthalma LINNANIEMI (AXELSON), 1911, p 13; 1912, p. 113.—
    WAHLGREN, 1919, p 745.—SCHÖTT, 1923, p. 11.—REMY, 1928, p 66.—
    HANDSCHIN, 1929, p 58
Isotoma (Folsomia) diplophthalma FOLSOM, 1919b, p. 276.

Description—Elongate. White, with a slight amount of pigment
in the form of scattered minute blackish dots, or without pigment
except that of the eyes; or pale gray with patches of pigment irregular
in size and distribution. Eyes (pl. 6, figs. 59, 60) one on each side,
appearing as round black spots. Postantennal organ (pl. 6, figs.
59, 60) close to the eye, large, four to seven times as long as the
diameter of the eye, subelliptical, often but not always constricted
near the middle, with thick chitinous wall. Antennae slightly longer
than the head, with segments in relative lengths about as $4:9:8:16$.
Sense organ of third antennal segment (pl. 6, fig. 61) with a pair of
slender feebly curving rods and a chitinous ridge Fourth antennal
segment with terminal tubercle, subapical papilla, and several
olfactory setae, somewhat shorter and stouter than the other setae.
Body subcylindrical, abdomen but slightly dilated. Unguis (pl. 6,
figs. 62, 63) simple, without lateral or inner teeth. Unguiculus
extending half as far as the unguis (first pair) or almost two-thirds
as far (third pair), lanceolate, untoothed. Tenent hairs absent.
Fourth, fifth, and sixth abdominal segments ankylosed dorsally;
either without sutures or, in some instances, with a suture between
the fourth and fifth. Anus ventrocaudal. Furcula appended to
the fourth abdominal segment, short, extending not quite to the
posterior edge of the second abdominal segment Manubrium stout,
longer than dentes. Manubrium:dens·mucro about as $48:37:10$.
Dens (pl. 6, fig. 64) stout, with a few minute dorsal crenulations
near the middle, and a long erect dorsal proximal seta. Between
the bases of the dens are two pairs of strong chitinous hooks (pl. 6,
figs. 64, 65). Mucro (pl. 6, fig. 66) three-fifths as long as hind
unguis, bidentate; apical tooth slightly hooked; anteapical tooth
usually larger than the first tooth, suberect or feebly hooked. Rami
of tenaculum quadridentate; corpus with a single stout curving seta.
Clothing (pl. 6, fig 67) of dense short stiff simple setae, absent on
the anterior and posterior parts of most of the body segments.
Sensory setae long, outstanding, simple. Length, 1.3 mm.

Remarks—All the specimens that I have seen have been white,
with little pigment at most, though Linnaniemi (1912) mentions also

dull grayish forms with the pigment distributed as in *quadrioculata*. According to him the dentes vary in length from somewhat shorter to somewhat longer than the manubrium.

In two individuals taken in colonies of *diplophthalma* (Homer, Ill., March 31, April 13), the eyes were absent; no ocular pigment was present, and I could distinguish no corneae.

F. diplophthalma is almost exactly like *quadrioculata*, the essential difference between the two species being in respect to the number of eyes. If traces of posterior eyes were present, *diplophthalma* should be regarded as a variety of *quadrioculata*, but neither Linnaniemi (1912, p 114) nor I have seen any clear evidence of such eyes. As further evidence of the distinctness of the two species Linnaniemi observes that the olfactory setae of the fourth antennal segment in *diplophthalma* (as many as eight of which may be present) are clearly differentiated; while in *quadrioculata* they are difficult to distinguish from ordinary setae.

Though *diplophthalma* has been found in company with *quadrioculata*, it occurs also alone. In one locality where I have several times taken *diplophthalma* in abundance, I have not been able to find *quadrioculata*.

F. diplophthalma is found on the ground under wood or dead leaves and in moss. I have taken hundreds of specimens in Illinois under damp logs and damp dead leaves in swampy places.

Distribution.—European authors have reported the species from Norway, Sweden, Finland, England, Russia, and Nova Zembla.

Illinois: Homer, March 24, 31, April 6, 7, 13, May 3.
Greenland: Saunders Island, June 15, M. C. Tanquary (American Museum of Natural History).

FOLSOMIA FIMETARIA (Linnaeus)

PLATE 7, FIGURES 68–79

Podura fimetaria LINNAEUS, 1758, p 609
Isotoma alba TULLBERG, 1871, p 152.—VON DALLA TORRE, 1895, p 9
Isotoma fimetaria TULLBERG, 1872, p. 48; 1876, p. 37.—UZEL, 1890, p. 66.—
    MacGILLIVRAY, 1891, p. 273; 1896, p. 58.—SCHOTT, 1894, p. 75; 1896a, p.
    184, 1902, p. 21.—REUTER, 1895, p. 28.—LIE-PETTERSEN, 1896, p. 18;
    1898, p 13.—MEINERT, 1896, p 169.—SCHÄFFER, 1896, p. 183; 1900a, p.
    217.—POPPE and SCHAFFER, 1897, p. 268.—SCHERBAKOV, 1898a, p. 58;
    1898b, p 12; 1899a, p. 47; 1899b, p. 5.—CARL, 1899, p. 310.—CARPENTER
    and EVANS, 1899, p. 251.—ABSOLON, 1900a, p. 29.—CARPENTER, 1900, p.
    274.—BÖRNER, 1901a, p. 46; 1903, p. 171.—EVANS, 1901b, p. 153; 1908,
    p. 197.—FOLSOM, 1902a, p. 92; 1902b, p. 364.—KRAUSBAUER, 1902, p.
    68.—ÅGREN, 1903, p 143; 1904, p. 21.—GUTHRIE, 1903, p 64.—AXELSON,
    1906, p 11
Isotoma manubriata MacGILLIVRAY, 1896, p 49
Isotoma fimentaria WAHLGREN, 1900a, p. 356; 1906a, p. 223; 1906b, p. 255.
Folsomia candida WILLEM, 1902b, p 280
Isotoma (Folsomia) fimetaria BÖRNER, 1903, p 171.—AXELSON, 1905b, p. 29.

Folsomia fimetaria LINNANIEMI (AXELSON), 1907, p. 21; 1911, p. 14; 1912, p. 114 —COLLINGE, 1910, p. 9.—COLLINGE and SHOEBOTHAM, 1910, p. 109.— SHOEBOTHAM, 1914, p 62; 1917, p. 221 —BARTHOLIN, 1916, p. 168.—BROWN, 1918, p 186—DENIS, 1921, p. 125; 1922a, p. 111.—STACH, 1921, p. 125.— HANDSCHIN, 1924a, p 110; 1924b, p. 85; 1926, p 130; 1929, p. 58.—WOMERS-LEY, 1924a, p 32; 1927, p. 376—FOLSOM, 1927, p. 6 —REMY, 1928, p. 66.
Folsomia fimentaria WAHLGREN, 1919, p. 750

Description.—White, slender. Eyes and ocular pigment absent. Postantennal organs (pl. 7, figs. 68–71) narrowly elliptical to sub-reniform, occasionally oval or ovate, typically half as long as the basal width of the first antennal segment, but in some individuals considerably longer. Antennal base well developed. Antennae longer than the head, with segments in relative lengths about as 3:9:8:14 or 3 7·6.9. Second antennal segment subclavate or cylindrical; third clavate, fourth elliptical to subcylindrical. Sense organ of third antennal segment (pl. 7, fig. 72) with a pair of subreniform or subclavate sense rods, subtended by a chitinous ridge. Fourth antennal segment with terminal tubercle, subapical papilla, and several long pointed olfactory setae. Unguis (pl. 7, fig. 73) slender, slightly curving, untoothed. Unguiculus about half as long as unguis, broadly lanceolate, acuminate, untoothed. Hind claws larger than the others. Tenent hairs absent. Last three abdominal segments ankylosed (pl. 7, figs. 74, 75), without dorsal sutures. Abdomen rounded posteriorly. Anus ventrocaudal. Furcula appended to the fourth abdominal segment, extending to the posterior border of the first abdominal segment or only to that of the second. Manubrium with many ventral setae in adults but only two pairs (distal) in the young. Dentes almost or quite twice as long as the manubrium, gradually tapering, with very many dorsal crenulations except on the proximal third. Mucrones subequal in length to hind unguiculi, bidentate (pl. 7, figs. 76, 77); apical tooth feebly curving; second tooth subequal to, or larger than the first, conical, erect. Rami of tenaculum (pl. 7, fig. 78) quadridentate; corpus with a single stout ventral seta. Clothing (pl. 7, fig. 79) of dense short setae, absent in the intersegmental regions. Long stiff simple sensory setae occur in a transverse row of six across the middle of abdominal segments one to three, inclusive; about 16 such setae, much longer, however, are present on the ankylosed last three abdominal segments; and similar long outstanding setae occur also on the posterior border of the head, mesonotum, and metanotum, on the anterior border of the mesonotum, and sparingly on the legs. Maximum length, 2 mm.

Variation.—The postantennal organs vary considerably in form and size, as indicated in plate 7, figures 68 to 71; both European and North American specimens varying in these respects. In specimens from Massachusetts and New Jersey (pl. 7, fig. 70), the length of the postantennal organ is one-half to three-fifths the width of the base of the first antennal segment, while in many examples from Illinois (pl. 7, fig. 71) it almost or quite equals the basal width of that segment.

In both Europe and North America the mucrones are somewhat variable in length and slenderness (pl. 7, figs. 76, 77).

In small individuals the antennae are shorter than the head; in large specimens they are longer than the head. The antennal segments vary greatly in relative as well as absolute lengths, according to the size of the individual, and become more nearly cylindrical with age.

Rarely, the unguis bears an inner tooth.

In some individuals an obsolete dorsal suture between the fourth and fifth abdominal segments can be distinguished.

Some of the largest individuals have two setae on the tenaculum, one in front of the other.

In specimens from Washington, D. C. (Folsom, 1902b), the postantennal organs were ovate or oval, and the dentes were two and one-half times as long as the manubrium.

Specimens from Alaska (Folsom, 1902a) had somewhat shorter antennae and stouter claws than those from Massachusetts.

According to Börner (1901), European examples sometimes vary to yellowish, and rarely show a little blackish pigment.

Determination.—Massachusetts specimens of this species agree in every essential with European examples, as Doctor Schaffer and I found, through an exchange of material, many years ago. Some European writers describe the postantennal organ as being long and narrow, but my European specimens show all variations from long and narrow to short and broad. The sensory rods of the third antennal segment are slenderer in European than in North American examples of the species.

Synonymy.—MacGillivray's (1896) description of *I. manubriata* applies evidently to *fimetaria*, and a cotype of *manubriata* that he gave me proved to be a small individual of *fimetaria*.

Schött (1896) was inclined to regard Packard's *nivalis* as this species. Such is not the case, however, as I found by an examination of Packard's cotypes.

Habitat.—*Folsomia fimetaria* belongs to the fauna of the soil and is one of our commonest species, being found among the roots of plants, under damp wood, stones, or bark, in moss, and not infrequently on well water. It occurs often in flowerpots in dwelling houses or greenhouses, having been brought in with the soil; and has been found in caverns and in graves.

Distribution.—In northern and middle Europe *F. fimetaria* is one of the commonest and best known of collembolans. It is known also from Siberia, Spitsbergen, Franz Josef Land, Greenland, Mexico, and Guatemala.

Maine: Waterville, October 6, C. W. Dunning.

Massachusetts· Cambridge, March 15, in a greenhouse, April 21, 24, May 7 (indoors in flowerpots on these dates), June 5. Longmeadow, December 3, L. R. Arneluxen.

New York: Ithaca, March 3, in a milk waste filter, J. G. Needham. New York City, May 17, in a flowerpot, Miss Mabel Minton.

New Jersey: New Brunswick, February 9, breeding abundantly in husks of English walnuts, A. Peterson.

District of Columbia: Washington, from graves, M. G. Motter (U. S. National Museum).

Ohio: Yellow Springs, April 15, in a flower pot.

Michigan: Holland, May 31, W. W. Wood.

Illinois: Bloomington, March 31, in a cistern, Mary B. King. Chicago, September, C. A. Hart. Homer, March 14, 25, 31, April 2, 3, 5, 6, 7, 9, 11, 13, 16, 18, 23, 25, 27, May 12, 13, 16, October 15. Urbana, January 30, March 11, 14.

Iowa: Ames, March 25, J. E. Guthrie.

Kansas: Manhattan, May 14, P. S. Welch.

Louisiana: Baton Rouge, H. A. Morgan (Cornell University). March 27, in cane trash, C. L. Stracener.

Minnesota: J. E. Guthrie (University of Minnesota).

California: San Francisco, G. Eisen (California Academy of Sciences).

Alaska: Sitka, June, T. Kincaid (U S. National Museum).

FOLSOMIA FIMETARIA (Linnaeus) variety CALDARIA (Axelson)

PLATE 8, FIGURE 80

Isotoma fimetaria var. *caldaria* AXELSON, 1905a, p. 790.
Isotoma (Folsomia) fimetaria var. *caldaria* AXELSON, 1905b, p. 29.
Folsomia fimetaria var. *caldaria* LINNANIEMI (AXELSON), 1912, p. 116.—STACH, 1921, p 160.—WOMERSLEY, 1924a, p. 32.

Description.—Clothing long. The long erect sensory setae, which may be three-fourths as long as the segments that bear them, are distally feebly feathered on one side. Antennae evidently longer than the head (as 8:7); fourth segment at least twice as long as the third, slender, subcylindrical. The furcula extends almost to the ventral tube, and always as far as the first abdominal segment. Dentes up to two and one-half times as long as manubrium. Maximum length, 3 mm. Intergrades with typical *fimetaria*. Finland, in dwelling houses and hothouses; under flowerpots (Linnaniemi).

Remarks.—Stach (1921) described from Poland a variety intermediate between *caldaria* and *fimetaria* proper, and noted the presence of a strong or weak tooth on the inner margin of the unguis, near the middle.

From Ithaca, N. Y., I received seven specimens, which agree with Linnaniemi's diagnosis but have a strong inner tooth on the unguis (pl. 8, fig. 80).

This variety *caldaria* differs in several respects from the variety *dentata* Folsom (1927).

Distribution.—Recorded as follows:

New York: Ithaca, November 5, working in decayed tissue due to work of a tortricid larva near bases of stems of *Impatiens pallida*, Mrs. L. A. Hausman.

FOLSOMIA NIVALIS (Packard)

PLATE 8, FIGURES 81–88

Isotoma nivalis PACKARD, 1873, p. 31.—MACGILLIVRAY, 1891, p 273; 1896, p 53.—VON DALLA TORRE, 1895, p 10

Description.—White throughout; a slender species Eyes absent. Postantennal organs (pl. 8, figs. 81, 82) long and narrow, about nine times as long as broad, four-fifths as long as the basal width of the first antennal segment, straight or slightly curving, with usually a minute notch at the middle of the anterior margin Antennal base well developed. Antennae as long as, or slightly longer than, the head (about as 31·29) with segments in relative lengths about as 5:7.6:10 or 8:12:11:22. Sense organ of third antennal segment (pl 8, fig. 83) with a pair of subclavate rods subtended by a thick chitinous ridge. Fourth antennal segment with slender olfactory setae. Unguis (pl. 8, fig. 84) long, slender, curving, unidentate near the middle of the inner margin; lateral teeth absent Unguiculus one-third (first pair of feet) to one-half (second and third pair) as long as unguis, broadly lanceolate, acuminate, untoothed. Tenent hairs absent. Last three abdominal segments ankylosed. Anus ventrocaudal. Furcula appended to the fourth abdominal segment, and extending to the middle of the second. Dentes one and one-half times as long as manubrium, slender, crenulate dorsally, the crenulations absent on the distal fifth. Mucrones a little longer than hind unguiculi, bidentate (pl. 8, figs. 85–88); apical tooth sub-horizontal or slightly hooked; second tooth erect or suberect, conical, stouter and usually longer than the apical tooth. Tenaculum quadridentate, with one stout ventral seta General clothing of short curving simple setae. Long stiff simple sensory setae occur in a transverse row across the middle of the first three abdominal segments, and numerously on the ankylosed segments. Usual length, 1 mm; maximum, 1.7 mm

The tooth of the unguis, usually strong, is sometimes reduced or absent. The apical tooth of the mucro is reduced occasionally; the anteapical tooth rarely (pl. 8, figs. 87, 88).

Remarks—The foregoing description is based on six of Packard's cotypes from Brunswick, Maine, supplemented by an abundance of specimens collected at Orono, Maine, by Prof. F. L. Harvey.

The specimens from Salem, Mass., referred to by Packard (1873) were missing from the collection in the Museum of Comparative Zoology.

Folsomia nivalis is closely related to *F. fimetaria*, from which it is distinguished chiefly by the long narrow postantennal organs, the tooth of the unguis, and the shorter dentes.

Distribution.—Recorded as follows:

Maine: Brunswick, September 10, under bark, common, A. S. Packard (Museum of Comparative Zoology). Orono, January, several hundred in a cellar in decaying beets; May, F. L. Harvey. April, Edith M. Patch (J. E. Guthrie).

New York: New York City, July, F. Silvestri.

Genus GUTHRIELLA Börner

Isotoma GUTHRIE, 1903, p. 72.
Guthriella BÖRNER, 1906, p. 172.

Genotype—Isotoma muskegis Guthrie.

Body and appendages robust. Body segments bulging, with deep intersegmental constrictions. Sclerites weakly chitinized, not sharply demarcated from one another. Tergites not imbricate; without well-developed intersegmental membranes. Prothorax not greatly reduced, pigmented and tuberculate, not membranous. Abdominal segments without ankylosis. Fourth abdominal tergite longer than the third. Third urotergite simple in form; the ventrolateral region not prolonged posteriorly. Anus not directed ventrally. Eyes 16 (in the three known species). Postantennal organs present, simple. Fourth antennal segment with olfactory setae and a terminal hemispherical sensory tubercle. Tibiotarsus with a distal subsegment. Unguis without lateral teeth. Unguiculus with a pair of inner lamellae. Tenent hairs present or absent. Ventral tube with a pair of rounded vesicles. Furcula long. Manubrium naked ventrally. Dentes stout, subcylindrical, not tapering. Mucrones bidentate, with equal inner and outer dorsal lamellae. Clothing of short equal curving simple setae; long sensory setae absent. Pigment dark blue (in the known species). Integument tuberculate.

The male of the species *muskegis* exhibits secondary sexual dimorphism.

On each side of the base of the furcula, between the fourth and fifth urotergites, there is an accessory sclerite (pl. 9, fig. 89), rounded ventrally, pigmented, and tuberculate. This sclerite occurs in all three species of this genus and in a few other generalized species of Isotomidae, but it is absent in the more specialized forms.

KEY TO SPECIES OF GUTHRIELLA

1. Furcula extending to the ventral tube. Unguis with an inner tooth. Postantennal organ with a notch in the middle of the anterior margin _____ muskegis (p. 36)
   Furcula not extending to the ventral tube. Unguis untoothed. Postantennal organ without a notch in the anterior margin_____2

2. Tenent hairs absent. Manubrium longer than dentes. Dentes
   rounded apically. Ventral margin of mucro not strongly
   curving, in lateral aspect_____ **antiqua** (p. 34)
   Tenent hairs present. Manubrium equal to, or shorter than,
   the dentes. Dentes not rounded apically. Ventral margin
   of mucro strongly curving_____ **vetusta** (p. 35)

GUTHRIELLA ANTIQUA, new species

PLATE 9, FIGURES 89–99

Description.—Dark blue, with bulging segments (pl. 9, fig. 89), the intersegmental constrictions being deeper than in other Isotomidae, except *G. muskegis*. Body stout. Antennae blue; legs white distally, pigmented basally; manubrium pigmented; dentes usually white. Eyes (pl. 9, fig. 90) eight on each side, on black patches. Postantennal organ (pl. 9, fig. 90) elliptical, one and one-half to three times as long as the diameter of an adjacent eye. Antennae subequal to head or a little shorter (as 7:8); segments in relative lengths about as 8:12:13:19. Sense organ of third antennal segment (pl. 9, fig. 91) with a pair of curving rods subtended by a thick ridge, and with two linear curving rodlike accessory setae. Fourth antennal segment with many olfactory setae (as many as 16) and an apical hemispherical sensory tubercle. Pronotum with folds, tuberculate, not membranous. Terga not imbricate. Abdominal segments without ankylosis; abdomen dilated. Fourth abdominal segment longer than the third (as 3·2). Tibiotarsus with a distal subsegment. Unguis (pl. 9, fig. 92) slender, without lateral or inner teeth. Unguiculus (pl. 9, fig. 93) extending two-fifths to three-fifths as far as the unguis, broadly lanceolate, acute, untoothed, with two inner lamellae. Tenent hairs absent. Furcula appended to the fifth abdominal segment, extending not quite to the ventral tube. Manubrium stout, but not swollen basally, with several dorsal setae but naked ventrally, with a pair of ventral subapical hooks and a pair of ventroapical paramedian teeth (pl. 9, fig. 94). Dentes (pl. 9, fig. 95) shorter than manubrium (as 5:6 or 5:7), stout, subcylindrical, not bowed or convergent, not tapering, apically rounded, with few dorsal setae, with stiff ventral and lateral setae on distal half, dorsally without transverse folds, but with numerous low tubercles, larger than the other cuticular tubercles. Mucro (pl. 9, figs. 96–98) one-third as long as dens, bidentate, bilamellate; apical tooth short, upcurved; anteapical tooth median dorsal; the outer and inner lamellae extend from the anteapical tooth to the base of the mucro. Rami of tenaculum quadridentate; corpus with a single curving ventral seta. Clothing of abundant minute curving setae (pl. 9, fig. 99) with a few setae longer than the others on the anal segment; long erect sensory setae absent. Integument finely tuberculate. Length, 0.9 mm.

Remarks.—In this species the achorutoid (see pp. 4–5) characters of the genus *Guthriella* are especially pronounced.

G. antiqua occurred in great abundance in a depression in a creek bed where the water had dried up.

Cotypes.—U.S.N.M. no. 42995.

Distribution.—Recorded as follows:

Missouri. Mountain Grove, March 29, E. P. Taylor.

GUTHRIELLA VETUSTA, new species

PLATE 10, FIGURES 100–106

Description.—General color blackish blue; head and body with close minute round pale spots and larger pale spots, rounded or elongate. Pigment deep blue; antennae blue; praecoxae and coxae dark blue; remaining leg segments more or less strongly pigmented; manubrium blue; dentes unpigmented, yellow in alcohol, possibly whitish in life. Prothorax heavily pigmented, tuberculate. Body and appendages stout. Body segments strongly bulging, with deep intersegmental constrictions. Eyes (pl. 10, fig. 100) on black patches, eight on each side, the two inner proximal eyes much smaller than the others. Postantennal organ (pl. 10, fig. 100) remote from eyes, near base of antenna, elliptical, one and one-half times as long as the diameter of an adjacent eye. Antennae shorter than the head (as 7:8) or subequal to it, with segments in relative lengths about as 10·17·15·25. First antennal segment cylindrical, second subclavate, third clavate, fourth elliptical. Sense organ of third antennal segment (pl. 10, fig. 101) with a pair of free subcylindrical rods and three guard setae. Fourth antennal segment with short stout curving olfactory pegs. Abdominal segments without ankylosis; fourth segment longer than the third (as 3:2). Tibiotarsus with a distal subsegment. Unguis (pl. 10, fig. 102) slender, not strongly curving, without lateral or inner teeth. Unguiculus extending two-thirds as far as the unguis on the hind feet; one-half as far on the other feet; sublanceolate, acuminate, untoothed, with a pair of inner lamellae. Tenent hairs two or three, as long as ungues. Furcula appended to the fifth abdominal segment, extending not quite to the second. Manubrium short and stout, naked ventrally, with a few stiff setae dorsally, and with a pair of subapical hooks. Dentes (pl. 10, fig. 103) longer than manubrium (as 3·2) or subequal to it, subcylindrical, narrowing but slightly, not rounded apically, with only the usual cuticular tubercles dorsally, with 9 or 10 dorsal setae, and naked ventrally. Mucrones (pl. 10, figs. 104, 105) one-fifth to one-fourth as long as dentes, bidentate, bilamellate, both teeth erect, the apical tooth being the smaller; lamellae equal, extending on each side from the anteapical tooth to the base of the mucro. Rami of tenaculum quadridentate; corpus with two anterior setae. General clothing of short curving setae of uniform length (pl. 10, fig. 106), on the middle regions of the body segments; long outstanding setae absent. Integument tuberculate. Length, 1.2 mm.

Cotypes.—U.S.N.M. no. 42996.

Distribution.—Recorded as follows:

California· Palo Alto, V. L. Kellogg and L. Bremner.

GUTHRIELLA MUSKEGIS (Guthrie)

PLATE 11, FIGURES 107–112; PLATE 12, FIGURES 113–119

Isotoma muskegis GUTHRIE, 1903, p. 72.
Guthriella muskegis BÖRNER, 1906, p. 172.

Description.—A robust species (pl. 11, figs. 107, 108). Blue-black, with small pigmentless spots dorsally. Tergites often edged posteriorly with blackish. Tubercles and abdominal horns of the male "light yellowish brown, giving to the body a yellow, floured appearance to the naked eye." Antennae dark blue; legs pale, mottled with blue, with dark coxae; manubrium pigmented; dentes white or slightly pigmented. Eyes eight on each side, subequal, on black patches. Postantennal organ (pl. 11, fig. 109) subelliptical, about as long as the diameter of an eye, with a deep notch at the middle of the anterior margin, and situated in a shallow groove at the base of the antenna. Antennae about one and one-half times as long as the head; first and second segments subcylindrical; third subclavate; fourth subelliptical or subclavate. Sense organ of third antennal segment with two linear feebly curving rods. Tibiotarsus with a distal subsegment (pl. 11, fig. 110). Unguis (pl. 11, fig. 110) slender, without lateral teeth, strongly unidentate near the middle of the inner margin. Unguiculus extending one-half to three-fifths as far as the unguis, longest on the hind feet, sublanceolate, acute or acuminate, untoothed, with a pair of inner lamellae. Tenent hairs 2 or 3; commonly 2, 3, 3. Abdominal segments without ankylosis. Furcula appended to the fifth abdominal segment, extending to the ventral tube, stout. Manubrium naked ventrally, with a pair of subapical hooks as in *antiqua.* Dentes one-fifth longer than manubrium, bowed (pl. 11, figs. 107, 108), convergent, not tapering, without dorsal crenulations, with only the fine primary cuticular tubercles, and with a few setae dorsally and ventrally, the latter on the distal half. Mucrones (pl. 11, figs. 111, 112; pl. 12, figs. 113, 114) as long as hind ungues, bidentate, bilamellate; apical tooth hooked; outer and inner lamellae similar, extending from the base of the mucro to the anteapical tooth. Rami of tenaculum quadridentate; corpus bisetose. Long erect sensory setae absent. Integument finely tuberculate. Length, 2.5 mm.

Female: Body segments relatively simple, not laterally dilated (pl. 11, fig. 107). Antennal segments in relative lengths about as 4.9:6.10. Fourth antennal segment with long strongly curving olfactory setae distally. Body segments in relative lengths as 9:19:21:20.18 20.24:12 6; fourth abdominal segment thus one-fifth longer than the third. Clothing of numerous short curving simple setae (pl. 12, fig. 115) with larger fringed setae across the posterior region of segments 2 to 7, inclusive. Setae of appendages simple.

In two females the lamellae of the mucrones showed lateral ribs (pl. 12, fig. 113), not visible, however, in specimens mounted in balsam.

Male: Body segments 2 to 7, inclusive, laterally dilated (pl. 11, fig. 108), particularly the fourth abdominal segment, of which each lateral dilatation bears a stout curving horn (pl 11, fig. 108; pl. 12, fig. 116) and several clavate fringed tubercles (pl 12, fig. 117). Segments 2 to 6, inclusive, have each a posterior row of large clavate fringed tubercles, and bear abundant small subclavate fringed setae. The fifth and sixth abdominal segments and the posterior part of the fourth have numerous small capitate setae (pl. 12, fig 118) Few of the body setae are simple, except on the genital and anal segments, though many simple setae occur on head, antennae, and legs. A few clavate fringed setae are present on the legs and the first two antennal segments, and antennae and tibiotarsi bear a few tubercles. In the male there is a long seta on each side of the prothorax (pl. 11, fig. 108). Antennal segments in relative lengths about as 3:6:4:8. Fourth antennal segment with stout lateral olfactory setae (pl. 11, fig. 119). Fourth abdominal segment but slightly longer than the third (as 16:15). Anal segment small, almost concealed from above by the genital segment.

Remarks.—*Guthriella muskegis* exhibits secondary sexual dimorphism to an extent that is unapproached in other known species of Collembola.

"* * * There seems no doubt that the tubercles are merely modified hairs, for one finds on the same individual nearly all gradations from the thick, stout hair with a very few short hairs at its end to the much swollen tubercles with their haired areas greatly distended" (Guthrie).

"I found this species twice during the summer of 1901 in marshes along the shore of Lake Vermillion, on Pine Island in St. Louis Co. (Minn). On both occasions they were on the upper ends of partially submerged roots, or other decaying pieces of wood. They seem to live socially, hundreds being seen together. They resemble the heavier species of *Achorutes* in habits, being rather slow in their movements. When exposed to the light, they become restless, and move about uneasily seeking for dark corners Unless considerably disturbed they prefer not to jump, and are not particularly strong leapers when they do" (Guthrie).

Through the courtesy of Profs H F. Nachtrieb and J. E. Guthrie I obtained for study 14 cotypes of this interesting species In addition, I examined several specimens from the Cornell University collection and others that were given to me by Professor Guthrie

Distribution.—Recorded as follows

Minnesota: St. Louis County, July 13. 1901, J E Guthrie (University of Minnesota).

Genus PROISOTOMA Borner

Isotoma TULLBERG, 1871, p. 150.
Proisotoma BORNER, 1901a, p. 134; 1903, p 171; 1906, p 172 —LINNANIEMI, 1912, p. 121.

Genotype.—Isotoma minuta Tullberg.

Fourth abdominal segment almost always longer than the third; the two subequal, however, in a few species. Third urotergite not ventrolaterally prolonged backward to any material degree Paratergite of fourth abdominal segment distinct, not united to the tergite of the genital segment. Genital and anal segments sometimes ankylosed. Furcula not attaining the ventral tube in most of the species Manubrium often longer than the dentes, rarely with many ventral setae, naked ventrally in a few species, but usually with one subapical pair of ventral setae, rarely two or three pairs Dentes usually stout, with relatively few coarse transverse dorsal folds, but smooth or with dorsal lobes or coarse tubercles in a few species The dentes when slender and tapering are longer than the manubrium and have many fine dorsal crenulations. Mucrones commonly bidentate or tridentate, lamellate in some of the species. Tibiotarsus often with a distal subsegment. Unguiculus often with a pair of inner lamellae. Tenent hairs present or absent. Postantennal organ often with a notch in the middle of the anterior margin or notched on both sides. Clothing of simple setae, usually very short. Integument almost always smooth, but tuberculate or reticulate in a few species.

KEY TO SUBGENERA OF PROISOTOMA

1. Dentes stout, dorsally smooth or with rounded lobes, never with
    transverse folds. Manubrium naked ventrally. Mucrones
    lamellate, bidentate. Tibiotarsus with a distal subsegment
    Unguiculus with a pair of inner lamellae_____**Ballistura** (p 39)
   Dentes dorsally with few or many transverse folds, or crenulations, with rare exceptions. Manubrium with ventral setae,
    usually few and subapical in position. Mucrones usually not
    lamellate. Tibiotarsus rarely with a distal subsegment. Unguiculus rarely with a pair of inner lamellae_____**Proisotoma** (p. 43)

Subgenus BALLISTURA Börner

Ballistura BÖRNER, 1906, p. 172.

Subgenotype.—Isotoma schötti Dalla Torre.

KEY TO SPECIES OF SUBGENUS BALLISTURA

1. Dentes dorsally smooth. Eyes 16_____2
   Dentes with dorsal lobes   Eyes 12.   Tenent hairs absent   Un-
      guiculus with an apical filament_____3
2. Dentes rounded apically.   Tenent hairs absent.   Postantennal
      organ slightly longer than the diameter of an adjacent eye.   Un-
      guiculus subulate apically.   Dark violet, bluish, reddish, or
      brownish_____schötti (p. 39)
   Dentes not rounded apically.   Tenent hairs present.   Post-
      antennal organ three times as long as the diameter of an ad-
      jacent eye.   Unguiculus not subulate.   Bluish or grayish___ewingi (p. 40)
3. Dentes with several dorsal lobes.   Fourth abdominal segment
      more than twice as long as the third.   Antennae telescopic.
      Apical filament of unguiculus short.   Yellowish; the body
      segments bordered posteriorly with blackish_____excavata (p. 41)
   Dentes with about 10 dorsal lobes.   Fourth abdominal segment
      less than twice as long as the third.   Antennae not telescopic.
      Apical filament of unguiculus long, extending as far as the
      unguis.   Olive-green_____laticauda (p. 42)

PROISOTOMA (BALLISTURA) SCHÖTTI (Dalla Torre)

PLATE 12, FIGURES 120–125

Isotoma litoralis SCHÖTT, 1894, p. 75.—REUTER, 1895, p. 29.
Isotoma schöttii VON DALLA TORRE, 1895, p. 10.—CARPENTER, 1900, p. 277.
Isotoma schotti SCHÄFFER, 1896, p. 183; 1900a, p. 248.—POPPE and SCHAFFER, 1897,
      p. 267.—CARPENTER and EVANS, 1899, p. 252.—SKORIKOW, 1900, p. 196.—
      BÖRNER, 1901a, p. 43.—CARL, 1901, p. 259.—SCHÖTT, 1902, p 21.—ÅGREN,
      1903, p. 131.—WAHLGREN, 1906b, p. 254.
Isotoma lacustris SCHÖTT, 1896a, p. 185.
Proisotoma schotti LINNANIEMI (AXELSON), 1907, p. 64; 1912, p. 123.—COLLINGE
      and SHOEBOTHAM, 1910, p. 109.—HANDSCHIN, 1919, p. 76; 1924a, p.
      111; 1929, p. 60.—WAHLGREN, 1920, p 8.—CARPENTER and PHILLIPS,
      1922, p. 18.—DENIS, 1924b, p. 228.

Description.—Color variable; commonly dark violet or dark blue;
sometimes more or less reddish or brownish; intersegmental regions
appearing as pale bands.   Antennal segments blue apically or blue
throughout; legs unpigmented beyond coxae; furcula unpigmented;
prothorax pigmented.   Body short and stout.   Eye spots half-moon
shaped, more posterior than is usual in the genus.   Eyes eight on
each side, equal.   Postantennal organ broadly elliptical, slightly
longer than the diameter of an eye, situated far from the eyes and
close to the antennal base.   Antennae a little shorter than the head,
with segments in relative lengths about as 4:7:8:10.   Sense organ
of third antennal segment with two curving rods protected by an
integumentary fold.   Special olfactory setae absent on the fourth

antennal segment. Fourth abdominal segment longer than the third (as 3:2). Genital and anal segments not ankylosed. Tibiotarsus with a distal subsegment. Unguis (pl. 12, figs. 120, 121) slender, curving, without lateral or inner teeth. Unguiculus scarcely more than one-third as long as the unguis, subulate apically, with a pair of rounded inner lamellae, untoothed. Tenent hairs absent. Furcula extending to the ventral tube. Manubrium equal to dentes in length, with numerous dorsal setae but naked ventrally. Dentes stout, not narrowing distally, rounded apically, without dorsal tubercles or folds, with many dorsal and ventral setae. Mucro (pl. 12, figs. 122–124) stout, somewhat longer than hind unguiculus, in lateral aspect strongly rounded ventrally, bidentate, with equal outer and inner lamellae. Rami of tenaculum tridentate; corpus with one seta. Clothing (pl. 12, fig. 125) of dense short equal simple setae, a little longer on the posterior part of the abdomen. Long erect sensory setae absent. Integument smooth but minutely pseudo-granulate. Length, 2 mm.

Remarks.—This active species is found usually on or near water. It occurs on the seashore under seaweed, stones, or débris, and inland on the surface of water or on damp soil.

Distribution.—*P. schötti* has been recorded from Sweden, Spitsbergen, Finland, Germany, France, Switzerland, Rumania, Great Britain, Tripoli, and French Guiana.

New York: Lakeville, November 13, under board on lake shore, E. A. Maynard.
California: Vicinity of Lake Chabot, G. Eisen (California Academy of Sciences).

PROISOTOMA (BALLISTURA) EWINGI, new species

PLATE 13, FIGURES 126–130

Description.—Body stout. Bluish or grayish, with white intersegmental bands. Pigment mottled dark blue, in the form of rounded granules, frequently surrounding hypodermal nuclei, which then appear as pale rounded spots. Sternum pale. Antennae spotted with blue. Legs unpigmented beyond the coxae. Furcula unpigmented. Pronotum pigmented. Eyes (pl. 13, fig. 126) eight on each side, equal. Ocular patch more elongate than is usual in the subgenus. Postantennal organ (pl. 13, fig. 126) broadly elliptical, almost three times as long as the diameter of an adjacent eye. Antennae slightly shorter than the head (about as 23:26), with segments in relative lengths about as 8·9·10:18; first segment cylindrical; second and third subclavate; fourth elliptical. Sense organ of third antennal segment with a pair of subcylindrical pegs, freely exposed, and with three guard setae. Fourth antennal segment with numerous curving olfactory setae. Third abdominal segment shorter than the fourth (as 5:6 or 5:7). Genital and anal segments not ankylosed. Anus directed ventroposteriorly. Tibiotarsus with a distal subsegment. Unguis (pl. 13, fig. 127) unusually stout, without lateral or inner teeth. Unguiculus extending three-fifths as far as the unguis, broadly lanceolate, acute, untoothed, with a pair of inner lamellae. Tenent hairs short; 2,2,2, or 3,3,3. Furcula appended apparently to the fifth abdominal segment, short, extending only as far as the second abdominal segment. Manubrium longer than dentes (as 5·4), stout, with short curving dorsal setae, but naked ventrally. Dentes (pl. 13, fig. 128) subcylindrical, narrowing but slightly, smooth dorsally, without dorsal tubercles or folds, with short curving dorsal setae and a few stiff ventral setae. Mucrones (pl. 13, fig. 128) almost one-half as long as dentes, bidentate, with outer and inner lamellae well developed, similar and equal; apical and anteapical teeth approximate, subequal, directed dorsally; ventral contour of mucro not strongly rounded, in lateral aspect. Rami of tenaculum bidentate (pl. 13, fig. 129); corpus with a single stout curving anterior seta. Clothing (pl. 13, fig. 130) of minute curving equal setae, absent on the intersegmental regions, erect sensory setae absent. Integument smooth. Length, 1 mm.

Cotypes.—U.S.N.M. no. 42981.

Distribution.—Recorded as follows·

Mississippi: Vicksburg, October 2, in decaying leaves and twigs, Dr. Henry E. Ewing, for whom the species is named.

PROISOTOMA (BALLISTURA) EXCAVATA, new species

PLATE 13, FIGURES 131–136; PLATE 14, FIGURES 137, 138

Description.—A stout, compact species. Pale yellowish (in alcohol); body segments bordered posteriorly with narrow blackish bands; legs pale; dentes pale; manubrium pigmented. Head large; oral region strongly protuberant. A wide ∧-shaped marking extends forward from the eye spots (pl. 13, fig. 131), and on each side of this marking the head is excavate around the base of the antenna. Eyes (pl. 13, fig. 132) six on each side, on black patches, the two inner proximal eyes smaller than the others. Postantennal organ (pl. 13, fig. 132) ovate to elliptical, one-fourth to one-half longer than the diameter of the nearest eye. Antennae approximate, stout, with strongly telescopic segments (pl. 13, fig. 133), in relative lengths about as 9 13:18:38; basal segment immersed in a pit and ringed basally with pigment; second and third segments ringed apically; fourth pigmented throughout. Sense organ of third antennal segment (pl. 13, fig. 134) close to distal end of segment, with a pair of slender linear rods and two guard setae. Fourth antennal segment with slender curving olfactory setae. Prothorax relatively small, concealed under the head and mesonotum. Abdominal segments without ankylosis. Fourth abdominal segment two and one half times as long as the third. Tibiotarsus with a distal subsegment (pl. 13, fig. 135). Unguis (pl. 13, fig. 135) stout, untoothed. Unguiculus extending three-fourths as far as unguis, broadly lanceolate, setaceously prolonged apically, untoothed, with a pair of inner lamellae. Claws of first pair of feet smaller than the others. Tenent hairs absent. Furcula appended to the fifth abdominal segment, extending to the ventral tube. Manubrium stout, longer than dens (as 11:7), with many stiff dorsal setae and without ventral setae. Dentes (pl. 13, fig. 136) stout, not tapering, with many strong dorsal setae, with five long subapical setae, two of which are ventral, and with several large rounded dorsal tubercles. Mucro (pl. 13, fig. 136; pl. 14, fig. 137) not quite one-half so long as dentes, bidentate, with narrow inner and outer lamellae extending from the base of the mucro to the anteapical tooth. Rami of tenaculum quadridentate; corpus with one ventral seta (occasionally two, one above the other). Clothing (pl. 14, fig. 138) of dense simple setae, slightly longer toward the end of the abdomen; long erect sensory setae absent. Integument smooth. Maximum length, 1 mm.

Remarks —This species evidently may occur in enormous numbers. The type material, consisting of thousands of individuals, was in the collection of Prof. F. L. Harvey. It has been collected in Florida by P. H. Rolfs

Cotypes.—U.S.N.M. no. 42988.

PROISOTOMA (BALLISTURA) LATICAUDA, new species

PLATE 14, FIGURES 139–146

Description.—General color olive-green, the combined effect of dark blue mottlings and pale yellow spots. Body segments narrowly edged posteriorly with blackish. Head with dorsal yellow spots. Legs and furcula pigmented basally; antennae bluish. Body short and stout. Eyes (pl. 14, fig. 139) six on each side, the two inner proximal eyes much smaller than the others. Postantennal organ (pl. 14, fig. 139) subelliptical, twice as long as broad, two and one-half to three times as long as the diameter of an adjacent eye. Antennae subequal to head in length, with segments in relative lengths about as 8:10:13:26. Sense organ of third antennal segment as in plate 14, figure 140. Fourth antennal segment without special olfactory setae. Unguis (pl. 14, fig. 141) stout, curving, with inner margin strongly unidentate two-fifths from the apex. Unguiculus subovate, untoothed, apically produced as a fine filament extending in some specimens almost as far as the opposite claw; inner lamellae two. Hind claws the largest. Tenent hairs absent. Tibiotarsus with a distal subsegment. Third abdominal segment shorter than the fourth (as 5.8). Abdominal segments without ankylosis. Furcula appended to the fifth abdominal segment, just reaching the ventral tube. Manubrium longer than dentes (as 3:2 or 4:3), setigerous dorsally, naked ventrally. Dentes (pl. 14, fig. 142) stout, not rounded apically, subcylindrical, each with two dorsal longitudinal rows of large rounded lobes, about 10 in number; several curving dorsal setae are present, and six subapical setae arranged in a circle around the dens; ventral surface naked except for a pair of subapical setae. Mucro (pl. 14, figs 143, 144) one-third or one-half as long as dens, stout, bidentate, bilamellate; the two lamellae extending from the base of the mucro to the anteapical tooth, apical tooth small, upturned, anteapical tooth larger, suberect or slightly hooked. Rami of tenaculum (pl. 14, fig. 145) tridentate; corpus with one stout curving ventral seta General clothing (pl. 14, fig 146) of short dense curving simple setae, becoming a little longer toward the end of the abdomen. Long outstanding sensory setae apparently absent. Integument smooth. Length, 1 3 mm.

The apical filament of the unguiculus is long in some individuals and short in others.

Cotypes.—U.S.N.M. no. 42982.

Distribution.—Recorded as follows:

Massachusetts: Arlington, April 8, May 1, in an old pile of horse manure and under boards near by.

Subgenus PROISOTOMA Borner

Proisotoma BORNER, 1901a, p 134

Subgenotype.—Isotoma minuta Tullberg.

KEY TO SPECIES OF SUBGENUS PROISOTOMA

1. Dentes dorsally smooth or with tubercles. Furcula attaining the ventral tube. Third abdominal segment a little longer than the fourth or subequal to it. Unguiculus with a pair of inner lamellae. Tenent hairs absent_____2
   Dentes dorsally with transverse folds Furcula rarely attaining the ventral tube. Third abdominal segment shorter than the fourth_____4
2. Dentes subcylindrical, apically rounded, dorsally smooth, subequal to, or only slightly longer than, the manubrium. Manubrium with many ventral setae Mucrones complexly lamellate, 3-toothed. Third abdominal segment slightly longer than the fourth Purple to brown_____ **schafferi** (p 46)
   Dentes narrowing more or less, not rounded apically, dorsally coarsely tuberculate, much longer than manubrium_____3
3. Mucrones complexly lamellate, 5-toothed. Manubrium more than half as long as dentes, with three ventral subapical setae Third and fourth abdominal segments subequal in length. Olive-green_____ **rainieri** (p. 45)
   Mucrones not lamellate, 4- (or 5-) toothed. Manubrium half as long as dentes, with many ventral setae. Third abdominal segment longer than the fourth. Dark blue_____ **communa** (p. 48)
4. Dentes usually shorter than manubrium, the two rarely subequal, stout, with relatively few transverse dorsal folds (up to 10 or 12, rarely as many as 20), which are usually coarse. Mucro with three teeth (four in *bulbosa*), lamellate in only two species_____5

44   BULLETIN 168, UNITED STATES NATIONAL MUSEUM

Dentes longer than manubrium, slender and tapering, with a
great many fine transverse dorsal crenulations. Mucro bidentate, not lamellate. Postantennal organ usually notched
or constricted at the middle. Unguiculus without a pair
of inner lamellae. Integument smooth, not tuberculate or
reticulate_____13
5. Mucrones lamellate. Dentes with 15 to 20 coarse dorsal folds.
Unguiculus with a pair of inner lamellae Tenent hairs one
or two. Postantennal organ usually notched or constricted
at the middle. Eyes 16. Genital and anal segments usually
ankylosed_____ 6
Mucrones not lamellate. Dentes with rarely more than 10
dorsal folds Unguiculus without a pair of inner lamellae
Tenent hairs present or absent. Postantennal organ with
or without a notch. Furcula not attaining the ventral tube_____7
6. Furcula extending not quite to the ventral tube. Integument
reticulate. Antennae not telescopic. Dark purple_____titusi (p. 49)
Furcula attaining the ventral tube Integument not reticulate
Antennae telescopic. Dark purple_____longispina (p 50)
7. Dens with a lateral subapical bladderlike appendage. Manubrium with three or many ventral subapical setae. Tibiotarsus not subsegmented. One tenent hair. Postantennal
organ with an anterior notch (sometimes absent) Integument more or less tuberculate or reticulate_____8
Dens without a bladderlike appendage. Manubrium with one
pair or four pairs of ventral subapical setae. Integument
not tuberculate or reticulate (except in *obsoleta*)_____9
8. Mucro tridentate. Dens with about 8 to 10 dorsal folds.
Manubrium slightly longer than dentes, with three ventral
subapical setae. Dark blue_____vesiculata (p 57)
Mucro quadridentate. Dens with about 8 dorsal folds. Manubrium slightly shorter than dentes, or subequal to them,
with many ventral subapical setae. Dark blue_____bulbosa (p. 58)
9. Dentes subcylindrical or swollen, rounded apically_____10
Dentes not rounded apically_____11
10. Manubrium longer than dentes. Tenent hairs one or two.
Integument not reticulate. Dark purple_____brevipenna (p. 56)
Manubrium shorter than dentes. Tenent hairs absent. Integument reticulate. Dark violet_____obsoleta (p 56)
11. Eyes present. Manubrium with one pair of ventral subapical
setae_____12
Eyes absent Manubrium with four pairs of ventral subapical
setae. One tenent hair. White, with gray or black mottlings_frisoni (p 55)
12. Eyes 16. Tenent hairs one, two, or none. Dens typically with
five or six dorsal folds. Genital and anal segments not
ankylosed. Anus caudal. Grayish or bluish_____minuta (p. 51)
Eyes 10 (sometimes 8). Tenent hairs absent. Dens with 8 to 10
dorsal folds. Genital and anal segments ankylosed occa-
sionally_____sepulcralis (p 54)
13. Furcula not attaining the ventral tube Manubrium with one
pair or three pairs of ventral subapical setae_____14
Furcula attaining the ventral tube Manubrium with two
pairs of ventral subapical setae. Genital and anal segments
not ankylosed. One tenent hair. Bluish or greenish____immersa (p 63)

14. Manubrium with one pair of ventral subapical setae Genital
    and anal segments almost always ankylosed_____15
    Manubrium with three pairs of ventral subapical setae. Genital
    and anal segments not ankylosed One tenent hair. White,
    mottled with gray or black_____simplex (p. 61)
15. Eyes 16_____16
    Eyes 10. Tenent hairs absent. White_____decemoculata (p. 60)
16. Unguis with an inner tooth. Tibiotarsus with a distal subseg-
    ment_____17
    Unguis without an inner tooth. Unguiculus untoothed. Ten-
    ent hairs absent. Genital and anal segments ankylosed_____18
17. Eye spots one on each side. One tenent hair. Mucro relatively
    shorter and stouter, with ventral contour strongly rounded,
    in lateral aspect Grayish or blackish_____tenelloides (p. 62)
    Eye spots usually two on each side Tenent hairs absent.
    Mucro relatively slenderer, with ventral contour not strongly
    rounded, in lateral aspect. Genital and anal segments anky-
    losed. Bluish or greenish gray_____aquae (p. 59)
18. Manubrium three-fifths as long as dentes. Teeth of mucro
    subequal Mucro relatively long, in lateral aspect not strongly
    rounded ventrally Yellow to purplish_____constricta (p. 64)
    Manubrium less than half as long as dentes. Apical tooth of
    mucro larger than the anteapical. Mucro relatively short,
    in lateral aspect strongly rounded ventrally. Bluish, green-
    ish, or blackish_____cognata (p 65)

PROISOTOMA (PROISOTOMA) RAINIERI, new species

PLATE 16, FIGURES 160–168

Description.—Olive-green throughout; darker dorsally. Body and
appendages stout. Eyes (pl. 16, fig. 160) eight on each side, subequal. Postantennal organ (pl. 16, fig. 160) broadly elliptical, from
two to three times as long as the diameter of an eye. Antennae one-
fourth longer than the head, with segments in relative lengths about
as 7.8:8·14. Sense organ of third antennal segment (pl. 16, fig 161)
with a pair of stout curving rods subtended by an evident chitinous
ridge. Fourth antennal segment with slender strongly curving olfactory setae. Third and fourth abdominal segments equal in length.
Genital and anal segments not ankylosed. Tibiotarsus without a
distal subsegment. Unguis (pl. 16, fig 162) not strongly curving, with
a pair of small lateral teeth one third from the base, and without inner
teeth. Unguiculus (pl 16, fig. 163) extending two-thirds as far as
unguis, sublanceolate, untoothed, with a pair of rounded inner
lamellae. Tenent hairs absent. Furcula appended to the fifth abdominal segment, extending about as far as the ventral tube. Manubrium: dens: mucro as 36:56 5. Manubrium subcylindrical, with
many short dorsal setae and three small subapical ventral setae.
Dentes (pl. 16, fig. 164) stout, slightly narrowing distally; with many
coarse hemispherical dorsal tubercles, larger proximally and gradually
becoming smaller distally; with many ventral setae, numerous short

stiff dorsal setae, and a long dorsal subapical seta extending to the middle of the mucro. Mucrones (pl. 16, figs. 165–167) stout, 5-toothed, bilamellate. A lamella on each side extends from the base of the mucro to the anteapical tooth. Apical tooth relatively small, almost straight or slightly hooked. Anteapical tooth large, subconical, erect. Of the three remaining teeth, one is lateral and stout. The two others are dorsal, equal, subconical, and usually almost opposite each other; the anterior of the two being the more lateral. The mucro bears a strong lateral seta extending almost to the apex of the mucro. Rami of tenaculum (pl. 16, fig. 168) quadridentate; corpus with four ventral setae. General clothing of sparse short setae, with longer stiff slender sensory setae, all the setae being simple. Integument smooth. Length, 1.7 mm.

Cotypes—U.S.N.M. no. 42980.

Distribution—Recorded as follows:

Washington: Nisqually Glacier, Mount Rainier, March 31, April 5, P. S. Welch.

PROISOTOMA (PROISOTOMA) SCHÄFFERI (Krausbauer)

PLATE 16, FIGURES 169, 170; PLATE 17, FIGURES 171–176

Isotoma schafferi KRAUSBAUER, 1898, p 495.—SCHÄFFER, 1900b, p. 260.—CARL, 1901, p 258.—BÖRNER, 1901a, p. 40.—KRAUSBAUER, 1902, p 70.

Description.—"Light purple to brownish, often whitish at the borders of the segments. Not infrequently the segments are mostly whitish weakly pigmented with purple. Head whitish with a little purple pigment. Antennae purple. The living insect has a silvery luster" (Krausbauer). "Gray-purple to greenish brown" (Schäffer).

Specimens from Massachusetts are yellowish green or brownish green, spotted with pale yellow; dorsum blackish purple. Eyes connected anteriorly by a broad purple mark; occiput with a median purple spot. Eye spots large, black, approximate, close behind the antennae. Eyes (pl. 16, fig. 169) eight on each side, subequal, or the two anterior eyes larger than the others. Postantennal organ (pl. 16, fig. 169) elliptical, small, in length shorter than, or equal to, the diameter of an adjacent eye. Antennae about one and one-half times as long as the head; segments cylindrical, in relative lengths about as 18:26:23:27; first and second segments greenish with purple apices; third and fourth purplish. Sense organ of third antennal segment (pl. 16, fig 170) with a pair of swollen curving rods, and an inner accessory rod, which is slender and subcylindrical or subclavate. Fourth antennal segment with olfactory setae, but slightly differentiated, however, from the other curving setae. Abdomen gradually dilating. Third abdominal segment a little longer than the fourth (as 16:15). Genital and anal segments not ankylosed. Legs stout, pale green tinged with purple. Tibiotarsi subcylindrical, not subsegmented. Unguis (pl. 17, fig. 171) exceptionally long and slender, curving, without lateral teeth, with a minute inner tooth (which may be absent) about one-third from the apex. Unguiculus (pl. 17, fig. 172) broad basally, acute, untoothed, with a pair of inner lamellae; on first feet, one-third as long as unguis; on second and third feet, two-fifths as long. Tenent hairs absent, represented by a very long simple hair. Furcula pale green, appended to the fifth abdominal segment, attaining the ventral tube. Manubrium a little shorter than dentes, densely and minutely setaceous, ventrally with many short stiff setae, most numerous distally. Dentes stout, subcylindrical, not tapering, rounded apically, neither crenulate, nor tuberculate dorsally, with dense short curving setae on all sides; distally with long stiff setae on the mesal sides, those of one side crossing those of the other. Mucro (pl. 17, figs. 173, 174) stout, equal to, or a little longer than, hind unguis, tridentate and complexly lamellate. The three teeth are dorsal and in longitudinal alinement, the third, or proximal, tooth, being large and conspicuous. There are four lamellae (pl. 17, figs. 173, 174) as follows: Dorsal, ventral, outer, and inner. The dorsal lamella extends from the base of the mucro to the proximal tooth (*ad*, anterodorsal) and from the proximal tooth to the anteapical tooth (*pd*, posterodorsal); but this posterior portion of the dorsal lamella is deeply notched just behind the proximal tooth, and thus consists of two lobes. The ventral lamella (*v*) extends from the base of the mucro to the apical tooth. The outer, or lateral, lamella (*o*) extends only a little beyond the middle of the mucro. The inner, or mesal, lamella (*i*) extends from the base of the mucro to the anteapical tooth. Rami of tenaculum (pl. 17, fig. 175) quadridentate; corpus with many curving setae. General clothing (pl. 17, fig. 176) of dense short equal simple setae, slightly longer posteriorly, sensory setae, longer than the others, outstanding, simple. Integument smooth. Length, 2.3 mm (Massachusetts specimens).

Young individuals that I received from New York State are purple above, white intersegmentally, with yellow head, purple antennae, purplish-white legs, and white furcula.

In specimens from Illinois the anterior body segments are dark purple, and the last four abdominal segments and the head olive-green.

Remarks.—This species was determined for me by Dr C. Schäffer, to whom I once sent specimens collected in Massachusetts.

I formerly found this to be a common species in eastern Massachusetts on ponds and brooks and in sphagnum moss—always in wet situations. It skips about in a lively manner on water, owing its ability as a leaper to its strong furcula, which, like that of *Podura aquatica*, is structurally adapted for use on the surface of water. The dense bristles of the furcula, the long stiff crossing mesal setae of the dentes, and particularly the highly developed lamellae of the mucrones—all enable the furcula to take advantage of the resistance of the surface film. This species is exceptionally tolerant of cold, being active in February or March in Massachusetts on days when the temperature is that of winter rather than spring. Krausbauer found specimens in Germany among moist leaves on the shore of a stream under ice at a temperature of −10° or −11° C.

In Massachusetts, partly grown individuals were common in February, but by April most of the specimens were full grown.

Distribution.—Recorded as follows:

Massachusetts. Arlington, February 21, March 1, 10, April 13. Brookline, April 11, R. W. Hall. Waverley, April 19, 21.

New York. Voorheesville, November 9, M. D. Leonard (New York State Museum).

Illinois. Harrisburg, March 6, T. H. Frison and H. H. Ross (Illinois State Natural History Survey) Herod, March 6, T H Frison and H. H. Ross (Illinois State Natural History Survey) Mermet, March 8, T. H. Frison and H. H. Ross (Illinois State Natural History Survey)

PROISOTOMA (PROISOTOMA) COMMUNA (MacGillivray)

PLATE 17, FIGURES 177–180

Isotoma communa MacGillivray, 1896, p. 50.

Description.—Blackish blue in alcohol. Head with large pale rounded or elongate spots. First three antennal segments whitish basally, blue apically; fourth segment dark blue. Legs white, tinged with blue basally. Manubrium blue above; dentes white. Eyes (pl. 17, fig. 177) eight on each side, equal, on black spots Postantennal organ (pl. 17, fig. 177) near eyes, elliptical, about three times as long as the diameter of an eye. Antennae longer than the head (as 7:5); segments stout, as 10:18:16:27; second and third segments clavate. Sense organ of third antennal segment (pl. 17, fig. 178) with a pair of stout, subcylindrical, slightly curving sense rods, apparently without a basal ridge. Tibiotarsus not subsegmented. Unguis (pl. 17, fig. 179) with a pair of strong lateral teeth, without an inner tooth Unguiculus relatively large, extending three-fourths as far as the unguis, broadly lanceolate, untoothed, with a pair of inner lamellae. Tenent hairs absent. Third abdominal segment longer than the fourth (as 5:4). Genital and anal segments not ankylosed. Furcula appended to the fifth abdominal segment, extending to the ventral tube. Manubrium slender, with many dorsal and ventral setae. Dens twice as long as the manubrium, slender, tapering, with many dorsal and ventral setae, and with large dorsal tubercles except apically. Mucro (pl. 17, fig. 180) stout, with strongly rounded ventral contour in lateral aspect, quadridentate; all the teeth being dorsal First and second teeth subequal. Third and fourth teeth almost opposite each other, the lateral tooth being slightly oblique and either more proximal or more distal than the other. On my single specimen a minute proximolateral fifth tooth occurs on the left mucro but not on the right. Rami of tenaculum quadridentate; corpus with a few ventral setae (four observed). General clothing of dense short curving setae; sensory setae longer, curving, becoming still longer and more numerous on the last three abdominal segments. Antennae densely clothed with short curving setae interspersed with long stiff setae. Integument smooth. Length, 1.5 mm.

Remarks.—This description was made from one cotype, given to me by Dr. MacGillivray, taken by him at Salem, Ohio.

PROISOTOMA (PROISOTOMA) TITUSI, new species

PLATE 18, FIGURES 181–189

Description.—Dark purple, with many rounded pale spots. Antennae, legs, and manubrium purplish. Eyes (pl. 18, fig. 181) eight on each side, subequal. Postantennal organ (pl. 18, fig. 181) elongate, three to five times as long as the diameter of an eye, four or five times as long as broad, usually slightly constricted near the middle. Antennae subequal to head in length, or a trifle longer, with segments in relative lengths about as 8:11:9:18. Sense organ of third antennal segment (pl. 18, fig. 182) with a pair of subclavate curving rods under a cuticular fold, and an accessory pair of linear rods. Fourth antennal segment with long olfactory setae. Prothorax pigmented, not greatly reduced; terga of remaining segments imbricate. Tibiotarsus with a distal subsegment. Unguis (pl. 18, fig. 183) slender, curving, without lateral teeth, with a weak tooth near the middle of the inner margin. Unguiculus extending three-fifths as far as unguis on hind feet, broadly lanceolate, acuminate, untoothed, with a pair of inner lamellae. Tenent hairs 1, 2, 2. Genital and anal segments ankylosed, with an obsolete dorsal suture. In young individuals the dorsum of the fifth abdominal segment bears numerous tuberculate protuberances, as in plate 18, figure 184; in old individuals only traces of these remain. Fourth abdominal segment slightly longer than the third (as 14:13). Furcula appended to the fifth abdominal segment, not attaining the ventral tube, but extending to the middle of the second abdominal segment, gradually tapering. Manubrium with many strong dorsal setae and with one pair of ventral subapical setae. Dentes four-fifths as long as manubrium, rather stout proximally (fig. 185) but gradually narrowing from base to apex, coarsely crenulate dorsally, there being about five large proximal folds and ten smaller distal folds; dens with long dorsal and ventral setae. Mucro (pl. 18, figs. 186–188) short and stout, about as long as hind unguiculus, tridentate, bilamellate; apical tooth longitudinal, curving upward apically; anteapical tooth subequal to first or larger, suberect; third tooth lateral, close to second tooth and slightly more proximal than the latter, curving. The inner lamella extends from the base of the mucro to the apex of the second tooth; the outer lamella, from the base to the lateral tooth. Rami of tenaculum quadridentate; corpus with one curving ventral seta. Clothing (pl. 18, fig. 189) of dense, short, curving, simple setae; sensory setae outstanding, relatively short, curving or straight, simple. Integument of the adult smooth but reticulate. Length, 1.4 mm.

Remarks.—At the base of the furcula is the same accessory sclerite that occurs in *Guthriella* (pl. 9, fig. 89).

The cotypes came from Prof. E. G. Titus, for whom the species is named.

From Prof. E. O. Essig I received a large number of specimens of this species, all of which were, however, young individuals, ranging up to 0.6 mm in length. These specimens, in alcohol, were purple-lake in color, with the terga bordered narrowly with darker purple; antennae purple, legs pale purple, furcula white. Ungues relatively stouter than in the adults, with the inner tooth often obscure or undeveloped. Dentes dorsally with about ten evident semicircular transverse intermediate folds, running into larger irregular folds proximally and distally.

Cotypes.—U.S.N.M. no. 42987.

Distribution.—Recorded as follows:

Utah: Petersboro, October 24, E. G. Titus.
California: San Luis Obispo County, February 26, on surface of water, E. O. Essig.

PROISOTOMA (PROISOTOMA) LONGISPINA (MacGillivray)

PLATE 18, FIGURES 190, 191; PLATE 19, FIGURES 192–197

Achorutes longispinus MacGILLIVRAY, 1893, p. 315.

Description.—General color blackish purple; alcoholic specimens show a violaceous tinge; legs and furcula pale. Head and second to seventh segments, inclusive, each bordered posteriorly with a blackish band. Head relatively large, one-third as long as body, with a subtriangular frontal projection, laterally pigmented, between the antennae (pl. 18, fig. 190). Eyes (pl. 18, fig. 191) eight on each side, equal, on black patches near the antennae. Postantennal organ (pl. 18, fig. 191) narrowly subelliptical or subreniform, three to four times as long as the diameter of an eye. Antennae inserted in excavations on each side of the frontal projection, slightly longer than the head, with all the segments telescopic, and in relative lengths about as 2:4:3:5; second and third segments dilated distally; fourth subclavate, rounded apically; first three segments ringed with black apically; fourth black apically. Sense organ of third antennal segment with a pair of linear curving sense rods subtended by a chitinous ridge. Fourth antennal segment with olfactory setae. Body subcylindrical; prothorax concealed from above. Fourth abdominal segment longer than the third (as 7:4). Genital and anal segments ankylosed dorsally, but separated by a suture ventrolaterally. Tibiotarsus with a distal subsegment. Unguis (pl. 19, fig. 192) slender, without lateral or inner teeth. Unguiculus extending half as far as the unguis on the second and third pairs of feet, shorter on the first pair; lanceolate, acuminate, untoothed, with a pair of inner lamellae. Tenent hairs one or two; often 1, 2, 2. Furcula appended to the fifth abdominal segment, long, extending to the ventral tube. Manubrium a little longer than dentes, with many short dorsal setae and a pair of ventral subapical setae. Dentes stout, with about 20 coarse, somewhat irregular, transverse, dorsal folds, except on the proximal third; with many ventral setae and fewer dorsal setae. Mucro short, tridentate (pl. 19, figs. 193–196), first and second teeth subequal, in longitudinal alinement; third tooth lateral; apical tooth almost straight or slightly hooked; anteapical tooth suberect or slightly inclined; third tooth close to second and subequal to it, though somewhat variable in size; outer and inner lamellae present. Rami of tenaculum quadridentate; corpus with one stout curving ventral seta. Clothing (pl. 19, fig. 197) of dense stiff simple setae, becoming longer toward the end of the abdomen; erect sensory setae apparently absent. Integument smooth, not reticulate. Maximum length, 1.4 mm.

Remarks.—The writer has redescribed this species from four cotypes and a large amount of type material received from Dr. MacGillivray. It has been taken in immense numbers at Alameda, N. Mex., by E. Van Patten.

Type and cotypes.—U S.N.M. no. 42986.

PROISOTOMA (PROISOTOMA) MINUTA (Tullberg)

PLATE 19, FIGURES 198–207

Isotoma minuta TULLBERG, 1871, p. 152; 1872, p. 47; 1876, p 36.—SCHÖTT, 1894, p. 74; 1902, p. 21.—VON DALLA TORRE, 1895, p. 10.—SCHAFFER, 1896, p. 183; 1900a, p. 248; 1900b, p. 255.—SCHERBAKOV, 1898a, p. 59; 1898b, p 11.—AXELSON, 1900, p. 113; 1905b, p. 29; 1906, p. 13.—BÖRNER, 1901a, p. 45; 1903, p. 171.—KRAUSBAUER, 1902, p. 41.—WAHLGREN, 1906b, p. 254.—EVANS, 1908, p. 197.

Isotoma clavipila AXELSON, 1903a, p. 7.

Proisotoma minuta LINNANIEMI (AXELSON), 1907, p. 21; 1911, p. 14; 1912, p. 130.—BAGNALL, 1909, p. 501.—STACH, 1922a, p. 17.—WOMERSLEY, 1924a, p 32; 1925, p 219.—HANDSCHIN, 1929, p. 61.

Description.—Grayish or bluish; largest individuals heavily pigmented with blue, interspersed with pale spots; specimens of medium size bluish gray, with scattered mottled blue pigment and with intersegmental white bands; small individuals white. Eye spots black. Eyes (pl. 19, fig. 198) eight on each side, equal. Postantennal organ (pl. 19, fig. 198) near the eyes, elliptical to ovate-elliptical, two and one-half to three times as long as the diameter of an eye. Antennae a little longer than the head; segments in relative lengths about as 4:5:5:12. Sense organ of third antennal segment (pl. 19, fig.

199) with a pair of approximate subclavate rods subtended by a thick chitinous ridge. Fourth antennal segment without special olfactory setae. Unguis (pl. 19, figs. 200, 201) simple, untoothed. Unguiculus extending one-half (first pair) to two-thirds (third pair) as far as unguis, broadly lanceolate, acute, untoothed. Knobbed tenent hairs one, two, or none (see beyond). Abdominal segments without ankylosis. Fourth abdominal segment one-fourth longer than the third. Furcula appended to the fourth abdominal segment, short (not reaching the ventral tube), but variable in length, extending to the middle of the third abdominal segment or to the middle of the second. Manubrium usually longer than dens (as 9:7), sometimes equal to dens, stout (pl. 19, fig. 202), with a pair of stout ventral subapical setae and many smaller dorsal setae. Dentes (pl. 19, fig. 202) stout, not tapering, with five or six (as many as 10 in large individuals) dorsal crenulations near the middle. Mucrones (pl. 19, figs. 203–206) slightly shorter than hind ungues, elongate, tridentate; apical tooth slender, almost straight or slightly hooked; second tooth suberect, third subequal to second, or smaller, lateral in position, inclined caudally. Rami of tenaculum (pl. 19, fig. 207) quadridentate; corpus with one strong curving ventral seta (the number varying, however, from one to four). Clothing of minute stiff simple setae, with short erect simple sensory setae. Integument smooth. Length, 0.9 mm; maximum, 1.3 mm.

Variations.—Specimens from Pennsylvania that I studied had a black body pigment in the form of minute points, outlining the hypodermis cells.

The eyes, particularly of small individuals, may be pigmented separately, instead of occupying a common pigment spot on each side of the head

In small specimens the antennae may be slightly shorter than the head.

The third antennal segment is sometimes shorter than the second.

The tibiotarsus has occasionally a distal subsegment.

In addition to the five or six dorsal crenulations near the middle of the dens, there are several smaller and less evident folds

The variation in the mucro occurs chiefly in respect to the lateral tooth, which varies mostly in size and form, though slightly in position. In an occasional specimen this tooth is present on one mucro but absent on the other.

I have seen but one ventral seta on the tenaculum, though the number varies from one to four, according to Linnaniemi.

The typical form of *minuta* has no tenent hairs (Axelson, Borner). Some of my European specimens have no tenent hairs; others have two or even three; this being true of North American specimens also. The second tenent hair (pl. 19, fig. 200) arises a little to one side of the principal tenent hair, but is shorter and weaker than the latter.

This variety with two knobbed hairs has been named *clavipila* by Axelson (1903a; 1912). There is often present also a third tenent hair, not mentioned by other writers, on the opposite side of the tibiotarsus, above the unguiculus; it is weak, like the second hair, and may easily be overlooked.

Remarks.—My North American material of this species agrees with numerous examples sent to me from Finland by Linnaniemi and from Germany by Schäffer.

Proisotoma minuta is essentially a soil-frequenting species, occurring often in large colonies, and occasionally in dense masses. In Europe it has been taken under dead leaves, wood, cow manure, in heaps of sawdust, under bark, under stones, on pools of fresh water, on the seashore under seaweed or stones, in wells and cisterns, and under flowerpots in dwelling houses or greenhouses.

In regard to specimens from Red Hook, N. Y., sent to Dr. E. P. Felt and referred to the writer for determination, Dr. Felt wrote: "The large number sent, a teaspoonful or so of practically undiluted insects, indicated that the species must have been enormously abundant, probably as a result of an unusually prolonged moist spell. They were on the ground and plants in and about a hotbed."

The number of specimens that I received from Pennsylvania—also indicated a similar abundance.

Distribution.—In Europe, *Proisotoma minuta* has been recorded from Norway, Sweden, Finland, Hungary, Russia, Siberia, Germany, Italy, Scotland, and England.

Massachusetts: Cambridge, May 24, great quantities in a greenhouse, E. L. Mark.

Connecticut: Warehouse Point, June 9, from soil of tobacco field, G. S. Phelps, from W. E. Britton (Connecticut Agricultural Experiment Station).

Pennsylvania: From H. A. Surface (Pennsylvania State College). Bustleton, July, C. A. Thomas.

New York: Nassau County, April 25, in masses in a greenhouse, C. R. Crosby (New York State Museum). Red Hook, June 7, from E. P. Felt (New York State Museum). Westport, May 18, immense numbers, F. C. Smith.

Illinois: Champaign, March 24. Chicago, November 7, P. S. Welch. Homer, March 31, April 5, 7, 11, 13. Oakwood, April 20, T. H. Frison (Illinois State Natural History Survey)

Iowa: Ames, March 28, April 3, J. E. Guthrie.

Kansas: Dodge City, January 6, in egg capsules of grasshoppers, P. S. Welch. Manhattan, November 12, in termite nest in a fencepost, P. S. Welch.

Louisiana: Baton Rouge, abundant, H. A. Morgan; March 9, abundant in cane trash, C. L. Stracener. Tallulah, April 17, abundant in damp spots under loose bark of a dead black locust tree

Texas: Waxahachie, February 6, thousands, M. C. Tanquary.

California: Claremont-Laguna region, G. A. Bacon.

Canada: Banff, Alberta, July 13, on surface of wooded swampy pool at base of Rundle Mountain; July 24, on soil in cold frame growing lettuce, C. G. Hewitt. St. Andrews, New Brunswick, May 26, from C. Macnamara (National Collection, Ottawa).

PROISOTOMA (PROISOTOMA) SEPULCRALIS (Folsom)

PLATE 20, FIGURES 208-215

Isotoma sepulcralis FOLSOM, 1902b, p. 364.

Description.—White; sometimes slightly pigmented with minute scattered round black spots. Eye spots black. Eyes (pl. 20, fig. 208) five on each side, equal; occasionally four on each side. Postantennal organ (pl. 20, fig. 208) distant from eyes, elliptical, oval or ovate, twice as long as the diameter of an eye. Antennae subequal to the head in length; segments stout, in relative lengths about as 6:10:9:19. Sense organ of third antennal segment (pl. 20, fig. 209) with a pair of subcylindrical or subclavate feebly curving rods, subtended by a weak cuticular ridge. Fourth antennal segment with terminal tubercle, subapical papilla, and slender curving olfactory setae. Abdominal segments normally without ankylosis. Anus ventro-caudal. Femur and tibiotarsus each with a distal subsegment. Unguis (pl. 20, fig. 210) simple, untoothed. Unguiculus extending two-thirds as far as unguis, on hind feet, ovate-lanceolate, acute, untoothed. Front claws smallest, the other pairs successively larger. Tenent hairs absent; instead, a long simple seta. Fourth abdominal segment one-third longer than the third segment, and bearing the furcula. Furcula short, extending as far as the posterior margin of the second abdominal segment. Manubrium stout, with a pair of stout ventral subapical setae and several smaller dorsal setae. Dens stout, narrowing distally, two-thirds as long as manubrium, with eight to ten coarse, rather irregular, oblique, dorsal crenulations, and six ventral setae. Mucrones (pl. 20, figs. 211-214) one-third as long as dens, slightly longer than hind unguiculus, elongate, subequally tridentate; apical tooth sharp, feebly hooked or, rarely, falcate; second tooth conical, erect; third tooth slightly smaller than the second, erect or feebly inclined, lateral in position. The mucro is narrowly bilamellate: An inner lamella extends from the base of the mucro to the anteapical tooth, and an outer lamella from the base to the′ third (or lateral) tooth. Rami of tenaculum (pl. 20, fig. 215) quadridentate; corpus with a single strong curving ventral seta. Clothing of numerous short stiff simple setae, absent on the anterior and posterior parts of most of the body segments; with longer erect simple sensory setae. Integument smooth. Maximum length, 1.8 mm.

Remarks.—In an occasional individual the genital and anal segments are ankylosed without suture.

The mucrones vary considerably in minor details, as shown in plate 20, figures 211-213. In one case, the third tooth was absent on the left mucro but present on the right one; and in a single instance (among more than 5,000 individuals) each mucro had a proximal fourth tooth (pl. 20, fig. 214).

This species comes close to *Isotoma minima* Absolon (1900a, 1900b, 1901), in which, however, the eyes are isolated on separate pigment spots, the third abdominal segment is almost as long as the fourth, and the third tooth of the mucro is close to the second.

Proisotoma sepulcralis is a species of the soil. Though the specimens that I examined in preparing the original description numbered more than 5,400, they are the only examples of the species that I have ever seen. They were collected from graves in Washington, D. C., during the summers of 1896 and 1897, by Dr. Murray Galt Motter.

Cotypes.—U.S.N.M. no. 6144.

PROISOTOMA (PROISOTOMA) FRISONI, new species

PLATE 20, FIGURES 216–219; PLATE 21, FIGURES 220–222

Description.—White. Eyes absent. Postantennal organ (pl. 20, figs. 216, 217) elliptical, with a thick wall, in length one-half the basal width of the first antennal segment. Antennal base strongly developed (pl. 20, fig. 216), about one-half as long as the first antennal segment. Antennae longer than the head (as 9:8), with segments in relative lengths about as 4:7:6:13. First segment cylindrical, second and third subclavate, fourth elliptical. Sense organ of third antennal segment (pl. 20, fig. 218) with a pair of slender, rather long rods, a chitinous ridge and two setae. Fourth antennal segment without special olfactory setae. Abdominal segments without ankylosis. Fourth abdominal segment longer than the third (as 6:5). Unguis (pl. 20, fig. 219) without lateral or inner teeth. Unguiculus extending two-thirds as far as the unguis on the hind feet; one-half as far on the fore feet. Tenent hairs 1, 1, 1. Furcula short, extending only to the posterior part of the second abdominal segment. Manubrium (pl. 21, fig. 220) longer than dentes (as 5:3), with four pairs of ventral subapical stout setae. Dens stout (pl. 20, fig. 220), but narrowing gradually, with six short stiff ventral setae; dorsally with about 10 or 12 small, somewhat irregular intermediate crenulations. Mucro (pl. 21, figs. 221, 222) elongate, one-third or two-fifths as long as dens, tridentate; apical tooth almost straight or slightly curving; anteapical about as long as apical, but stouter, erect or slightly inclined; third tooth the smallest, as a rule (though sometimes subequal to second), proximal, lateral, oblique. Rami of tenaculum quadridentate; corpus with three stout curving anterior setae. Clothing of dense minute stiff reclinate setae; erect sensory setae absent. Integument smooth. Maximum length, 1.1 mm.

Cotypes.—U.S.N.M. no. 42978.

Distribution.—Recorded as follows:

Illinois: Cahokia, May 8, T. H. Frison (Illinois State Natural History Survey).

PROISOTOMA (PROISOTOMA) BREVIPENNA (MacGillivray)

PLATE 21, FIGURES 223–225

Isotoma brevipenna MacGILLIVRAY, 1896, p. 53

Description —Dark purple, mottled with small pale spots; antennae, legs, and furcula paler. Eyes and postantennal organs, not studied. Antennae slightly shorter than the head, with segments in relative lengths about as 2:3:3:8 First two segments cylindrical, third gradually dilating apically, fourth elliptical. Body stout Third abdominal segment shorter than the fourth (as 13:18). Genital and anal segments ankylosed, with an obsolete dorsal suture. Unguis (pl. 21, fig. 223) largest on the hind feet, comparatively slender, curving, with a pair of strong lateral teeth, and inner margin unidentate about one-third from the apex. Unguiculus lanceolate, acuminate, unidentate. Tenent hairs 1, 2, 2. Furcula appended to the fourth abdominal segment, short, not reaching the ventral tube, but extending about to the middle of the third abdominal segment. Manubrium longer than dentes (as 4:3) Dentes stout, swollen, tapering gradually, rounded apically. Mucro (fig. 224) as long as hind unguiculus, stout, tridentate; apical tooth small, hooked; second and third subequal, inclined slightly forward; ventral margin in lateral aspect almost straight except distally. Corpus of tenaculum with several curving setae. General clothing (pl 21, fig. 225) of dense short curving setae, sensory setae long, outstanding Length, 1.5 mm.

Remarks —The preceding description, in some respects incomplete, was made from a single type in the Museum of Comparative Zoology, Cambridge, Mass., taken at Salineville, Ohio, by A. D. MacGillivray.

PROISOTOMA (PROISOTOMA) OBSOLETA (MacGillivray)

PLATE 21, FIGURES 226–228

Isotoma obsoleta MacGILLIVRAY, 1896, p. 54

Description.—Blackish violet Eyes eight on each side, unequal, the two inner proximal eyes on each side being smaller than the others. Postantennal organs situated near the bases of the antennae, narrowly elliptical, with thick wall, and about twice as long as the diameter of an adjacent eye. Antennae slightly longer than the head, with segments in relative lengths about as 4.5:6:12; second and third segments dilated apically Third abdominal segment shorter than the fourth (as 6:7). Genital and anal segments ankylosed. Tibiotarsus without a distal subsegment. Unguis (pl 21, fig. 226) stout, strongly curving, with a pair of small lateral teeth, without an inner tooth. Unguiculus more than half as long as unguis, broadly lanceolate, aciculate, with a strong inner tooth (sometimes absent). Tenent hairs absent; represented by a single long simple hair. Furcula short, extending only about as far as the middle of the third abdominal segment. Dentes longer than manubrium, stout, subcylindrical, rounded apically, with coarse intermediate dorsal crenulations, with a few short dorsal setae and a few lateral and subapical ventral setae. Mucrones (pl. 21, fig. 227) tridentate; apical tooth the smallest, almost straight or slightly hooked; second and third subequal, subconical, erect; third more lateral than the second; ventral margin in lateral aspect almost straight except distally. Clothing (pl. 21, fig. 228) of short curving reclinate setae, longer posteriorly, sensory setae long, outstanding. Integument smooth but reticulate. Length, 1.1 mm.

Remarks.—The only examples of this species that I have seen are three cotypes: One belonging to the Museum of Comparative Zoology, Cambridge, Mass.; one to Cornell University; and one given to me by Dr. MacGillivray. In the first-mentioned cotype the legs and furcula are white; in the other two they are marked with pale violet, and the antennae are whitish with more or less purple, especially distally.

Distribution.—Recorded as follows:

Ohio: Salineville, February 2, A. D. MacGillivray (Museum of Comparative Zoology; Cornell University).

PROISOTOMA (PROISOTOMA) VESICULATA, new species

PLATE 21, FIGURES 229–232; PLATE 22, FIGURES 233–237

Description.—Head and body blackish blue; body with narrow white intersegmental bands; appendages paler blue; coxae blackish. Less heavily pigmented individuals may be mottled with white spots, with antennae and legs yellow distally and blue proximally. Body and appendages stout. Eyes (pl. 21, fig. 229) eight on each side, the two inner proximal eyes smaller than the others. Postantennal organ (pl. 21, fig. 229) situated close to the antennal base, subelliptical, about one-fourth longer than the diameter of one of the largest eyes, with a notch near the middle of the anterior margin. Antennae subequal to head in length, or slightly longer than head, with segments in relative lengths about as 8:10:11:21, or 6:7:7:16; third segment occasionally slightly shorter than the second. Sense organ of third antennal segment as in figure 230. The curving setae of the fourth antennal segment are strong, but not evidently modified to form olfactory setae. Tibiotarsus without a distal subsegment. Unguis (pl. 21, fig. 231) with a pair of strong lateral teeth and a tooth behind the middle of the inner margin. Unguiculus extending two-thirds as far as unguis on hind feet, acute, with an inner angle tooth. One long tenent hair, feebly knobbed, extends as far as the inner tooth of the unguis. Third abdominal segment shorter than the fourth (as 7:10). Genital and anal segments ankylosed, with in some cases a trace of a dorsal suture. Furcula (pl. 21, fig. 232) stout, appended to the fifth abdominal segment, not attaining the ventral tube, but extending to the middle of the second abdominal segment.

Manubrium setigerous dorsally; with three ventral subapical setae. Several long stiff erect simple setae occur dorsally on the manubrium and the bases of the dentes. Dentes (pl. 21, fig. 232) slightly shorter than manubrium, stout, with eight to ten coarse dorsal crenulations. At the extremity of the dens is a large lateral transparent bladderlike dilatation (pl. 22, figs. 233, 234) extending beyond the mucro. Mucrones (pl. 22, figs. 233, 234) stout, subequal to hind unguiculi in length, tridentate; apical tooth the smallest, more or less hooked; second and third teeth in line with the first, subequal or third smaller than second, suberect or inclined slightly forward. Ventral margin of mucro well rounded, in lateral aspect. Rami of tenaculum tridentate; corpus with two stout curving ventral setae. General clothing (pl. 22, fig. 235) of short stout curving simple setae of uniform length; erect sensory setae short, stout, simple; several long stout simple setae occur dorsally on the last two abdominal segments. The integument is smooth externally but the intersegmental membranes of the body are reticulate (figs. 236, 237), as are also the antennae, legs, furcula, and the ventral integument of head and body. Length, 1.3 mm.

Cotypes.—U.S.N.M. no. 42983.

Remarks.—The only examples of this species that I have seen are the cotypes, taken at Arnprior, Ontario, December 7 and 8, on snow, by Charles Macnamara.

PROISOTOMA (PROISOTOMA) BULBOSA, new species

PLATE 22, FIGURES 238-244

Description.—Blackish blue, including the appendages. A stout species. Eyes (pl. 22, figs. 238, 239) eight on each side, one or both of the inner proximal eyes on each side being smaller than the others. Postantennal organ (pl. 22, figs. 238, 239) subelliptical but somewhat irregular, twice as long as the diameter of an adjacent eye, with an exceptionally thick bordering ridge. Antennae slightly longer than the head (as 7:6), with segments variable in relative lengths; third segment usually a little shorter than the second, occasionally a little longer; fourth two to three times as long as second. Sense organ of third antennal segment (pl. 22, fig. 240) with a pair of feebly curving rods in a deep groove, with four guard setae. The curving setae of the fourth antennal segment are strong, but not evidently differentiated as olfactory setae. Tibiotarsi not subsegmented. Unguis (pl. 22, fig. 241) weakly curving, with a pair of lateral teeth two-fifths from the base, and an inner tooth one-third from the apex. Unguiculus extending three-fifths to four-fifths as far as the unguis, sublanceolate, acute, untoothed. One tenent hair, weakly knobbed. Third abdominal segment shorter than the fourth (about as 19:22). Genital and anal segments ankylosed, with the dorsal suture often indicated, however; dorsally with coarse tuberculate ridges. Furcula appended to the fifth abdominal segment, not attaining the ventral tube but extending as far as the second abdominal segment, stout. Manubrium about seven-eighths as long as dentes, setigerous on all sides. Dentes stout, not tapering, broad apically, each with a lateral protuberance one-fourth from the base, and with about eight large dorsal semicircular folds. Dentes with a few setae dorsally, and many stiff setae laterally and ventrally. At the end of the dens is a conspicuous lateral expansion in the form of a transparent bladder (pl. 22, figs. 242, 243) extending half the length of the mucro. Mucro (pl. 22, figs. 242, 243) stout, quadridentate. Apical tooth small, slightly curving or almost straight; second and third teeth in line with the first, subequal, directed slightly forward; fourth tooth lateral, oblique. Ventral contour of mucro in lateral aspect almost straight proximally. Rami of tenaculum quadridentate; corpus with three ventral setae. General clothing (pl. 22, fig. 244) of short strong curving simple setae, becoming longer on the genital and anal segments. Erect sensory setae apparently absent. Integument minutely tuberculate, becoming smooth and reticulate on the posterior regions of the body segments and on the intersegmental membranes. The coarse dorsal tubercles of the anogenital segment form several crenulate ridges. Length, 1.2 mm.

Cotypes.—U.S.N.M. no. 42989.

Distribution.—Recorded as follows:

Maine: Orono, March 10, in moss in pine woods, F. L. Harvey.

PROISOTOMA (PROISOTOMA) AQUAE (Bacon)

PLATE 22, FIGURES 245, 246; PLATE 23, FIGURES 247-252

Isotoma aquae BACON, 1914, p. 147.

Description.—General color gray, with a bluish or greenish tinge; mottled blue and yellow. The pigment forms a reticulation around the borders of the hypodermis cells. Intersegmental regions unpigmented, appearing as white bands. Antennae and bases of legs mottled with pigment; manubrium pigmented. Eyes (pl. 22, fig. 245) eight on each side, unequal. Ocular patches black, usually two on each side (pl. 22, fig. 246); an anterior, with five eyes, and a posterior, with three eyes. Postantennal organ (pl. 22, figs. 245, 246; pl. 23, fig. 247) subelliptical, constricted near the middle, thick-walled, three to three and one-half times as long as the diameter of an adjacent eye. Antennae slightly longer than the head (as 8:7), with segments varying in relative lengths but frequently as 16:25:27:50. Sense organ of third antennal segment (pl 23, figs 248, 249) with a pair of subclavate, slightly curving, oblique sense rods immersed in a pit and subtended by a thick cuticular fold. Olfactory setae of fourth antennal segment not clearly differentiated from ordinary setae. Third abdominal segment shorter than the fourth (as 6:7 or 7:8). Genital and anal segments ankylosed, without a suture. Tibiotarsus with a distal subsegment. Hind claws the largest. Unguis (pl. 23, fig. 250) stout, without lateral teeth, with inner margin unidentate two-thirds from the base. Unguiculus lanceolate, acute, untoothed, extending half as far as the unguis on the hind feet, two-fifths as far on the other feet. Knobbed tenent hairs absent. Furcula attached between the fourth and fifth abdominal segments, relatively short, extending to the middle of the second abdominal segment. Manubrium with several dorsal setae, and without ventral setae excepting a subapical pair. Dens one-third longer than manubrium, slender, gradually tapering, with many fine dorsal crenulations: absent basally and ending distally at a distance from the mucro equal to twice the length of the latter. Dentes with several long proximal dorsal setae and many stiff ventral setae. Mucro (pl. 23, fig. 251) small but relatively stout, three-fifths as long as hind unguis, or a little longer than hind unguiculus, subequally bidentate; apical tooth curving, attaining almost the height of the second tooth, which is erect. Rami of tenaculum quadridentate; corpus with one stout stiff ventral seta. General clothing (pl. 23, fig. 252) of dense, short, stiff, simple setae; erect sensory setae short and simple. Integument smooth. Maximum length, 1.5 mm.

Remarks.—In 85 percent of the specimens there are two eye patches on each side of the head; in 15 percent the two patches are confluent, sometimes broadly, but usually by means of a narrow connection.

My redescription of *P. aquae* has been made from a large number of specimens given to me by the author of the species.

Distribution.—This species is known as yet only from California, where it was found "in great abundance on pools of water in a newly plowed field after a hard rain." It was taken also under rocks.

California: Claremont–Laguna region, G. A. Bacon. Indian Hill, February, A. K. Payne.

PROISOTOMA (PROISOTOMA) DECEMOCULATA, new species

Plate 23, Figures 253–255

Description.—White to the naked eye. Slightly pigmented with minute dark points and patches. Antennae slightly pigmented; legs white, pigmented basally; manubrium pigmented, dentes white. Eyes (pl. 23, fig. 253) five on each side, equal. The two anterior eyes occupy a single elliptical spot of pigment; the three posterior eyes are pigmented separately, each being on a round black spot. Postantennal organ (pl. 23, fig. 253) subelliptical, about three times as long as the diameter of an eye, with a trace of a constriction near the middle of the anterior margin. Antennae subequal to head in length, with segments as 14:18:20:37. Fourth abdominal segment longer than the third (as 15:13). Unguis (pl. 23, fig. 254) simple, curving, without lateral or inner teeth. Unguiculus lanceolate, extonding half as far as the unguis, untoothed. Tenent hairs absent. Furcula extending only to the middle of the second abdominal segment. Manubrium two-thirds as long as dentes, with many short dorsal setae and one pair of stout subapical ventral setae. Dentes slender, gradually tapering, crenulate dorsally, with many ventral setae. Mucro (pl. 23, fig. 255) a little longer than hind unguiculus (as 13:11), subequally bidentate; apical tooth upcurving, second suberect. Rami of tenaculum quadridentate; corpus with a single stout seta. General clothing of abundant rather stiff simple setae of moderate length; sensory setae outstanding, stiff, relatively stout, simple. Length, 0.5 mm.

Remarks.—This species is close to *angularis* Axelson (1905), from which it differs as shown in table 3.

TABLE 3.—*Comparison of* Proisotoma angularis *and* P. decemoculata

Species	Manu-brium dentes as—	Antennal formula	Extent of furcula	Ventral setae of manubrium
angularis	2·1	2.3·3½·5	Not quite to abdominal segment 2	None.
decemoculata	2·3	14·18·20·37	To middle of abdominal segment 2	One pair.

Cotypes.—U.S N.M. no. 42990
Distribution —Recorded as follows·
Illinois: Homer, April 6 and 9, under a stone on grass.

PROISOTOMA (PROISOTOMA) SIMPLEX new species
PLATE 23, FIGURES 256–258

Description.—White, mottled with gray or black pigment. Body segments bordered posteriorly with black. Antennae mottled with black; legs and furcula white. A black Λ-shaped mark extends forward from the eyes. Eyes eight on each side, subequal. Post-antennal organ (pl. 23, fig. 256) subelliptical, a little more than twice as long as the diameter of an adjacent eye. Antennae one-fifth longer than the head, with segments in relative lengths about as 3:6:5:10. Sense organ of third antennal segment with a pair of minute linear naked rods. Fourth antennal segment without special olfactory setae. Third abdominal segment shorter than the fourth (as 5:6). Genital and anal segments not ankylosed. Tibiotarsus with a trace of a distal subsegment. Unguis (pl. 23, fig. 257) feebly curving, untoothed. Unguiculus lanceolate, untoothed, extending three-fifths as far as the unguis on the hind feet, and half as far on the other feet. One tenent hair. Furcula not attaining the ventral tube, but extending to the middle of the second abdominal segment. Manubrium stout, with a few dorsal setae and three pairs of ventral subapical setae. Dentes scarcely longer than the manubrium, stout, tapering, with numerous dorsal crenulations, which are coarse proximally and finer distally, with stiff ventral setae and a few outstanding dorsal setae Mucro (pl. 23, fig. 258) bidentate; apical tooth smaller than the anteapical. Rami of tenaculum quadridentate; corpus with a single seta. General clothing of short simple setae; erect sensory setae short, simple. Integument smooth. Maximum length, 1.1 mm.

Cotypes.—U S N.M. no. 42976.

Distribution.—Recorded as follows:

Pennsylvania: Kennett Square, in a mushroom house. Concordville, September 24, in a manure pile, C. A. Thomas.

PROISOTOMA (PROISOTOMA) TENELLOIDES, new species

PLATE 23, FIGURES 259–261

Description.—General color grayish or blackish, with close pale spots of various sizes. Pigment black, in the form of minute granules, which outline the hypodermis cells. Intersegmental regions banded narrowly with white. Head with a dark interocular area containing minute round pale spots, uniform in size and distribution. Antennae stout, segments spotted with blackish pigment; first three segments unpigmented basally. Coxae pigmented; legs otherwise white. Furcula white, with a little dorsal pigment at the base of the manubrium Eyes eight on each side, equal Postantennal organ (pl 23, fig. 259) large, subelliptical, constricted at the middle, with wide border, and three times as long as the diameter of an eye. Antennae stout, a little longer than the head, with segments about as 12:17:14.29; third segment thus slightly shorter than the second, and fourth twice as long as the third. Sense organ of third antennal segment present, of the usual type. Fourth antennal segment without special olfactory setae. Third urotergite shorter than the fourth (as 4:5 or 6:7). Genital and anal segments ankylosed. Tibiotarsus and femur each with a distal subsegment. Unguis (pl. 23, fig. 260) stout, almost straight, without lateral teeth, with a small tooth near the middle of the inner margin. Unguiculus extending not quite half as far as unguis on hind feet, lanceolate, untoothed One tenent hair, as long as the unguis. Furcula arising between the fourth and fifth abdominal segments, short, extending a little beyond the posterior margin of the second abdominal segment. Manubrium three-fifths as long as dentes, dorsally and laterally with a few short stiff setae; ventrally naked except for one subapical pair of setae. Dentes ventrally with relatively few short stiff setae; dorsally with numerous fine crenulations (25 to 35), which are absent proximally and end distally at a distance from the mucro equal to twice the length of the latter. Mucro (pl 23, fig 261) one and one-half times as long as hind unguiculus, bidentate, with both teeth directed dorsally; apical tooth larger than the anteapical; ventral margin strongly rounded in lateral aspect. Rami of tenaculum quadridentate; corpus with one long straight anterior seta.

General clothing of rather dense short simple setae, becoming considerably longer on the anogenital segment. Outstanding sensory setae simple, short and stiff, much longer on the ano-genital segment. Integument smooth. Maximum length, 1.1 mm.

Remarks.—This species agrees in most respects with the European species *tenella* Reuter, types of which were redescribed by Linnaniemi (1912). In *tenella* there is, however, no ankylosis of the genital and anal segments; the unguiculus is narrow; the dorsal folds of the dens are present apparently as far as the mucro; and the latter is relatively slender and not strongly rounded ventrally.

This species may prove to be synonymous with *Isotomina thermophila* var. *anomala*, for it differs only in minor respects from the description and figures of that form as given by Linnaniemi (1912, p. 136).

Cotypes.—U.S.N.M. no. 42984.

Distribution.—Recorded as follows:

Illinois: Homer, April 23, 24, and 29, under boards on grass.

PROISOTOMA (PROISOTOMA) IMMERSA (Folsom)

PLATE 24, FIGURES 262–268

Isotoma immersa FOLSOM, 1924, p. 1.

Description.—Ground color pale yellow in alcohol (possibly white in life); pigment purple, becoming blackish where dense. Head and body coarsely mottled with irregular spots dorsally; body segments bordered posteriorly with broad bands of blackish. First three antennal segments each with an apical band; fourth segment dark apically. Legs pale yellow, the segments mottled with more or less pigment. Furcula and ventral region unpigmented. Head (pl. 24, fig. 262) large in proportion to the body, and two-fifths as long as the latter. A blackish Λ-shaped mark extends forward from the eyes. Eyes (pl. 24, fig. 263) eight on each side, unequal. Postantennal organ (pl. 24, fig. 263) close to eyes, elliptical to oval, usually constricted at the middle, and two to three times as long as the diameter of an adjacent eye. Antennae stout, approximate, subequal to, or slightly longer than, the head, with segments in relative lengths about as 11:14:22:45. Antennal segments strongly telescopic (pl. 24, fig. 264). Basal antennal segment cup-shaped, immersed in a pit (pl. 24, fig. 262); second subcylindrical; third subclavate; fourth elliptical. Sense organ of third antennal segment (pl. 24, fig. 265) with a pair of feebly curving rods subtended by a chitinous ridge. Fourth antennal segment without special olfactory setae. Prothorax concealed from above by the head and mesonotum. Abdominal segments without ankylosis. Body segments (excepting prothorax) in relative lengths about as 10:6:4:5.6:8:5:4. Fourth abdominal segment longer than the third (as 2:1 or 3:2). Anal segment relatively long and broad;

suranal and subanal valves (pl. 24, fig. 266) relatively large, subtriangular. Tibiotarsus with a distal subsegment (pl. 24, fig. 267). Hind claws the largest. Unguis (pl. 24, fig 267) curving, without lateral teeth, unidentate at the middle of the inner margin. Unguiculus half as long as unguis, lanceolate, untoothed. One long tenent hair, extending almost to apex of unguis. Furcula appended to the fifth abdominal segment, long, attaining the ventral tube. Manubrium with many dorsal setae and two pairs of ventral subapical setae. Dentes one-fourth longer than manubrium, rather stout, slightly narrowing distally, with 20 to 25 coarse dorsal folds, which become successively smaller from the base toward the apex of the dens, and end before the apex at a distance equal to the length of the mucro. Dentes with several dorsal setae and stiff ventral setae. Mucro (pl. 24, fig. 268) as long as hind unguiculus, with narrow outer and inner lamellae, and subequally bidentate; apical tooth feebly curving; anteapical tooth slightly larger, suberect. Rami of tenaculum quadridentate; corpus with one ventral seta (sometimes two). General clothing of short dense simple setae, longer on the posterior part of the abdomen; erect sensory setae a little longer than the others, simple. Integument smooth. Maximum length, 0.7 mm.

Remarks—The apical tooth of the mucro is, in rare instances, reduced. Especially characteristic of this species are the strongly telescopic antennae, inserted in foveae, and the large anal segment.

The only specimens of this species that I have seen were those given to me many years ago by Samuel Henshaw. They were taken from a vial (Museum of Comparative Zoology) containing practically innumerable individuals, found in a mushroom cellar.

Cotypes.—U.S.N.M. no. 42977. Some of the cotypes are in the American Museum of Natural History.

Distribution.—Recorded as follows:

New York: Long Island, Dr. J. A. Lintner.

PROISOTOMA (PROISOTOMA) CONSTRICTA, new species

PLATE 24, FIGURES 269–272

Description.—Pale yellow, marked with a fine network of minute black specks. In heavily pigmented individuals, however, this network becomes obscured, and the general color is purple or blackish purple. Antennal segments mottled with purple. Legs white beyond coxae, or mottled throughout with purple. Furcula white. Eyes eight on each side, unequal. Postantennal organ (pl. 24, fig. 269) large, elliptical, strongly constricted at the middle, thick-walled, three times as long as the diameter of an adjacent eye. Antennae subequal to head in length, or a little longer, with segments in relative lengths about as 11:19:19:34; third segment sometimes slightly longer than the second. Sense organ of third antennal segment (pl. 24, fig 270) with a pair of linear feebly curving rods, a thick chitinous ridge, and a pair of guard setae. Third abdominal segment shorter than the fourth (as 5:6). Genital and anal segments ankylosed. Unguis (pl 24, fig 271) simple, without lateral or inner teeth. Unguiculus broadly lanceolate, acuminate, extending about half as far as the unguis. Tenent hairs absent. Furcula slender, gradually tapering, extending only as far as the middle of the second abdominal segment. Manubrium three-fifths as long as dentes; dorsally with a few short stiff setae; ventrally naked except for one subapical pair of long setae. Dentes slender, tapering; dorsally with a few basal setae and many crenulations, ending far from the apex; ventrally with many stiff appressed setae. Mucro (pl. 24, fig. 272) about as long as hind unguiculus, subequally bidentate; apical tooth hooked, anteapical erect. Rami of tenaculum quadridentate; corpus with a single seta. General clothing of short stiff simple setae; erect sensory setae short, simple. Maximum length, 1.9 mm.

Cotypes.—U.S N.M. no. 42979.

Distribution.—Recorded as follows·

Florida: Gainesville, January 12, in decaying leaves; Gainesville, February 20, D. M. Bates. Camp Torreya, April 4; Rock Bluff, April 4, T. H. Hubbell.

PROISOTOMA (PROISOTOMA) COGNATA, new species

PLATE 24, FIGURES 273–275

Description.—General color bluish, greenish, or blackish; pigment blue or blackish, mottled; anterior borders of body segments white; posterior borders edged narrowly with blackish; antennae blue; legs pale, feebly pigmented; furcula white. Eyes eight on each side, on black patches, the two inner proximal eyes of each side smaller than the others. Postantennal organ (pl. 24, fig 273) subelliptical, constricted at the middle, thick-walled, two and one-half times as long as the diameter of an adjacent eye. Antennae a little longer than the head, with segments in relative lengths about as 6:11:10:22. Sense organ of third antennal segment with a pair of slender curving rods, subtended by a chitinous ridge. Fourth antennal segment without special olfactory setae; with a terminal tubercle. Fourth abdominal segment longer than the third (as 3:2). Genital and anal segments ankylosed. Unguis (pl. 24, fig. 274) slender, weakly curving, without lateral or inner teeth. Unguiculus broadly lanceolate, acuminate, untoothed, extending half as far as the unguis on the hind feet; two-fifths as far on the other feet. Tenent hairs absent. Furcula extending to the middle of the second abdominal segment. Manubrium stout, dorsally with numerous short stiff setae, ventrally with one pair of stout subapical setae. Dens not quite twice so long as manubrium, slender, tapering, dorsally with numerous fine crenulations except proximally and distally, and a few stiff setae; ventrally with numerous short stiff setae. Mucro (pl. 24, fig. 275) as long as hind unguiculus, in lateral aspect strongly rounded ventrally, bidentate; apical tooth relatively long, hooked; anteapical smaller, suberect. Rami of tenaculum quadridentate; corpus with a single seta Clothing of short setae; outstanding sensory setae also short. Integument smooth. Maximum length, 1 2 mm.

Cotypes.—U.S.N.M. no. 42985.

Distribution.—Recorded as follows:

Louisiana: Baton Rouge, March 9, in cane trash, C L Stracener.

Genus ARCHISOTOMA Linnaniemi

Isotoma PACKARD, 1877, p. 52 (part).
Archisotoma LINNANIEMI, 1912, p. 118.

Genotype.—*Isotoma besselsii* Packard.

Head broad and long; front low-arched. Eyes and postantennal organs present. Fourth antennal segment relatively short, with a terminal lobe, a subapical papilla and a few olfactory setae. Third and fourth abdominal segments subequal in length. Genital and anal segments ankylosed. Anus caudal. Hind femur with a distal outer thornlike process. Tibiotarsus with a distal subsegment. Outer lamella of unguiculus absent. Tenent hairs absent. Manubrium longer than dentes, with a long coxal, or basal, segment, and naked ventrally. Dentes stout, subcylindrical, smooth dorsally. Mucrones tridentate, not lamellate. Rami of tenaculum quadridentate; corpus with a large anterior accessory lobe, and without setae. Bothriotricha present. Integument smooth.

ARCHISOTOMA BESSELSI (Packard)

PLATE 14, FIGURES 147–149; PLATE 15, FIGURES 150–155

Isotoma besselsii PACKARD, 1877, p. 52.—MACGILLIVRAY, 1891, p. 273; 1896, p 52.—VON DALLA TORRE, 1895, p 10.—DAVENPORT, 1903, p 6.—BACON, 1912, p 841; 1914, p 148.
Isotoma pulchella MONIEZ, 1890, p 431.—DENIS, 1923, p 221.
Isotoma besselsi SCHAFFER, 1900a, p. 248.—FOLSOM, 1901, p. 162.—AXELSON, 1905b, p. 30.—WAHLGREN, 1906c, p. 16.
Isotoma spitzbergensis LUBBOCK, 1898, p. 616.—CARPENTER and EVANS, 1899, p 252.—SKORIKOW, 1900, p. 193.
Isotoma arctica SCHERBAKOV, 1899a, p 47; 1899b, p 5.
Isotoma janmayensis WAHLGREN, 1900a, p. 354
Proisotoma besselsi LINNANIEMI (AXELSON), 1907, p. 73; 1911, p. 14.
Archisotoma besselsi LINNANIEMI (AXELSON), 1912, p 119.—BROWN, 1918, p. 186; 1925, p. 157.—FOLSOM, 1919b, p 277.—DENIS, 1923, p. 221; 1924c, p. 562; 1926, p 16.—WOMERSLEY, 1924a, p 32; 1924b, p. 169.—REMY, 1928, p. 65.—HANDSCHIN, 1929, p 59

Description.—Gray, bluish gray, blue, or blackish; in alcohol more or less greenish. Borders of body segments pale or white, giving the insect a banded appearance. Posterior region of head and sides of body with unpigmented spots. Body slender. Head broad, long and low arched; oral region elongate. Eye spots elongate. Eyes (pl. 14, fig. 147) eight on each side, the two inner proximal eyes much smaller than the others. Postantennal organ (pl. 14, fig. 147) elongate, narrowly elliptical, one and one-half to four times as long as the diameter of the adjacent eye. Antennae usually as long as, or slightly longer than, the head, in some individuals 1.7 times as long, however. Antennal segments in relative lengths about as 3:4:5.4 or 8 10.9:12; the last segment being, therefore, relatively short. Sense organ of third antennal segment with two feebly curving rods subtended by a chitinous ridge, which is sometimes absent, however. Fourth antennal segment with two or three dorsolateral curving blunt olfactory setae, with terminal lobe and subapical papilla. Femur and tibiotarsus each with a distal subsegment (pl. 14, figs. 148, 149) on all the legs. Hind femur with a distal outer thornlike process (pl. 14, fig. 149). Unguis (pl. 14, fig. 148) narrow, curving, without lateral teeth and without an inner tooth (often with a small inner tooth according to Linnaniemi, 1912). Unguiculus extending three-fourths as far as unguis, broadly sublanceolate, apically setaceous, untoothed, with outer lamella absent, and with a pair of inner lamellae. Tenent hairs absent. Third and fourth abdominal segments subequal, or third a little shorter than fourth (as 7.8). Fifth and sixth abdominal segments almost or completely ankylosed; there being, however, in some specimens, particularly in small individuals, a faint short dorsal suture between the two segments. The last two abdominal segments project conspicuously beyond the base of the furcula, which arises (apparently) from both the fourth and fifth abdominal segments. Furcula stout, of almost uniform thickness, extending not quite to the ventral tube. Manubrium long, slender, with a long coxal, or basal, segment; with many longer or shorter stiff dorsal setae and naked ventrally. Manubrium equal to dens plus mucro in length. Dentes stout, not tapering distally, rounded apically, not crenulate or tuberculate dorsally, with many short setae dorsally and ventrally. Mucrones (pl. 15, figs. 150, 151) about as long as hind unguiculi, tridentate, with a large apical tooth and a pair of large dorsolateral basal teeth subtriangular in lateral aspect. Mucrones strongly asymmetrical in dorsal aspect (pl. 15, figs. 152, 153). Lateral mucronal seta present. Rami of tenaculum (pl. 15, fig. 154) quadridentate; corpus with a large subconical anterior accessory lobe, and without setae. General clothing of dense short simple setae (pl. 15, fig. 155), becoming longer on the posterior part of the abdomen. Long outstanding simple setae occur also on all the body segments. Abdominal bothriotricha (exceptionally long, slender, naked hairs) at least two pairs (see beyond). Integument smooth. Length, usually 1–1.5 mm, maximum, 2.1 mm.

Remarks.—Denis (1924c) found two pairs of bothriotricha on the anal segment. I note two pairs situated as follows: (1) A pair on the anterodorsal region of the genital segment, close to the suture between the fourth and fifth urotergites; (2) a pair on the anterodorsal region of the anal segment, close to the obsolete suture between the genital and anal segments.

Denis (1926) says that in males longer than 1.1 mm the antennae are longer in relation to the head than in females.

In specimens from Massachusetts some of the stiff outstanding setae of body, legs, and antennae are thickened and spinelike, as in plate 14, figure 149—a condition that I have not yet found in Arctic material.

Through the courtesy of Dr. A. S. Packard I once examined 18 cotypes of this species from Polaris Bay, latitude 81°20′ to 81°50′ N.

A. besselsi is a littoral species, limited to the seashore or its vicinity, and commonly found between tide marks, where it occurs under stones, seaweed, or driftwood, or burrowing in the sand, or exposed on the shore. It is an agile species and a vigorous jumper, as mentioned by Davenport (1903) in his interesting account of the distribution and movements of littoral Collembola.

Cotypes.—U.S.N.M. no. 43002.

Distribution.—There are records of the occurrence of this species in Jan Mayen Island, Spitsbergen, Nova Zembla, Russia (Kola Peninsula), Finland, Norway, France, Scotland, England, and Tierra del Fuego. The species ranges from northern Greenland almost to the Antarctic Circle, and probably owes its exceptional distribution to marine currents.

Greenland: Polaris Bay, July 5, Dr. Bessels (U.S. National Museum). Umanak, June 28, July 26, M. C. Tanquary (American Museum of Natural History; University of Illinois).

Massachusetts: Neponset, May 4, October 7, 10.

New York: Cold Spring Harbor, Long Island, July, C. B. Davenport.

California: Laguna Beach, G. A. Bacon.

Genus ÅGRENIA Borner

Isotoma TULLBERG, 1876, p. 34 (part).
Ågrenia BORNER, 1906, p. 171.—LINNANIEMI, 1912, p. 173.

Genotype.—Isotoma bidenticulata Tullberg.

Unguis with a basal membrane connecting the strong lateral teeth. Dentes twice as long as manubrium, stout, slightly narrowing distally, not crenulate dorsally, but with coarse rounded tubercles, with a very long subapical seta. Furcula long, attaining the ventral tube. Manubrium with many ventral setae. Mucrones lamellate. Corpus of tenaculum with very many setae. Third and fourth abdominal segments subequal in length, or third a little longer. Genital and anal segments ankylosed. Tibiotarsus without a distal subsegment. Unguiculus with a pair of inner lamellae. Tenent hairs absent. Clothing of short simple setae.

ÅGRENIA BIDENTICULATA (Tullberg)

PLATE 15, FIGURES 156–159

Isotoma bidenticulata TULLBERG, 1876, p. 35.—STUXBERG, 1887, p. 42.—MAC-
GILLIVRAY, 1891, p. 273; 1896, p. 50.—SCHAFFER, 1894, p. 129.—SCHOTT,
1894, p. 67.—VON DALLA TORRE, 1895, p. 10.—SCHERBAKOV, 1899a, p. 47;
1899b, p. 5.—WAHLGREN, 1899b, p. 337; 1906a, p. 224; 1906b, p. 257.—
CARPENTER, 1900, p. 274.—SKORIKOW, 1900, p. 205.—ÅGREN, 1904, p. 17.—
EVANS, 1908, p. 200.
Isotoma lanuginosa CARL, 1899, p. 307.
Ågrenia bidenticulata BÖRNER, 1906, p. 171.—LINNANIEMI (AXELSON), 1907,
p. 74; 1909, p. 9; 1912, p. 173.—CARPENTER, 1908, p. 176.—HANDSCHIN,
1919, p. 77; 1924a, p. 116; 1924b, p. 85; 1929, p. 71.—WAHLGREN, 1919,
p. 751; 1920, p. 8.—CARPENTER and PHILLIPS, 1922, p. 15.—SCHÖTT, 1923,
p. 13.—DENIS, 1924b, p. 231; 1925, p. 145.—REMY, 1928, p. 65.

Description.—Coloration variable; purple or green with pale legs
and furcula; or yellowish green, brownish dorsally; sometimes dark
brown with more or less of a greenish luster. A median dorsal black
spot occurs behind the eyes; anteriorly a transverse black band connects the eye spots; or instead of this there may be three black spots;
one immediately behind the base of each antenna, and a median spot;
these spots being less evident in heavily pigmented individuals.
Eyes (pl. 15, fig. 156) eight on each side, on black spots, the two inner
proximal eyes much smaller than the others. Postantennal organ
(pl. 15, fig. 156) roundish, oval or broadly elliptical, slightly longer
than the diameter of the adjacent eye. Antennae almost or quite
twice as long as the head, with segments in relative lengths about as
11:13:15:19. Sense organ of third antennal segment (pl. 15, fig. 157)
with two curving rods, usually freely exposed. Fourth antennal segment with small olfactory setae, three ventroapical finely granulate
papillae, and a subapical pit with a central tubercle. Unguis (pl. 15,
fig. 158) long and narrow, with a small tooth near the middle of the
inner margin, and a pair of large basal lateral teeth, between which a
delicate membrane extends closely over the base of the unguis. Unguiculus two-fifths to one-half as long as the opposite unguis, with a pair
of inner lamellae. Tibiotarsus without a distal subsegment and without tenent hairs or other long distal hairs. Third and fourth abdominal segments subequal, or third a trifle longer than the fourth (as
25:24). Genital and anal segments ankylosed. Furcula appended to
the fifth abdominal segment and attaining the ventral tube. Manubrium with abundant short stiff ventral setae. Dens almost or quite
twice as long as manubrium, subcylindrical, slightly narrowing distally, not rounded apically, not crenulate, but dorsally covered with
small rounded turbercles; dorsally with a few short proximal setae;
laterally and ventrally with abundant stiff setae. An exceptionally
long and strong subapical seta on the mesal side of the dens extends
far beyond the mucro (pl. 15, fig. 159). Mucro (pl. 15, fig. 159)
about one-third as long as hind unguis, bilamellate, with strongly

convex ventral margin (in lateral aspect) and three approximate teeth, the proximal tooth being lateral in position, weakly developed and sometimes absent. Rami of tenaculum quadridentate; corpus stout, with abundant (20 to 30) ventral setae. Clothing exclusively of dense short stiff simple setae; a very long simple seta projecting from the inner side of the femur. Integument smooth. Length, 2 mm (Ågren); 2.5 mm (Carpenter).

In some individuals an obsolete dorsal suture occurs between the genital and anal segments.

Remarks.—The basal membrane of the unguis has been described in detail by Denis (1924b), who holds that it is not the equivalent of the *tunica* of certain Sminthuridae, but is an expansion of the lateral teeth of the unguis.

European examples of this species were kindly given to me by Dr. C. Schäffer, Dr. E. Handschin, Dr. Jan Stach, and Dr. R. Denis.

This species occurs under stones on the seashore, under partly submerged stones in streams, and on the snow. It is distinctively an arctic and alpine species (Carpenter); in arctic regions being abundant and, in some places, the dominant species of its order.

Distribution.—*Ågrenia bidenticulata* has been recorded from Greenland, Spitsbergen, Bear Island, King Charles Island, Franz Josef Land, Nova Zembla, Siberia, Norway, Sweden, Finland, Lapland, Russia, Switzerland, Scotland, and Ireland.

Colorado: Ghost Glacier, August 31, G. W. Goldsmith.

Wyoming: Yellowstone National Park, August 28, S. A. Forbes (Illinois State Natural History Survey).

British Columbia: Watershed of Franklin River, August 2, on surface of water and snow at 10,500 feet, Mr. and Mrs. D. Mundy.

Genus ISOTOMURUS Borner

Podura MULLER, 1776, p. 183 (part).

Isotoma BOURLET, 1839, p. 399 (part).—TULLBERG, 1872, p. 44 (part).

Isotomurus BÖRNER, 1903, p. 171; 1906, p. 162.—LINNANIEMI, 1912, p. 186.

Genotype.—*Podura palustris* Muller.

Fourth urotergite a little shorter than the third (subequal). Third urotergite ventrolaterally prolonged backward. Paratergite of fourth abdominal segment as in *Isotoma*. Genital and anal segments not ankylosed. Furcula attaining the ventral tube. Manubrium about one-half as long as dentes, with many ventral setae. Dentes long, slender, tapering, and dorsally with very many transverse crenulations. Mucrones quadridentate (tridentate), lamellate. Tenaculum with many ventral setae. Tibiotarsus without a distal subsegment. Tenent hairs absent. Clothing of relatively long setae, sometimes fringed. Fringed abdominal bothriotricha present. Integument smooth.

The qualifications in parentheses apply to foreign species of the genus.

Only the bothriotricha and the type of mucro distinguish *Isotomurus* from *Isotoma*.

KEY TO SPECIES OF ISOTOMURUS

1. Unguis extremely slender (pl. 25, fig. 277), without lateral teeth
   Yellowish green_____retardatus (p. 71)
   Unguis not conspicuously slender (pl. 26, fig. 285) and with a
   pair of lateral teeth_____2
2. Unguiculus setaceously prolonged.　Clothing of short setae
   fringed on all sides.　Violet_____palustroides (p. 77)
   Unguiculus not setaceously prolonged.　Clothing of simple setae.
   Coloration variable_____palustris (p. 72)

ISOTOMURUS RETARDATUS, new species

PLATE 25, FIGURES 276–280

Description.—Yellowish green.　Appendages pale green.　Head with two median dorsal roundish black spots; one anteocular, the other postocular.　Eyes (pl. 25, fig. 276) eight on each side, the two inner proximal eyes of each side somewhat smaller than the others. Postantennal organ (pl. 25, fig. 276) elliptical, slightly shorter to one-third longer than the diameter of an adjacent eye.　Antennae longer than the head (as 7:5), with segments in relative lengths about as 10:19:21:27; segments more or less blackish apically; third segment subclavate; fourth elliptical, petiolate.　Sense organ of third antennal segment with a pair of subcylindrical rods subtended by a thick chitinous ridge; fourth segment without special olfactory setae. Unguis (pl. 25, figs. 277, 278) exceptionally long and slender, uniformly tapering and curving, untoothed.　Unguiculus sublanceolate, acuminate, untoothed; on first and second pairs of feet extending one-third as far as the unguis; on third pair, larger, extending more than half as far as the unguis, aciculate.　Tenent hairs absent.　Third abdominal segment equal to fourth or longer (as 7:6).　Genital and anal segments not ankylosed.　Furcula appended to the fifth abdominal segment, attaining the ventral tube.　Manubrium with dense short stiff setae dorsally and ventrally.　Dentes almost twice as long as manubrium (as 7:4), slender, tapering, crenulate dorsally, with numerous short stiff dorsal setae except on distal third, and dense short stiff ventral setae.　Mucro (pl. 25, fig. 279) quadridentate, lamellate.　Apical tooth of mucro small, at the base of the second tooth, blunt or pointed, reduced or absent in some individuals; second and third teeth large, in longitudinal alinement with the first; fourth tooth proximolateral, oblique, blunt or acute; base of mucro with a median dorsal rounded lobe.　Outer and inner dorsal lamellae extend from the base of the mucro to the second and third teeth, respectively; a narrow median ventral lamella is also present. Rami of tenaculum quadridentate; corpus with many ventral setae. General clothing of dense short stiff simple setae of irregular length, becoming slightly longer posteriorly; with longer erect simple sensory setae; spinulate setae (pl. 25, fig. 280) occur on the genital and anal segments. Length, 1.7 mm.

Cotypes.—U.S.N.M. no. 42998.

Distribution.—Recorded as follows:

New Mexico: Las Vegas Hot Springs, February 16, W. P. and T. D. A. Cockerell.

ISOTOMURUS PALUSTRIS (Muller)

PLATE 25, FIGURE 281; PLATE 26, FIGURES 284-290

Podura palustris MULLER, 1776, p. 184.—GMELIN, 1778-93, p. 2911.—BOURLET, 1841-42, p. 117.

Isotoma palustris LUBBOCK, 1873, p. 169.—REUTER, 1876, p. 82 (part), 1890, p. 20; 1891, p. 228; 1895, p. 26.—REUTER, L. and O. M., 1880, p. 207.—TOMÖSVÁRY, 1882, p. 124.—PARONA, 1885, p. 45; 1895, p. 699.—VON DALLA TORRE, 1888, p. 156; 1895, p. 10.—UZEL, 1890, p. 62; 1891, p. 920.—PARFITT, 1891, pp. 342-343.—SCHOTT, 1891b, p. 22; 1894, p. 63; 1896a, p. 184; 1902, p. 22.—LIE-PETTERSEN, 1896, p. 17; 1898, p. 13; 1907, p. 65.—MACGILLIVRAY, 1896, p. 48.—SCHÄFFER, 1896, p. 186; 1898, p. 401; 1900a, p. 246; 1900b, p. 256.—POPPE and SCHÄFFER, 1897, p. 268.—SCHERBAKOV, 1898a, p. 58; 1898b, p. 7.—CARL, 1899, p. 311; 1901, p. 262.—CARPENTER and EVANS, 1899, p. 247.—ABSOLON, 1900a, p. 30.—BÖRNER, 1901a, p. 50; 1902a, p. 105.—EVANS, 1901b, p. 153.—BECKER, 1902, p. 26.—KRAUSBAUER, 1902, p. 40.—ÅGREN, 1903, p. 132.—GUTHRIE, 1903, p. 70.—PHILIPTSCHENKO, 1905, p. 3.—WAHLGREN, 1906b, p. 255; 1907a, p. 5.—COLLINGE, 1910, p. 11.—COLLINGE and SHOEBOTHAM, 1910, p. 112.—BACON, 1914, p. 153.—FOLSOM, 1919a, p. 11.

Isotoma tricolor PACKARD, 1873, p. 34 (part).—MACGILLIVRAY, 1891, p. 274 (part); 1896, p. 48.

Isotoma aquatilis LUBBOCK, 1873, p. 170 (part).—PARONA, 1879, p. 600; 1882, p. 463.

Isotoma stuxbergii TULLBERG, 1876, p. 35 (part).

Isotoma tullbergi MONIEZ, 1889, p. 28.

Isotoma stuxbergi MONIEZ, 1891, p. 70.

Isotoma aequalis MACGILLIVRAY, 1896, p. 49.

Isotomurus palustris BORNER, 1903, p. 171; 1906, p. 173.—AXELSON, 1905b, p. 35; 1906, p. 16.—LINNANIEMI (AXELSON), 1911, p. 19; 1912, p. 186.—IMMS, 1912, p. 93.—SHOEBOTHAM, 1917, p. 221.—BROWN, 1918, p. 186; 1926, p. 206.—WAHLGREN, 1919, p. 751.—DENIS, 1921, p. 126; 1922a, p. 111; 1924b, p. 232, 1927, p. 196.—STACH, 1922a, p. 23, 1922b, p. 117.—HANDSCHIN, 1924a, p. 121; 1924b, p. 85; 1925a, p. 232; 1927, p. 110; 1928a, p. 542; 1928b, p. 6; 1928c, p. 129; 1929, p. 72.—WOMERSLEY, 1924a, p. 33, 1927, p. 377.

Description.—Very variable in coloration. The typical form (pl. 25, fig. 281) is yellowish or greenish with blue, purple, or blackish pigment; having a median dorsal stripe with irregular margins; and frequently lateral spots, which may coalesce to form a stripe on each side of the body. Head often with a dorsal lunate or anchor-shaped spot.

Legs of the body color, dark basally, furcula unpigmented or with some pigment on the manubrium. Eyes (pl. 26, fig 284) eight on each side of the head, subequal; or the two inner proximal eyes of each group a little smaller than the others. Postantennal organ (pl. 25, fig. 284) near the eyes, elliptical, slightly longer than, to twice as long as, the diameter of an adjacent eye. Antennae one and one-half to two times as long as the head, with segments in relative lengths about as 3:4:5:6; first segment pale, or bluish apically; second and third pale, bluish apically; fourth bluish throughout. Sense organ of third antennal segment with a pair of linear feebly curving rods, a thick basal ridge, and two guard setae. Very short curving sensory setae occur on all the antennal segments as follows: Segment 1, 2–5; 2, 3–7; 3, 3–7; 4, 10–15. On the first three segments these are on the under side near the distal outer end; on the fourth segment they occur on the distal half along the outer side (Ågren, 1903). Mesonotum almost covering the pronotum. Third abdominal segment a little longer than the fourth (about as 5:4). Abdominal segments without ankylosis. Unguis (figs. 285, 286) stout, curving, with a pair of small lateral teeth, and with inner margin untoothed. Unguiculus broadly lanceolate, with inner lamella roundly dilated basally, untoothed as a rule, extending about half as far as the unguis on the hind feet, shorter on the other feet. Tenent hairs absent, represented by a single long simple hair. Furcula appended to the fifth abdominal segment, and extending to the anterior border of the ventral tube. Manubrium with many stiff ventral setae. Dentes twice as long as manubrium, slender, gradually tapering, crenulate dorsally. Mucro (pl 26, figs. 287, 288) two-thirds as long as hind unguis, quadridentate. Apical tooth of mucro small, at the base of the second tooth; second and third teeth dorsal, large, subequal, subconical, in line with the first tooth; fourth tooth lateral, oblique, acute; a membrane extends on each side from the apex of the third tooth to the base of the mucro; basolateral mucronal seta present. Rami of tenaculum quadridentate (pl. 26, fig. 289); corpus with many (15 or more) ventral setae. General clothing of abundant short simple setae. The second to fourth abdominal segments, inclusive, bear on each side three long attenuate feathered bothriotricha (pl. 26, fig. 290). Length, 3 mm

Remarks.—The ungues vary in stoutness (pl. 26, figs. 285, 286).

The statement regarding bothriotricha is from Börner. They vary somewhat in number and position, and may occur on the last five abdominal segments.

North American examples of *palustris* agree accurately with the European specimens that I have received from Dr C. Schäffer and Dr Jan Stach.

Packard's six cotypes of his *Isotoma tricolor*, from Waco, Tex., in the Museum of Comparative Zoology, Cambridge, Mass , for which

MacGillivray (1896) retained the name of *tricolor*, I found to be *palustris;* the remaining five specimens, from Salem, Mass., being *viridis.*

I. aequalis MacGillivray is also *palustris*, as I have found from a cotype given to me by MacGillivray.

The form with three stripes is *trifasciata* Bourlet (1839) as Handschin (1929) notes.

I. palustris lives in moist places, and is especially abundant along the edges of ponds and streams, frequenting the vegetation in preference to the water, though it is quite at home on the surface of the water, where it leaps vigorously and repeatedly. The species occurs on the seashore also, under seaweed, driftwood, or stones, and is sometimes found on the snow.

In a collection of Collembola taken from the stomachs of young trout at Ithaca, N. Y., by H. J. Pack, I found 38 specimens of *I. palustris*. This collection comprised more than 600 collembolans, representing 9 species. Mr. Pack found that Collembola formed from 20 to 25 percent of the bulk of the stomach contents of the young trout, which were mostly 25 to 30 mm in length.

This is one of the dominant species of its order. It is cosmopolitan in distribution, everywhere common, and highly variable in coloration, several varieties having received names.

Distribution.—The typical form of *I. palustris* is known from all parts of Europe, from Siberia, Nova Zembla, Spitsbergen, Bear Island, Greenland, Ellesmere Land, Azores Islands, Sicily, Sardinia, Algeria, Mesopotamia, Bismarck Archipelago, Argentina, Costa Rica, and Mexico.

Maine: Orono, February, F. L. Harvey.

Massachusetts: Arlington, January 16, March 10, April 6, 8, 13, May 2, 14, July 6, 10, August 2, November 6. Belmont, October 23. Cambridge, February 9, March 1, April 22, 29, 30, May 14, December 9 Lexington, April 17, May 7, 10, 16. Norwood, August 26. Waverley, March 27, April 4, 19, 21. Winchester, April 15.

New York: Ithaca, May, June, October, R. M. Hughes (Cornell University), May, June, H. J. Pack (Cornell University). Lakeville, October 7, E. A. Maynard. Pine Plains, June 14, D. B. Young (New York State Museum). Riverhead, Long Island, May 25, S. C. Bishop (New York State Museum) Rochester, March 11, E A Maynard Sodus Point, June 29, J. D. Hood Voorheesville, August 30, M. D. Leonard (New York State Museum).

Ohio: Salem, March 21, A. D. MacGillivray. Yellow Springs, February 9, March 4, April 3, August 28.

Indiana· La Fayette, J. J. Davis.

Illinois: Anna, May 6, 7, T. H. Frison (Illinois State Natural History Survey). Homer, April 5, 6, 9, 11, 16, 17, 24, 30, May 1, 5, 6, 9, June 9, 10, 11, 16. Urbana, January, C. A. Hart (Illinois State Natural History Survey); April 30. Volo, April 4, T. H. Frison and H. H. Ross (Illinois State Natural History Survey).

Iowa: Ames, March 31, April 7, J. E. Guthrie. Spirit Lake, April 7, J. E. Guthrie.

Wisconsin: Two Rivers, August, September.

Minnesota: Minneapolis, J. E. Guthrie (University of Minnesota).

Tennessee: Knoxville, February 18, C. N. and G. G. Ainslie.

Georgia: St. Simon Island, February 16, J. C. Bradley.

Florida: Gainesville, January 12, T. H. Hubbell. Marion County, February 20, T. H. Hubbell.

Louisiana: Tallulah, January 15, April 2, 7, 9, 18.

Texas: Waco, G. W. Belfrage (Museum of Comparative Zoology)

California: Palo Alto, V. L. Kellogg and L. M. Bremner (Stanford University). Claremont–Laguna region, January, December, G. A. Bacon.

Canada: Arnprior, Ontario, January 10, March, May, September, C. Macnamara. Toronto, Ontario, June 26, R. J. Crew.

ISOTOMURUS PALUSTRIS (Muller) variety PRASINUS (Reuter)

Isotoma stuxbergi var. *prasina* REUTER, 1891, p. 229.

Isotoma palustris var. *prasina* SCHÖTT, 1894, p. 66.—VON DALLA TORRE, 1895, p. 10.—REUTER, 1895, p. 26.—MACGILLIVRAY, 1896, p. 48.—SCHAFFER, 1896, p. 186; 1898, p. 403; 1900a, p. 246, 1900b, p. 256.—POPPE and SCHAFFER, 1897, p. 268.—CARL, 1899, p. 312; 1901, p. 262.—CARPENTER and EVANS, 1899, p. 247.—WAHLGREN, 1899c, p. 850; 1906b, p. 255; 1907a, p. 5.—BORNER, 1901a, p. 50.—BECKER, 1902, p. 26.—KRAUSBAUER, 1902, p. 40.—ÅGREN, 1903, p. 133.—FOLSOM, 1919a, p. 12.

Isotoma palustris var. *pallida* SCHAFFER, 1896, p. 186.—BORNER, 1901a, p. 50.—KRAUSBAUER, 1902, p. 66.

Isotomurus palustris var. *prasina* AXELSON, 1905b, p. 35; 1906, p. 16.—WAHLGREN, 1907a, p. 5.—LINNANIEMI (AXELSON), 1907, p. 30; 1911, p. 19; 1912, p. 187.—BROWN, 1918, p. 186.—DENIS, 1921, p. 126.—STACH, 1921, p. 164.—HANDSCHIN, 1929, p. 73.

Description.—Yellowish green or pale yellowish, varying sometimes into yellowish red or brownish; unicolorous, or with a trace of the median dorsal stripe. Length as great as 4.5 mm.

Specimens of this variety from Cuba are green, with narrowly elliptical postantennal organs twice as long as the diameter of an adjacent eye.

Distribution.—The variety *prasinus* has been recorded from Sweden, Finland, Poland, Germany, France, Switzerland, England, Scotland, Nova Zembla, Ellesmere Land, Siberia, and Bismarck Archipelago.

Massachusetts. Arlington, August 2.

New York: Lakeville, October 9, E. A. Maynard. Voorheesville, August 30, M. D. Leonard (New York State Museum).

Illinois: Anna, May 6, 7, T. H. Frison (Illinois State Natural History Survey). Glenview, December 27, A. R. Park (Illinois State Natural History Survey).

Alaska: Demarcation Point, May 16, F. Johansen (National Collection, Ottawa).

Canada: Bernard Harbour, Northwest Territories, May 25, June 16, 18, 25, July 9, F. Johansen (National Collection, Ottawa). Arnprior, Ontario, March 10, August, C. Macnamara.

Cuba: Habana, C. F. Baker.

ISOTOMURUS PALUSTRIS (Müller) variety BALTEATUS (Reuter)

Isotoma balteata REUTER, 1876, p. 82

Isotoma palustris var. *balteata* ABSOLON, 1900a, p. 30.—SCHOTT, 1894, p. 66;
    1896a, p. 184.—VON DALLA TORRE, 1895, p. 10.—REUTER, 1895, p. 26.—
    SCHAFFER, 1896, p 186, 1898, p. 402.—SCHERBAKOV, 1898a, p. 58; 1898b,
    p 7 —PHILIPTSCHENKO, 1905, p. 4.

Isotoma palustris var. *cincta* KRAUSBAUER, 1902, p. 40.

Isotomurus palustris var. *balteata* LINNANIEMI, 1912, p. 189.—HANDSCHIN, 1929,
    p. 73.

Description.—Ground color yellow, sometimes whitish. Body segments (except prothorax) broadly banded with dark blue or blackish; the unpigmented posterior region of each segment appearing as a yellow or white band. Vertex with a median black spot. Antennal base black. Antennae and legs variable in the amount of pigmentation. Sternum and furcula unpigmented, or latter pigmented basally. Length, 1.25 mm.

Remarks.—Some of my specimens from Louisiana show a trace of a median dorsal black line.

Small individuals from Florida are pale yellow, with pale purple antennae.

On one occasion I observed a coleopterous larva, determined by Dr. A. G. Boving as a species of *Stenus*, holding one of these collembolans between its jaws.

Distribution.—This well-marked variety of *palustris* has been recorded from Finland, Russia, Hungary, Bismarck Archipelago and California.

Maryland: College Park, March, in a greenhouse, E. N. Cory.

Florida: Gainesville, January 12, in decaying leaves in moist hammock, T. H. Hubbell.

Illinois: Homer, April 17, on rain-water pool on grass.

Iowa: Burlington, July, J. E. Guthrie.

Louisiana: Tallulah, March 31, April 2, 4, under a log on grass.

California: Lake Chabot, near Oakland, G. Eisen (California Academy of Sciences). Palo Alto, V L. Kellogg and L. M. Bremner (Stanford University).

British West Indies: Grenada, August 25, on grass growing through water, H. E. Summers.

ISOTOMURUS PALUSTRIS (Müller) TEXENSIS, new variety

PLATE 25, FIGURES 282, 283

Description.—Ground color yellow. Markings dark blue to black Antennal bases black, connected by a black line. Vertex with a median black spot. Body with a broad median dorsal black stripe, with irregular margins, extending back as far as the third abdominal segment; also a pair of broad irregular subdorsal stripes. Abdominal segments with lateral black markings. The last four abdominal segments have a dorsal pattern that is variable, but essentially as in plate 25, figures 282 and 283. First antennal segment pale, or dark apically; second and third dark apically or throughout; fourth dark. Precoxal segments and coxae more or less pigmented; femora often pigmented basally and apically; tibiotarsi dark blue; furcula unpigmented. Length, 2.3 mm.

Small individuals have very little pigment. Individuals about 1.5 mm in length have the black antennal bases, the spot on the vertex, and a little pigment at the bases of the legs; while the median dorsal line is represented by a series of black spots, and the subdorsal spots are ill-defined.

Remarks —This variety resembles var. *maculata* Schäffer (1896), examples of which I have received from him. The type of coloration is, however, rather different in the two forms, as may be seen by comparing my figures with those of Stach (1924, pl. 2, figs. 9–12). The median dorsal stripe in *texensis* is not narrow, as it is in *maculata*, but is always broad, with irregular margins.

Cotypes.—U.S.N.M. no. 42999.

Distribution.—Recorded as follows:

Texas: College Station, December 22, C. A. Hart.

ISOTOMURUS PALUSTROIDES, new species

PLATE 26, FIGURES 291–295

Description.—Dark violet with white spots. Legs, manubrium, and bases of dentes pale purple. Antennae purple; basal ring blackish purple. Eyes (pl. 26, fig. 291) eight on each side, subequal. Postantennal organ (pl. 26, figs. 291, 292) elliptical, slightly shorter than, or subequal to, the diameter of an adjacent eye. Antennae one and three-fourths times as long as the head, with segments in relative lengths as 4:8:9:7.5.

Abdominal segments without ankylosis. Third abdominal segment longer than the fourth (as 4:3). Unguis (pl. 26, fig. 293) slender, curving, with a pair of minute lateral teeth and with inner margin untoothed. Unguiculus sublanceolate, untoothed, apically setaceously prolonged, extending two-thirds as far as the unguis. Tenent hairs absent, represented by a single long simple hair. On each mid and hind tibiotarsus (fore legs also?) there is a long hair, minutely fringed on all sides (bothriotrix), inserted on the same side as the unguis (upper side), and almost half as long as the tibiotarsus. Furcula attaining the ventral tube. Dentes about twice as long as the manubrium. Mucrones (pl. 26, fig. 294) about as long as hind unguiculi, quadridentate, in form essentially as in *palustris*. Apical tooth small but evident, at base of second; second and third teeth dorsal, large, subequal, subconical, in longitudinal alinement; fourth tooth lateral, oblique, acute. Basolateral mucronal seta probably present normally, as indicated by the insertion pit in plate 26, figure 294. General clothing of abundant short tapering setae, fringed on all sides (pl. 26, fig. 295).

Abdominal bothriotricha were not seen in the single specimen available, but may have dropped off.   Length, 2.2 mm.

Cotypes.—U.S N.M. no. 42997.

Distribution.—Recorded as follows:

Canada: Arnprior, Ontario, October, C. Macnamara.

Genus ISOTOMA Bourlet

Isotoma BOURLET, 1839, p. 399 (part) —BORNFR, 1903, p 139; 1906, p. 171—
  LINNANIEMI, 1912, p. 138.
Desoria AGASSIZ, 1841, p. 384.—NICOLET, 1841, p 57.

Genotype.—*Isotoma viridis* Bourlet.

Fourth urotergite usually shorter than the third; the two seldom equal. Third urotergite ventrolaterally prolonged backward (pl. 38, fig 441). Paratergite of the fourth abdominal segment always united to the tergite of the genital segment, or the two ankylosed without suture. When the furcula is extended, the membrane between the paratergites of the third and fourth abdominal segments is exposed. Genital and anal segments rarely ankylosed. Furcula long, almost always attaining the ventral tube. Manubrium much shorter than dentes, with many ventral setae. Dentes long, slender, tapering, with very many dorsal transverse folds or crenulations. Mucrones tridentate or quadridentate, rarely lamellate. Tenaculum with many ventral setae. Tibiotarsus without a distal subsegment. Tenent hairs present or absent. Postantennal organ not notched or constricted. Clothing of relatively long setae, the largest of which are not infrequently unilaterally serrate or branched. Bothriotricha absent. Integument smooth.

KEY TO SUBGENERA OF ISOTOMA

1. Tibiotarsi with two or three tenent hairs_____ 2
   Tibiotarsi without tenent hairs_____ **Isotoma** (p 87)
2 Genital and anal segments not ankylosed. Furcula attaining
      the ventral tube or not. Dentes convergent_____ **Vertagopus** (p. 81)
   Genital and anal segments ankylosed. Furcula attaining the
      ventral tube. Dentes not convergent_____ **Pseudisotoma** (p. 78)

Subgenus PSEUDISOTOMA Handschin

Pseudisotoma HANDSCHIN, 1924a, p 111.

Subgenotype.—*Isotoma sensibilis* Tullberg.

ISOTOMA (PSEUDISOTOMA) SENSIBILIS Tullberg

PLATE 27, FIGURES 296–299

Isotoma sensibilis TULLBERG, 1876, p 36.—UZEL, 1890, p. 64.—SCHOTT, 1894,
  p 72; 1902, p 28.—REUTER, 1895, p. 27.—LIE-PETTERSEN, 1896, p. 18;
  1898, p 13, 1907, p 61—CARL, 1899, p 307; 1901, p. 264.—CARPENTER
  and EVANS, 1899, p 249—ABSOLON, 1900a, p. 30.—SCHAFFER, 1900a, p.
  247; 1900b, p 258—WAHLGREN, 1900a, p. 367; 1906b, p. 257—EVANS,

1901b, p. 153.—Krausbauer, 1902, p. 41.—Ågren, 1903, p. 139, 1904, p. 17.—Guthrie, 1903, p. 67.—Linnaniemi (Axelson), 1907, p. 30; 1911, p. 15.—Schille, 1906, p. 8.—Brown, 1918, p. 186; 1919, p 64; 1923, p. 262.—Denis, 1924a, p 260.

Isotoma dubia Reuter, 1895, p. 27.

Isotoma determinata MacGillivray, 1896, p 54.

Isotoma parva MacGillivray, 1896, p 50

Isotoma longidens Schaffer, 1896, p. 188.

Isotoma monstrosa Schäffer, 1896, p 189.

Isotoma inopinata Axelson, 1902, p. 108.

Isotoma (Vertagopus) sensibilis Linnaniemi, 1912, p 143.—Handschin, 1919, p. 76.—Stach, 1921, p. 161.—Schött, 1923, p. 11.—Womersley, 1924a, p. 32; 1925, p. 219.

Isotoma (Pseudisotoma) sensibilis Handschin, 1924a, p. 111.

Pseudisotoma sensibilis Handschin, 1924b, p 85; 1929, p. 64.—Remy, 1928, p. 65.

Description.—Bluish gray, greenish, clear blue, or blackish blue. A common form of the species under loose bark of dead trees (MacGillivray's *determinata*) is green, marked with blackish; with the ground color white; and, in individuals that are not too heavily pigmented, with minute round white spots distributed abundantly and uniformly throughout the green areas. Large irregular white spots occur dorsally on the head, mesonotum, metanotum, and the first five abdominal segments. A Λ-shaped black marking extends forward from the eyes. An irregular median black spot occurs midway between the eyes and the posterior border of the head. Second and third thoracic, and the first four or five abdominal segments bordered posteriorly with black, which extends also along the lateral margins of the tergites, particularly the mesonotum and metanotum. Sternum, legs, and furcula white; or manubrium pigmented slightly. Antennae pale green proximally, dull bluish green distally; or bluish throughout: first two segments green, ringed with black apically; last two segments green, mottled with blue. Other forms of the species have blue, instead of green, pigment. Young individuals may be almost white. Eyes (pl. 27, fig. 296) eight on each side; the two inner proximal eyes of each group smaller than the others. Postantennal organ (pl. 27, fig. 296) broadly elliptical, oval or subovate, varying from a little shorter than, to one and one-half times as long as, the diameter of an adjacent eye. Antennae a little longer than the head, stout: third segment slightly shorter to slightly longer than the second; fourth, one and one-half to two times as long as the third. Sense organ of third antennal segment with a pair of stout curving rods under an integumentary fold, and subtended by a chitinous ridge. Fourth antennal segment without special olfactory setae. Third abdominal segment subequal to fourth or a little longer (as 15:13). Genital and anal segments ankylosed. Unguis (pl. 27, fig. 297) with a small inner tooth one-fourth from the apex (sometimes absent, however) and a pair of small lateral teeth. Unguiculus extending almost half as far as the unguis, broadly lanceolate or subovate, acute or acuminate, with or without a tooth at the angle of the inner lamella. Hind claws the largest. Tenent hairs 2, 3, 3, strongly knobbed, distally bending. Furcula appended to the fifth abdominal segment, long, extending almost or quite to the ventral tube. Manubrium relatively short and stout, with many setae dorsally and ventrally. Dentes two and one-half to three times as long as the manubrium, not convergent, slender, gradually tapering, dorsally crenulate, with a strong ventral subapical seta that may extend as far as the apex of the mucro (pl. 27, fig. 298), or beyond it. Mucro (pl. 27, figs. 298, 299) shorter than hind unguiculus, tridentate, with the teeth somewhat variable in relative sizes: Apical tooth the longest, slender or stout, more or less hooked; second inclined caudally; third lateral, close to second, conical or slightly hooked, inclined caudally. Rami of tenaculum quadridentate; corpus with several (7 to 12) ventral setae, the largest of which (on the last three abdominal segments) are minutely and unilaterally branched; erect simple sensory setae are present also. Maximum length, 2 mm.

Remarks—In occasional individuals the genital and anal segments are not completely ankylosed.

European specimens may attain a length of 2 mm (Ågren); but the largest individuals that I have seen from this country (from Minnesota) were 1.2 mm in length.

Specimens that I collected in Massachusetts agree exactly with German examples received from Dr. C. Schäffer and with English specimens from J. M. Brown.

The types of MacGillivray's *parva* and *determinata* in the Museum of Comparative Zoology, Cambridge, Mass., are *sensibilis* Tullberg. In the original description of *parva* the third, or lateral, tooth of the mucro is not mentioned as being present.

Guthrie's specimens from Minnesota are evidently *sensibilis*.

In Europe, *I. sensibilis* lives primarily under loose bark and in moss, but occurs also under logs and stones, on the seashore under seaweed, and on the surface of pools of fresh water. It occurs at times in large masses, and has been taken abundantly on snow on mild winter days.

Most of my North American material of this species was taken under the loose dead bark of trees or logs: Chestnut, cedar, oak, basswood, maple, willow, and black locust.

Distribution.—Recorded as follows:

Massachusetts. Cambridge, May 7. Dedham, July 21. Dover, November 9, A. P. Morse (Museum of Comparative Zoology). Newton, June 22. Norwood, August 26. Waltham, July 29.

New York: Macedon, May 11, J. D. Hood.

Ohio: Salineville, A. D. MacGillivray (Museum of Comparative Zoology).

Illinois: Oregon, April 3, in moss on rocks, T. H. Frison and H. H. Ross (Illinois State Natural History Survey).

Minnesota: St. Louis County, July 6, 30, J. E. Guthrie (University of Minnesota).

Florida: Alachua County, March 20, T. H. Hubbell. Camp Torreya, Liberty County, April 3, T. H. Hubbell Marion County, February 20, in moss, T. H. Hubbell. Putnam County, March 19, T. H. Hubbell.

Louisiana: Tallulah, April 9, 25, May 3.

Canada: Arnprior, Ontario, April, October, C. Macnamara.

Subgenus VERTAGOPUS Borner

Vertagopus BÖRNER, 1906, p. 171—LINNANIEMI, 1912, p. 138.

Subgenotype.—Isotoma cinerea (Nicolet).

KEY TO SPECIES OF SUBGENUS VERTAGOPUS

1. Furcula extending almost or quite to the ventral tube. Mucro, in lateral aspect, with strongly curving ventral contour. Eyes unequal. Blackish or purplish, appendages white or yellowish_____ arborea (p 83)

   Furcula extending only as far as the posterior border of the second abdominal segment. Mucro, in lateral aspect, with ventral contour feebly curving or almost straight. Eyes equal. Variable in coloration: Yellowish, bluish, or greenish_____ cinerea (p. 81)

ISOTOMA (VERTAGOPUS) CINEREA (Nicolet)

PLATE 27, FIGURES 300–308

Desoria cinerea NICOLET, 1841, p 60.—GERVAIS, 1844, p. 429.

Isotoma cinerca NICOLET, 1847, p 372.—TULLBERG, 1872, p. 47.—LUBBOCK, 1873, p. 174.—PARONA, 1879, p. 602; 1882, p. 463.—TÖMÖSVÁRY, 1882, p 124.—VON DALLA TORRE, 1888, p. 157; 1895, p. 10.—UZEL, 1890, p. 66.—SCHOTT, 1894, p. 73; 1902, p. 28.—REUTER, 1895, p. 28.—LIE-PETTERSEN, 1896, p. 18.— CARL, 1899, p. 320.—CARPENTER and EVANS, 1899, p. 251.—SCHÄFFER, 1900a, p. 247; 1900b, p. 260.—BÖRNER, 1901a, p. 58.—EVANS, 1901b, p. 153.—ÅGREN, 1903, p. 142; 1904, p. 17.—AXELSON, 1904, p. 70; 1905b, p. 32; 1906, p. 13.—WAHLGREN, 1906a, p 223; 1906b, p. 257; 1919, p. 745.— LINNANIEMI (AXELSON), 1907, p. 21, 1909, p. 13; 1911, p. 15.—COLLINGE and SHOEBOTHAM, 1910, p 108.—BARTHOLIN, 1916, p. 168.—BROWN, 1918, p. 186.

Isotoma quadri-denticulata TULLBERG, 1871, p. 152.

Isotoma unica MACGILLIVRAY, 1896, p. 50.

Isotoma dilatata MACGILLIVRAY, 1896, p. 53.

Isotoma inclinata MACGILLIVRAY, 1896, p. 55.

Isotoma lateraria MACGILLIVRAY, 1896, p. 56.

Isotoma (Vertagopus) cinerea BÖRNER, 1906, p. 171.—COLLINGE, 1910, p. 9.— LINNANIEMI, 1912, p. 139.—DENIS, 1921, p. 125; 1922a, p. 111; 1924d, p. 210.—STACH, 1921, p. 161.—HANDSCHIN, 1924a, p. 113; 1929, p. 64.—WOMERSLEY, 1924a, p. 32; 1925, p. 219.

Vertagopus cinerea HANDSCHIN, 1924b, p. 85.

Description.—General color yellow, olivaceous, grayish, or bluish, according to the amount of blue pigment present; in alcohol, often greenish, the combined effect of the yellow ground color and minute spots of blue pigment. Body segments frequently edged with dark blue. In heavily pigmented individuals a median dorsal interrupted blackish stripe may be present; or there may be three dorsal stripes.

Head with an anteocular blue spot, often ill defined. An elongate species Eyes (pl. 27, fig. 300) eight on each side, subequal. Post-antennal organ (pl. 27, fig. 300) broadly elliptical, oval or ovate; about twice as long as the diameter of an eye. Antennae one and one-half to almost two times as long as the head; segments apically or entirely purplish, in relative lengths about as 6:9:10:20. Sense organ of third antennal segment (pl. 27, fig. 301) consisting of a pair of linear rods, basally curving, subtended by a chitinous ridge. Mesonotum with an anteromedian rounded emargination. Unguis (pl. 27, fig 302) with an inner tooth beyond the middle, one-third from the apex, and a pair of small lateral teeth one-third from the base. Unguiculus one-half to two-thirds as long as unguis, lanceo-late, acuminate, unidentate on the inner margin. Knobbed tenent hairs two or three on each tibiotarsus. Third abdominal segment a little longer than the fourth (as 17:14). Genital and anal seg-ments not ankylosed Furcula appended to the fifth abdominal segment; extending almost to, or slightly beyond, the posterior margin of the second abdominal segment. Dentes twice as long as manubrium, slender, tapering, apically convergent, dorsally crenu-late. Mucrones (pl. 27, figs. 303–307) a little shorter than hind unguiculi, quadridentate, with ventral margin straight to slightly convex in lateral aspect; apical tooth straight to subfalcate, some-times reduced; second and third teeth subequal, or the third smaller, conical, suberect or feebly hooked; first three teeth in longitudinal alinement; fourth tooth lateral, near the third, acute, oblique, or suberect, sometimes reduced or absent (pl. 27, fig. 307). Rami of tenaculum (pl. 27, fig. 308) quadridentate; corpus with six to nine ventral setae. Clothing of dense short curving reclinate setae, with a few long outstanding sensory setae, simple or weakly spinulate. Length, 1.6 mm.

Remarks.—The amount of blue pigment varies greatly but increases with the age of the individual as a rule. The antennae and furcula increase in relative length with age; and in small individuals the former may not be much longer than the head. In small individuals the inner tooth of the unguis and that of the unguiculus are small or absent. The common formula for the number of tenent hairs is 2, 3, 3; this occurring in 48 percent of the Massachusetts specimens that I examined; the other formulae found being 2, 2, 2 (23 percent), 2, 2, 3 (23 percent), and 3, 3, 3 (6 percent). The mucrones vary considerably in form, as is shown in figures 303 to 307, and many mucronal variations may be found in members of the same colony.

Two individuals, taken at Homer, Ill., are unusually long—2.7 mm.

At one time I sent Massachusetts specimens to Dr. C. Schäffer, who reported them to be the common European *I. cinerea* (Nicolet), and in return he sent me European examples of the species, enabling me to confirm his determination.

J. M. Brown sent me specimens of the species from England.

The specimens that I sent to Schäffer I had compared with, and found to agree with, a type of *lateraria* MacGillivray in the Museum of Comparative Zoology.

I. unica MacGillivray, of which I examined one cotype in the same museum, was evidently described from young individuals of *cinerea* (about 1 mm in length), in which the antennae were short and the claws as yet without teeth.

I. dilatata MacGillivray agrees with *cinerea* Nicolet. In the single type of *dilatata* in the museum at Cambridge, the tooth of the unguiculus is wanting and the small lateral tooth of the mucro is absent.

I. inclinata MacGillivray is also a synonym of *cinerea*, as I found from three cotypes in the Museum of Comparative Zoology, and two others given to me by A. P. Morse. In *inclinata* also the lateral tooth of the mucro is absent.

This species, one of our commonest collembolans, is found in colonies, chiefly under the loose damp bark of trees or logs, but occurs also on damp soil under sticks or dead leaves, and in moss. I have taken it on oak, apple, willow, elm, cherry, maple, and sycamore, and it doubtless occurs on other kinds of trees as well; once I found it on a fungus.

Distribution.—*Isotoma cinerea* is abundant in almost all parts of Europe and has been recorded from Siberia and Franz Josef Land also.

Maine: Orono, July 20, October, F. L. Harvey.

Massachusetts. Vicinity of Boston (Cambridge, Arlington, Lexington), January 16, March 20, April 12, 13, 17, 22, 23, May 7, 11, 13, 14, June 11. Dover, Beverly, A. P. Morse (Museum of Comparative Zoology).

New York: Albany, May 7, D. B. Young (New York State Museum). Ithaca, A. D. MacGillivray (Cornell University). Macedon, April 6, 13, 20, May 4, J. D. Hood.

Ohio: Salineville, A. D. MacGillivray (Museum of Comparative Zoology). Yellow Springs, February 4, 9, April 3.

Illinois: Homer, February 28, March 15, 31, April 2, 6, 9, 10, 12, 13, 16, 24, 25, May 12. Makanda, March 5, T. H. Frison and H. H. Ross (Illinois State Natural History Survey). Oakwood, February 11, April 20, T. H. Frison (Illinois State Natural History Survey). St. Joseph, February 11, H. H. Ross (Illinois State Natural History Survey). Urbana, February 13, March 11, 13, April 5, 11, 12, 14, 18, May 1, December.

Canada. Arnprior, Ontario, April, May 11, November, C. Macnamara. De Grassi Point, Ontario, September, E. M. Walker.

ISOTOMA (VERTAGOPUS) ARBOREA (Linnaeus)

PLATE 28, FIGURES 309–315

Podura arborea LINNAEUS, 1758, p. 609.

Isotoma arborea BOURLET, 1839, p. 402; 1841–2, p. 115.—ÅGREN, 1903, p. 140.—WAHLGREN, 1906b, p. 257.—BARTHOLIN, 1916, p. 169.—SHOEBOTHAM, 1917, p. 221.—BROWN, 1918, p. 186.

Isotoma reuteri SCHÖTT, 1894, p. 71; 1902, p. 23.—VON DALLA TORRE, 1895, p. 10.

Isotoma denticulata SCHAFFER, 1896, p. 189.—POPPE and SCHÄFFER, 1897, p. 268.—CARL, 1899, p. 321.—BORNER, 1901a, p. 57.—KRAUSBAUER, 1902, p. 43.—SCHILLE, 1906, p. 8.

Isotoma synonymica MACGILLIVRAY, 1896, p. 52.

Isotoma terminata MACGILLIVRAY, 1896, p. 56.

Isotoma (Vertagopus) arborea COLLINGE, 1910, p. 9.—WOMERSLEY, 1924a, p. 32; 1927, p. 376.

Vertagopus arborea STACH, 1922a, p. 19.—HANDSCHIN, 1929, p. 65.

Description.—Blackish purple, dorsally mottled with small unpigmented spots, which are round, oval, or elongate. Legs and furcula whitish or yellowish, except coxae and manubrium, which are usually pigmented. Antennae purplish. Young individuals are brown (Schaffer). Eyes (pl. 28, fig. 309) eight on each side, unequal, the two inner proximal eyes of each group being smaller than the others. Postantennal organ (pl. 28, fig. 309) elliptical to suboval, one to two times as long as the diameter of an adjacent eye. Antennae one and one-third times as long as the head; segments in relative lengths about as 5:9:7:13. or 5:9·8:16; second and third segments each with a short incomplete apical subsegment. Sense organ of third antennal segment (pl. 28, fig. 310) with a pair of subclavate sense rods, more or less curving (see beyond), under a thin integumentary fold. Fourth antennal segment without special olfactory setae; with a hemispherical apical papilla and an adjacent bluntly conical peg. Unguis (pl. 28, fig. 311) stout, curving, unidentate near the middle, or a little beyond the middle, of the inner margin, with a pair of small lateral teeth one-third from the base. Unguiculus one-half as long as the unguis, extending three-fifths as far as the latter, broadly lanceolate, with inner margin dilated and unidentate. Tenent hairs 2, 3, 3. Genital and anal segments not ankylosed as a rule (see beyond). Third abdominal segment equal to, or slightly longer than, the fourth (as 12:11). Furcula appended to the fifth abdominal segment and attaining the ventral tube. Dentes from two to two and one-half times as long as the manubrium, slender, gradually tapering, with numerous dorsal crenulations, and convergent. Mucro (pl. 28, figs. 312–315) shorter than hind unguiculus, quadridentate; apical tooth hooked, typically much shorter than the second tooth (pl. 28, fig. 312), but in specimens from the United States often becoming almost as large as the anteapical tooth, second tooth the largest, suberect or inclined slightly backward; third tooth a little smaller than the second, inclined backward or suberect; first three teeth in longitudinal alinement; fourth tooth lateral, more proximal than the third tooth or almost opposite the latter, inclined backward, sometimes reduced or absent (pl. 28, fig. 315). Rami of tenaculum quadridentate; corpus with several (as many as nine) setae. General clothing of short dense curving simple setae. Erect sensory setae occur in a transverse row across the middle of each of the first four abdominal segments, on the mesonotum anteriorly and posteriorly, and on the legs. The sensory setae are long and numerous on the genital and anal segments, where the largest setae are often minutely serrate. Length, 1 5 mm; maximum, 2 mm.

Remarks —The third antennal segment, usually shorter than the second, may become longer than the latter in large individuals The inner tooth of the unguis varies in size and is sometimes absent.

The tooth of the unguiculus is at times reduced to an angle The teeth of the mucro vary greatly in form and relative size. Thus, the first tooth may be as large as the second; and the lateral tooth may be long or short, pointed or blunt; sometimes all four teeth are subequal.

In some of my specimens from Oregon, Ill., the genital and anal segments are ankylosed; as they are also in some of the English examples that I received from J. M. Brown.

In plate 28, figure 310, the strong bending of the two sense rods is abnormal, being due to pressure from the cover glass used. The rods appear in their normal attitude in plate 28, figure 318.

My European material of this species consists of 9 specimens of *denticulata* from Germany, given to me by Schäffer, and 11 examples of *arborea* from England, from J. M. Brown.

In this species the convergence of the dentes is a striking character, and one known to Ågren (1903) in only one other species of *Isotoma*, namely, *cinerea* Nicolet. This convergence, as Ågren notes, is evident in living or stupefied individuals, but it sometimes does not show so plainly in alcoholic material. ·

The three cotypes of MacGillivray's *terminata* in the Museum of Comparative Zoology, Cambridge, Mass , as well as four others given to me by A P. Morse, agree exactly with the specimens of *denticulata* that I received from Schaffer.

I synonymica MacGillivray is also this species, as I have found from an examination of five cotypes: three in the museum just named and two given to me by MacGillivray.

Distribution.—*Isotoma arborea* is known from Sweden, Denmark, Germany, Switzerland, Hungary, Siberia, and England. In both Europe and North America it is most numerous in winter and spring, and in Europe is said to occur in large colonies, sometimes on the snow. The species lives primarily under the loose bark of trees or logs in colonies, but may be found scattered on the ground under damp leaves, and occurs in moss.

Maine· Orono, March 10, F. L. Harvey.

Massachusetts: Arlington, March 20, April 9 Cambridge, May 14, just hatched.

New York· Ithaca, February, March 20, 25, A. D. MacGillivray (Cornell University); March 8, in a crow's nest, I D. Dobroscky. Macedon, April 6, 20, May 11, J. D. Hood. Potsdam, May 26, D B. Young (New York State Museum).

Ohio: Salineville, February 17, 19, December 21, 25, A. D. MacGillivray (Museum of Comparative Zoology, Cornell University).

Illinois: Homer, April 29. Urbana, March 11, 13, April 5. Oregon, April 3, T. H. Frison and H. H. Ross (Illinois State Natural History Survey).

ISOTOMA (VERTAGOPUS) ARBOREA (Linnaeus) variety NIGRA MacGillivray

PLATE 28, FIGURES 316–319

Isotoma brunnea MacGillivray, 1896, p. 52.
Isotoma speciosa MacGillivray, 1896, p. 55.
Isotoma nigra MacGillivray, 1896, p. 56.

Description.—This variety differs from typical *arborea* only in having no knobbed tenent hairs; in place of these there being a single long simple hair. The color is blackish purple, with legs and furcula whitish, yellowish, or brownish. In this variety, as in the typical form also, the lateral tooth of the mucro may be reduced to a rounded knob (pl. 28, fig. 316).

Remarks.—My figures of *nigra* (pl. 28, figs. 316–319) would answer equally for typical *arborea*.

MacGillivray's *brunnea*, *speciosa*, and *nigra* are this variety. Except in lacking tenent hairs, his cotypes of these agree exactly with his cotypes of *terminata* and *synonymica* (synonyms of *arborea*); the slight differences given in the original descriptions being all within the range of individual variation of the species. *I. brunnea*, for example, has a blunt apical mucronal tooth and no lateral tooth (one cotype in Museum of Comparative Zoology; one from MacGillivray). *I. speciosa* has the lateral mucronal tooth absent in one cotype but present in another (one cotype, Museum of Comparative Zoology; one from A. P. Morse). Of *nigra*, I studied four cotypes (two in Museum of Comparative Zoology; one from A. P. Morse).

To designate this variety I have retained MacGillivray's name of *nigra*, preferring this for the reason that the descriptions of *brunnea* and *speciosa* were based on abnormal individuals.

The variety *nigra* may be found intermingled with the typical *arborea*. Thus, in two collections that I made under the loose bark of one log (Urbana, Ill., March 11, 13) both forms were present; and a vial of many specimens from F. L. Harvey (Orono, Maine, March 10, in moss) also contained both forms. On the other hand, *nigra* may occur by itself. Charles Macnamara, of Arnprior, Ontario, used to take *nigra* every winter on the snow, without ever finding typical *arborea*.

Distribution.—Recorded as follows:

Maine: Orono, March 10, April, October 28, F. L. Harvey.

Massachusetts: Arlington, March 20.

New York: Altamont, April 12, C. R. Crosby and S. C. Bishop (New York State Museum). Ithaca, March 20, 25, A. D. MacGillivray (Cornell University). Rochester, April 9, November 16, E. A. Maynard. Varna, November (Cornell University).

Ohio: Salineville, A. D. MacGillivray (Museum of Comparative Zoology).

Illinois: Homer, April 16. Urbana, March 11, 13, 21.
Canada: Arnprior, Ontario, January 4, 10, March, April 24, November, December 19, 25.

Subgenus Isotoma Borner

Isotoma BORNER, 1906, p. 171.—LINNANIEMI, 1912, p. 138.—HANDSCHIN, 1924a, p. 111.

Subgenotype.—Isotoma viridis Bourlet.

KEY TO SPECIES OF SUBGENUS ISOTOMA

1. Mucrones lamellate, quadridentate_____ 2
   Mucrones nonlamellate, tridentate or quadridentate_____ 3
2. Last three antennal segments almost equal in length. Lateral
   teeth of unguis dentate or fringed distally. Anal valves conspicuous, subtriangular_____ subaequalis (p. 107)
   Last three antennal segments unequal in length. Lateral teeth
   of unguis entire. Anal valves not conspicuous_____ gelida (p. 106)
3. Mucrones tridentate_____ 4
   Mucrones quadridentate (except a tridentate form of *olivacea
   grisea*)_____ 11
4. Large species (maximum length, 6 mm). Unguis with two
   strong inner teeth and with parallel basal folds_____ 5
   Small species (maximum length, 1.5 mm). Claws usually untoothed. Unguis without basal folds_____ 6
5. Teeth of mucro subequal, hooked, the two proximal teeth
   opposite each other in lateral aspect (pl. 38, fig. 437)_____ viridis (p. 109)
   Teeth of mucro unequal, the two proximal teeth not opposite
   each other (pl. 38, fig. 445)_____ subviridis (p. 115)
6. Postantennal organs present_____ 7
   Postantennal organs absent_____ 10
7. Eyes eight on each side_____ 8
   Eyes four on each side_____ eunotabilis (p. 92)
8. Unguis and unguiculus toothed. Postantennal organ elongate,
   narrow, in length five to seven times the diameter of an
   eye_____ difficilis (p. 89)
   Unguis and unguiculus untoothed. Postantennal organ oval,
   not more than twice as long as the diameter of an eye_____ 9
9. Antennae in foveae, and strongly telescopic. Anal lobes conspicuous, subtriangular_____ marissa (p. 80)
   Antennae not in foveae, not telescopic. Anal lobes not con-
   spicuous_____ trispinata (p. 91)
10. Eye spots and corneae absent. Fourth antennal segment with
    conspicuous sensory cones_____ minor (p. 94)
    Eye spots present but corneae absent. Fourth antennal
    sensory cones absent_____ finitima (p. 93)
11. Apical tooth of mucro minute, at the base of the anteapical;
    the three large teeth subequal, hooked; the two proximal
    teeth opposite each other_____ viridis catena (p. 112)
    Apical tooth of mucro well developed; the three remaining teeth
    varying in size, form, and position_____ 12
12. Purple or blue, sometimes blackish. Legs and furcula whitish,
    yellowish, or brownish throughout, or purplish, basally; in
    nigrifrons, tibiotarsi purple apically_____ 13
    Coloration various, but not as above; usually olivaceous,
    yellowish, gray, or white_____ 16

13. Postantennal organ subequal in length to the diameter of an eye
    (in var. *caeruleatra* one and one-half to three times as long).
    Unguis typically with a strong inner tooth. Unguiculus
    typically with a strong tooth. Crenulations of dens ending
    at a distance from the mucro equal to three times the length
    of the latter. Mucro a little shorter than hind unguiculus.
    Body setae moderately to very long Sensory setae long

    violacea (p. 101)

    Postantennal organ in length one and one-fourth to two times
    the diameter of an adjacent eye. Body setae short to mod-
    erately long_____ 14

14 Inner tooth of unguis strong Tooth of unguiculus strong
    Crenulations of dens ending at a distance from the mucro
    equal to three to four and two-thirds times the length of the
    mucro. Apical tooth of mucro not long and slender. Eyes
    unequal. Abdominal sensory setae long_____ 15

    Inner tooth of unguis small or absent Tooth of unguiculus
    minute or absent Crenulations of dens ending at a distance
    from the mucro equal to one and one-half times the length
    of the mucro. Mucro one and two-thirds times as long as
    hind unguiculus. Apical tooth of mucro relatively long and
    slender. Eyes subequal. Abdominal sensory setae short

    olivacea neglecta (p. 101)

15. Body uniformly blackish purple Legs and furcula whitish,
    yellowish, or brownish. Crenulations of dens ending at a
    distance from the mucro equal to four and two-thirds times
    the length of the mucro. Mucro three-fourths as long as hind
    unguiculus_____ arborea nigra (p. 86)

    First four body segments usually purple throughout; second,
    third, and fourth abdominal segments each with a broad
    white posterior band Crenulations of dens ending at a dis-
    tance from the mucro equal to three times the length of the
    mucro. Mucro one and one-half times as long as hind un-
    guiculus_____ nigrifrons (p. 105)

16. Head conspicuously large in proportion to the body, almost
    one-third as long as the latter. Olive-green_____ grandiceps (p. 108)

    Head not noticeably large_____ 17

17. Eye spots not greatly elongate (length: width as 5:3). Post-
    antennal organ variable in length. Inner tooth of unguis
    (occasionally absent) near the middle Unguiculus extend-
    ing one-half as far as the unguis. Furcula attaining the ven-
    tral tube Apical tooth of mucro not very long and slender.
    Coloration various_____ olivacea (p. 98)

    Eye spots elongate (2½ to 3 times as long as wide). Postanten-
    nal organ two to three times as long as the diameter of an eye.
    Inner tooth of unguis weak or absent, when present, one-third
    from the apex. Unguiculus extending two-thirds as far as
    the unguis. Furcula extending only to the middle of the
    second abdominal segment. Apical tooth of mucro very
    long and slender. White or snuff yellow_____ albella (p. 95)

ISOTOMA (ISOTOMA) DIFFICILIS, new species

PLATE 28, FIGURES 320–323

Description.—White, minutely spotted with black. Eye patches small and irregular. Eyes (pl. 28, fig. 320) eight on each side, equal. Postantennal organ (pl. 28, fig. 320) elongate, about as wide as the diameter of an eye, and five to seven times as long. Antennae longer than the head (as 4:3), with segments in relative lengths about as 6:9:10:15; first segment cylindrical; second subclavate, third clavate, fourth elliptical. Sense organ of third antennal segment with a pair of linear unprotected rods; fourth antennal segment without special olfactory setae. Third and fourth abdominal segments subequal in length. Genital and anal segments not ankylosed. Unguis (pl. 28, fig. 321) with a pair of small lateral teeth, and a strong tooth behind the middle of the inner margin. Unguiculus extending two-thirds as far as unguis on the hind feet, and half as far on the other feet, ovate, acuminate, unidentate. Tenent hairs absent. Furcula extending to the ventral tube. Manubrium short and stout, with many stiff setae dorsally and ventrally. Dentes three times as long as manubrium, slender, tapering, finely crenulate dorsally, with a few stiff setae dorsally and dense setae ventrally. Mucro (pl. 28, figs. 322, 323) about as long as hind unguiculus, tridentate; apical tooth long and hooked; anteapical smaller, conical, erect; third tooth lateral, oblique, large, almost straight or feebly hooked. Mucro in lateral aspect strongly rounded ventrally. Rami of tenaculum quadridentate; corpus with nine or ten setae. General clothing of dense short stiff setae. The outstanding sensory setae become very long on the posterior part of the abdomen, with a few spinules on the convex surface. Integument smooth. Length, 1.5 mm.

The number and position of the eyes were difficult to make out, by the method of depigmentation, but plate 28, figure 320, composed from studies of 10 individuals, is essentially correct.

Cotypes.—U.S.N.M. no. 42975.

Distribution.—Recorded as follows:

Illinois: Urbana, February 23, in the leaf stratum of a forest, I. H. Blake.

ISOTOMA (ISOTOMA) MARISSA, new species

PLATE 29, FIGURES 324–330

Description.—A stout species. General color bluish. White, mottled with purple pigment, and broadly banded with blackish purple. The broad transverse bands occur on the posterior border of the head and along the posterior borders of all the body segments except the prothorax and the genital and anal segments. Antennae mottled with purple; first three segments heavily pigmented apically.

Legs white, more or less pigmented basally. Furcula white, slightly pigmented basally. Head relatively large; front sharply demarcated anteriorly, forming a blunt obtuse angle projecting between the antennae, and broadly bordered with purple. Eye spots situated close to the bases of the antennae. Eyes (pl. 29, fig. 324) eight on each side, equal. Postantennal organ (pl. 29, fig. 324) close to eyes, oval, slightly longer than the diameter of an eye (as 9.8). Antennae a little shorter than the head, with segments in relative lengths about as 2:5·5:12; first three segments gradually expanding distally; fourth elliptical. The antennae are inserted in foveae under the projecting front, and their segments are strongly telescopic. Sense organ of third antennal segment (pl. 29, fig. 325) with two linear, feebly curving rods, subtended by a chitinous ridge. Special olfactory setae of fourth antennal segment apparently absent. The mesonotum conceals the pronotum. Abdominal segments without ankylosis. Fourth abdominal segment longer than the third (as 5:4). The anal segment terminates in three conspicuous subtriangular lobes: a suranal valve and a pair of subanal valves. Tibiotarsus without a distal subsegment. Unguis (pl. 29, fig. 326) stout, feebly curving, untoothed. Unguiculus extending two-thirds as far as unguis on the hind feet, broadly lanceolate, acuminate, untoothed. Tenent hairs absent. Furcula appended to the fifth abdominal segment, extending considerably beyond the ventral tube. Manubrium with many ventral setae, of which twelve are subapical in position. Dentes twice as long as manubrium, slender, tapering, strongly crenulate dorsally, densely setigerous. Mucro minute, slightly shorter than hind unguiculus, tridentate (pl. 29, figs. 327–330); apical tooth long, acute, upcurving; second tooth, small, conical, suberect or inclined backward; third tooth long, thornlike, proximolateral, directed obliquely backward. Dens with a long subapical ventral seta, which may extend beyond the apex of the mucro. Rami of tenaculum quadridentate; corpus with three (occasionally as many as five or six) setae. General clothing of dense short stiff unequal simple setae. Long erect sensory setae absent. Integument smooth. Length, 0.8 mm.

Remarks.—This species is to be added to the list of those collembolans that, under certain favorable conditions, occur in masses of countless numbers. I received from Prof. G. H. French hundreds of thousands of individuals, taken in cornrows in a garden at Marissa, Ill., by Thomas Keyworth, who wrote that they were in clusters by the millions; in fact, could be taken up by the shovelful on the ground. This is especially remarkable because the specimens averaged only half a millimeter in length, and a large proportion of them were almost invisible to the naked eye.

From Prof. P. S. Welch I received also an immense number of specimens taken at Kiowa, Kans., by J. M. Miller, who stated·

"They were in small piles or swarms lying on the ground. Could have secured a gallon of them."

Additional specimens numbering thousands of individuals were sent to me from Alabama by Prof. J. M. Robinson.

Cotypes.—U.S.N.M. no. 42968.

Distribution.—Recorded as follows:

Illinois: Marissa, June 24, T. Keyworth.
Kansas: Kiowa, June 18, J. M. Miller.
Alabama: Auburn, March 25, J. M. Robinson.

ISOTOMA (ISOTOMA) TRISPINATA MacGillivray

PLATE 29, FIGURES 331-336

Isotoma trispinata MacGillivray, 1896, p. 51.

Description.—General color grayish or bluish; blackish when heavily pigmented; finely mottled with blue pigment; with pale intersegmental bands. The posterior border of the head, and the mesonotum and metanotum, are narrowly edged with blue, as are also the posterior borders of the abdominal segments. Head with an anteocular blackish Λ-shaped mark; antennae bluish; legs and furcula white, slightly pigmented basally. Eye spots black, large, midway between antennae and base of head. Eyes (pl. 29, fig. 331) eight on each side, slightly unequal. Postantennal organ (pl. 29, fig. 331) close to eyes, oval, one and one-half to two times as long as the diameter of an adjacent eye. Antennae longer than the head (as 4:3) with segments in relative lengths about as 15:25:27:42; second and third segments subclavate; fourth stout, elliptical, without special olfactory setae. Third abdominal segment shorter than the fourth (as 3:4 or 4:5). Genital and anal segments not ankylosed. Unguis (pl. 29, fig. 332) stout, simple, without teeth. Unguiculus extending two-thirds as far as the unguis on the hind feet, relatively large, broadly lanceolate, acuminate, with inner basal margin strongly rounded and untoothed; shorter on fore and mid feet. Tenent hairs absent. Furcula appended to the fifth abdominal segment, extending to the anterior border of the ventral tube. Dorsal setae of manubrium numerous, short and erect; ventral setae numerous, stiff, and inclined backward. Dentes more than twice as long as manubrium, slender, tapering, finely crenulate dorsally; the crenulations ending at a distance from the mucro equal to one and one-half times the length of the latter; ventrally with many short stiff oblique setae, and with a strong subapical seta extending as far as, or beyond, the end of the mucro. Mucrones (pl. 29, figs. 333-336) minute, slightly longer than hind unguiculus, with strongly rounded ventral margin, tridentate; apical tooth large, upcurving; anteapical tooth smaller, conical, erect or oblique; third tooth proximal, ventrolateral, oblique, acute. Rami of tenaculum quadridentate; corpus with several (5 to 7) curving setae. Clothing of dense short stiff setae, unequal in length; erect sensory setae simple, not much longer than the other setae.   Length, 0.9 mm.

Remarks.—There is some variation in the form of the mucro, particularly in the size of the anteapical tooth, as shown in plate 29, figures 333 to 336.

My specimens agree with a cotype in the Museum of Comparative Zoology, Cambridge, Mass., and with a cotype received from Mac-Gillivray.

This species occurs in or near the soil.   I have found it to be rather common under damp logs lying on the ground, or under the loose bark of logs, and have taken it abundantly in pastures in decaying manure.

Distribution.—Recorded as follows:

Massachusetts: Arlington, May.
New York· Rochester, March 9, E. A. Maynard.
Ohio: Salineville, A D MacGillivray (Museum of Comparative Zoology).
Illinois: Champaign, March 13, 16, 17, 19 Homer, April 2, 17, 24, 27, 29, May 3, 13, October 10, 15
Louisiana: Baton Rouge, March 9, in cane trash, C. L Stracener.

ISOTOMA (ISOTOMA) EUNOTABILIS, new species

PLATE 29, FIGURES 337, 339; PLATE 30, FIGURES 340–344

Description.—General color grayish, greenish, or bluish. Head and body finely mottled with bluish-gray pigment interrupted by closely set, rounded, pale spots.   Body segments narrowly bordered posteriorly with blackish.   Eyes connected anteriorly by a narrow ∧-shaped mark.   Legs and furcula pale.   Antennae pale, with segments more or less purplish distally.   Young individuals may be white, with minute specks of blackish pigment.   Eyes four on each side, equal, arranged as in plate 29, figure 337, on a small roundish black patch.   Postantennal organ (pl. 29, fig. 337) relatively large, elliptical, close to eyes, three to four times as long as the diameter of an eye.   Antennae longer than the head (as 1.5·1), with segments in relative lengths about as 10:16:16:33.   Sense organ of third antennal segment with a pair of small, slightly curving rods, subtended by a chitinous ridge.   Fourth antennal segment with a few stout, slightly curving olfactory setae.   Unguis (pl. 29, fig. 339) simple, without lateral or inner teeth.   Unguiculus extending half as far as the unguis, broadly sublanceolate, pointed, untoothed.   Tenent hairs absent.   Third abdominal segment slightly shorter than the fourth (as 28:33).   Genital and anal segments ankylosed, with often a trace of the dorsal suture.   Furcula appended to the fifth abdominal segment, extending to the ventral tube.   Manubrium much shorter than dentes (as 6:17), with many stiff setae on all sides.   Dentes slender, gradually tapering, crenulate dorsally, with many ventral setae and a few erect dorsal proximal setae.   Mucro (pl. 30, figs.

340–343) small, tridentate. Apical tooth strong, hooked. Ante-apical tooth smaller than the apical, inclined or suberect. Third tooth proximolateral, curving dorsally more or less and projecting caudolaterally (pl. 30, fig. 343). Dens with a strong subapical ventral seta projecting as far as the end of the mucro or slightly beyond it. Rami of tenaculum quadridentate; corpus with two strongly curving ventral setae (rarely with three). General clothing (pl. 30, fig. 344) of numerous short setae, most of which are simple; the longest setae, near the extremity of the abdomen, are, however, feebly unilaterally spinulate. Sensory setae simple or with two or three branches unilaterally (pl. 30, fig. 344), erect, scarcely longer than the inclined setae. Length, 0.7 mm.

In moderately pigmented individuals the minute specks of pigment form a loose network, outlining the hypodermis cells.

Remarks.—This species is very close to the European *notabilis* Schäffer, of which I have studied three specimens from Finland, sent to me by Linnaniemi. Both species have four eyes on each side, but the arrangement of the eyes differs in the two species, as will be seen by comparing plate 29, figure 337 (*eunotabilis*), with plate 29, figure 338 (*notabilis*). In *notabilis* the third abdominal segment is to the fourth as 46:47; while in *eunotabilis* the ratio is 56:66. In *notabilis* the large posterior setae of the abdomen are more strongly feathered than in *eunotabilis*. I do not know whether *notabilis* ever has the interocular Λ-shaped mark, my specimens from Finland having very little pigment. In other respects this species agrees with *notabilis*, even to the presence of feathered setae on the bases of the legs.

Isotoma eunotabilis belongs to the fauna of the soil. It is common on damp ground under logs and among dead leaves. I have often taken it under damp boards on grass.

Cotypes.—U.S.N.M. no. 42967

Distribution.—Recorded as follows:

Illinois: Homer, February 28, March 3, 14, 25, April 2, 3, 11, 12, 14, 15, 16, 21, 25, May 2, 3, 14, 16, June 6
Wisconsin: Beloit, October, V. G. Davidson.
Canada: Arnprior, Ontario, November, C. Macnamara.

ISOTOMA (ISOTOMA) FINITIMA Scherbakov

Plate 30, Figure 345

Isotoma finitima SCHERBAKOV, 1899c, p. 80.—WAHLGREN, 1900a, p. 367.—REMY, 1928, p. 65.

Description.—Bluish white; young individuals are white. Eye spots black, but eyes absent. Postantennal organs absent. Antennae longer than the head, with segments in relative lengths as 10:15:-16:25. Fourth abdominal segment about as long as the third (as

16.18).   Unguis and unguiculus without teeth.   Tenent hairs absent.
Furcula appended to the fifth abdominal segment, attaining the
ventral tube.   Dentes twice as long as manubrium.   Mucro (pl. 30,
fig. 345) tridentate.   Dens with a long subapical seta extending
almost as far as the apex of the mucro.   Length, 0.6 mm to 0.8 mm.

Remarks.—Scherbakov found this species abundantly under
flowerpots and in boggy soil in southwestern Russia.   Wahlgren
recorded it from moss in eastern Greenland, and remarked that it is
easily overlooked on account of its minute size.

The preceding description and the figure are from Scherbakov.

ISOTOMA (ISOTOMA) MINOR Schaffer

PLATE 30, FIGURES 346–352

Isotoma minor SCHÄFFER, 1896, p. 182.—SCHERBAKOV, 1898a, p. 59; 1898b'
p. 10.—AXELSON, 1900, p. 113; 1901, p 71, 1905b, p. 34, 1906, p 13.—BORNER,
1901a, p 53—ÅGREN, 1903, p. 138.—BECKER, 1902, p. 28.—KRAUSBAUER,
1902, p 43—SCHOTT, 1902, p 23.—PHILIPTSCHENKO, 1905, p. 3.—WAHL-
GREN, 1906a, p. 225; 1906b, p. 256; 1919, p. 751.—LINNANIEMI (AXELSON),
1907, p. 21; 1909, p. 9; 1911, p. 19; 1912, p. 172.—COLLINGE and SHOE-
BOTHAM, 1909, p 88; 1910, p. 107.—BROWN, 1919, p. 64; 1923, p. 262.—
STACH, 1921, p. 163; 1922a, p. 23.—DENIS, 1924a, p. 260.—HANDSCHIN,
1924a, p. 113; 1924b, p. 85; 1928a, p. 542; 1929, p. 65.—WOMERSLEY,
1925, p. 219; 1927, p. 376.

Description.—White.   A slender species.   Eyes absent.   Postantennal organs absent.   Antennae longer than the head, with stout
segments, in relative lengths about as 16.21:23.41.   Sense organ of
third antennal segment (pl. 30, fig. 346) with a pair of slender straight
rods lying free, that is, not in a groove.   Fourth antennal segment
with five to eight (commonly six) distal, lateroventral, relatively
large sensory cones (pl. 30, fig. 347).   In addition to these there are
several "olfactory" setae of the usual type.   In dorsal aspect, six
outer and three inner setae of this type may be seen.   Unguis (pl. 30,
fig. 348) stout, without lateral or inner teeth.   Unguiculus broadly
lanceolate, acute, untoothed, extending more than half as far as the
unguis on the hind feet, and half as far or less on the remaining feet.
Tenent hairs absent.   Fourth abdominal segment a little longer than
the third (as 37:33).   Genital and anal segments ankylosed.   Furcula
appended to the fifth abdominal segment, extending not quite to
the ventral tube, slender and tapering.   Dentes slender, gradually
tapering, two and one-half to three times as long as the manubrium,
dorsally crenulate except on the distal third, with short stiff ventral
setae.   Mucrones minute, tridentate (pl. 30, figs. 349–351).   Apical
tooth relatively long, hooked; second smaller, in line with the first
tooth, suberect; third tooth lateral, opposite the second, oblique.
Dens with a strong subapical seta exceeding the mucro.   Rami of
tenaculum quadridentate; corpus with one ventral seta.   General
clothing of short simple setae.   Long, stout, more or less curving,

doubly fringed setae (pl. 40, fig. 352) occur on the body segments, becoming longer and stronger toward the extremity of the abdomen, and being numerous on the last three abdominal segments. Several such setae occur also on the bases of the legs, the number varying somewhat. Length, 0.8 mm.

Remarks.—My material of this well-marked species agrees with European descriptions of *minor* Schaffer and with five specimens sent to me from Finland by Linnaniemi. The peculiar expanded sensory setae of the fourth antennal segment are bluntly conical, as in plate 30, figure 347, not only in individuals from Illinois but also in those from Finland; they are represented as clavate by Borner (1901) and by Linnaniemi (1912). My specimens had been treated with potassium hydroxide.

Isotoma minor is a species of the soil. It occurs in the soil itself or on the surface under damp stones, wood, or fallen leaves, sometimes under loose bark and often in moss. It has been taken on the seashore under stones, wood, and seaweed, and in dwelling houses and greenhouses under flowerpots. As Linnaniemi notes, this species is frequent in occurrence but seldom taken in abundance, as the individuals occur singly or in sparse numbers. It is conspicuously lively, leaping rapidly and repeatedly when disturbed. The white color and small size render it difficult to detect.

Distribution.—*I. minor* has been recorded from almost all parts of Europe, and from Mexico.

Massachusetts: Norwood, August 26.
Illinois: Champaign, October 20, in soil among roots of red clover. Homer, April 6, 13, May 13, 16.

ISOTOMA (ISOTOMA) ALBELLA Packard

PLATE 31, FIGURES 353–361

Isotoma albella PACKARD, 1873, p. 32.—MACGILLIVRAY, 1891, p 273; 1896, p. 51.—SCHÄFFER, 1900b, p. 256.—AXELSON, 1905b, p 33; 1906, p 15 — LINNANIEMI (AXELSON), 1907, p. 30, 1909, p 11; 1911, p. 16; 1912, p 155 — WAHLGREN, 1906b, p 256.—STACH, 1921, p. 161.—HANDSCHIN, 1929, p. 70.
Isotoma nivea SCHÄFFER, 1896, p. 184.—AXELSON, 1900, p 114.—SCHOTT, 1902, p. 26

Description.—White throughout, or pigmented sparsely with blackish or grayish points or flecks, which may form broken outlines around the hypodermal nuclei An elongate species Eye spots black, long and narrow (pl. 31, fig 353), about two and one-half to three times as long as wide. Eyes (pl. 31, figs. 354, 355) eight on each side of the head, subequal. Postantennal organ (pl. 31, figs. 354, 355) broadly elliptical or subovate, one and one-half to two times as long as broad, and two to three times as long as the diameter of an adjacent eye. Antennae one and one-half to two times as long as the head, with segments in relative lengths about as 15:20:18:33 Sense organ of third antennal segment as in plate 31, figure 356.

Fourth antennal segment without special olfactory setae, with three unequal apical tubercles, and subapical pit with papilla. Unguis (pl. 31, fig. 357) rather narrow, feebly curving, with a pair of evident lateral teeth; inner margin untoothed or with a weak tooth one-third from the apex. Unguiculus extending two-thirds as far as the unguis, broadly lanceolate, acuminate, with inner lamella broadly rounded and untoothed. Tenent hairs absent; in place of these a long simple seta. Abdominal segments without ankylosis (pl. 31, fig. 358). Third abdominal segment slightly longer than the fourth (about as 37:35). Furcula appended to the fifth abdominal segment, and extending to the middle of the second. Manubrium with many dorsal and ventral setae. Dentes a little more than twice as long as manubrium, slender, gradually tapering, dorsally crenulate except basally and apically. Dens without a long subapical seta. Mucrones five-sevenths as long as hind unguiculi. Mucro (pl. 31, figs. 359, 360) quadridentate; apical tooth exceptionally long, slender, projecting obliquely upward and more or less hooked; anteapical tooth smaller, conical, erect or slightly inclined; proximal teeth smallest, subequal, almost side by side, one of them being lateral and more or less oblique. Rami of tenaculum quadridentate; corpus with many ventral setae (about 11 to 17). Clothing (pl. 31, fig. 361) of dense short simple setae; sensory setae short, erect, simple, in a row across the middle of each body segment except the prothorax, and becoming long on the genital and anal segments. Maximum length, 1.7 mm.

Remarks.—The inner tooth of the unguis is commonly absent, and when present is small.

The specimens that I have seen from this country have no angle-tooth on the unguiculus, there being at most a suggestion of a tooth; though such a tooth is usually present in European specimens.

As a variation, the apical tooth of the mucro may be stouter than usual.

My determination of this species is based on an examination of Packard's types in the Museum of Comparative Zoology, Cambridge, Mass. The types studied were three from Brunswick, Maine, those from Salem, Mass., being absent from the collection.

I sent Massachusetts specimens to Dr. C. Schäffer, who reported (Schäffer, 1900b) that his *nivea* was synonymous with *albella* Packard.

A specimen of *albella* from Finland, which I received from Dr. Linnaniemi, agrees essentially with our examples of the species. The specimens described by Linnaniemi (1912) as compared with ours have a narrower postantennal organ, stouter unguis with the tooth near the middle of the inner margin, shorter unguiculus with an evident tooth, and relatively longer third abdominal segment.

Specimens from Poland, received from Dr. Jan Stach, agree with North American material of this species.

This common corticolous species may be found in large colonies under the recently loosened bark of logs or stumps of many kinds of trees, and occurs sporadically in humus under logs or other objects.

Distribution —In Europe, *I. albella* has been recorded from Norway, Sweden, Finland, Estonia, Poland, and Germany.

Maine: Orono, October, F. L. Harvey.
Massachusetts: Arlington, April 13.
New York: Albany, February 16, J. H. Blatner (New York State Museum). Geneva, July 17, H. Glasgow. Ithaca, September 20, A. D. MacGillivray (Cornell University). Potsdam, May 23, D. B. Young (New York State Museum). Wells, July 21, D. B. Young (New York State Museum).
Illinois: Alto Pass, March 4, T. H. Frison and H. H. Ross (Illinois State Natural History Survey). Bloomington, March 24, T. H. Frison and H. H. Ross (Illinois State Natural History Survey). Homer, April 5, August 30. Makanda, March 5, T. H. Frison and H. H. Ross (Illinois State Natural History Survey). Mermet, March 8, T. H. Frison and H. H. Ross (Illinois State Natural History Survey). Monmouth, April 2, T. H. Frison and H. H. Ross (Illinois State Natural History Survey). Oakwood, April 20, T. H. Frison (Illinois State Natural History Survey).
Tennessee: Knoxville, April 5, H. E. Summers.
Canada: Arnprior, Ontario, April 25, C. Macnamara.

ISOTOMA (ISOTOMA) ALBELLA Packard variety LEONINA Packard

?*Isotoma walkerii* PACKARD, 1871, p 16; 1873, p. 34.—MACGILLIVRAY, 1891, p 274; 1896, p 54.
Isotoma leonina PACKARD, 1873, p. 32 —MACGILLIVRAY, 1891, p. 273 —GUTHRIE, 1903, p. 67.

Description.—Dull greenish, snuff yellow, or tawny-yellow. Appendages white or pale yellowish. Head sometimes with fine blackish dorsal mottlings. Young individuals are almost white.

Remarks.—Except in coloration, *leonina* is exactly like *albella*. Young white individuals in colonies of *leonina* are indistinguishable from those in colonies of *albella*.

This is possibly the form that Packard described as *walkerii*, but his description is insufficient, and the types of *walkerii* are lost, whereas those of *leonina* are preserved in the Museum of Comparative Zoology, Cambridge, Mass., where I had an opportunity to study them; *leonina* is here made a variety of *albella* because the latter name has page precedence (Packard, 1873).

This abundant variety occurs, like typical *albella*, in large colonies under the loose damp bark of trees, stumps, and logs of apple, oak, maple, elm, pine, cypress, and doubtless other trees. It appears as soon as the inner bark has begun to loosen from the sapwood, before much decay has occurred. Packard's specimens of his *walkerii* were taken on April 25, under the bark of an apple tree, where the eggs hatched until May 6; the form being abundant in spring and autumn and in the following spring under the bark of the same tree. In association with *albella* and its variety *leonina* under bark, *Isotoma cinerea* (Nicolet) often occurs Though belonging primarily to the fauna of the cortex, *leonina*, like typical *albella*, may occur individually in other situations, as under damp stones or wood, in moss, or on pools of water.

Distribution.—Recorded as follows:

Maine: Orono, October, F. L Harvey.

Massachusetts: Arlington, January 16 (full grown), April 13, 23, May 1

New York: Ithaca, A. D. MacGillivray (Museum of Comparative Zoology); A. P. Morse. Macedon, April 13, J. D. Hood. Varna, March 27 (Cornell University).

Pennsylvania: Hazleton, May 29, 31, W. G. Dietz.

Ohio: Yellow Springs, August 18.

Illinois: Homer, March 31, April 27, May 16. Makanda, March 5, T. H. Frison and H. H. Ross (Illinois State Natural History Survey). Mermet, March 8, T. H. Frison and H. H. Ross (Illinois State Natural History Survey). Urbana, March 18, 31, April 5, 12, May 3, August 11.

Minnesota: J E. Guthrie (University of Minnesota).

Canada: Arnprior, Ontario, April 25, C. Macnamara.

ISOTOMA (ISOTOMA) OLIVACEA Tullberg

PLATE 32, FIGURES 362–371

Isotoma olivacea TULLBERG, 1871, p. 151; 1872, p. 46.—UZEL, 1890, p. 64.— SCHÖTT, 1894, p 68; 1896b, p 116; 1902, p. 27.—REUTER, 1895, p. 27.— LIE-PETTERSEN, 1896, p 17.—SCHERBAKOV, 1898a, p. 59; 1898b, p 9.— WAHLGREN, 1900a, p. 367; 1906a, p. 225; 1906b, p 256; 1919, p. 746.— BORNER, 1901a, p. 54.—BECKER, 1902, p. 28.—AXELSON, 1904, p. 74; 1905b, p. 32, 1906, p. 15 —LINNANIEMI (AXELSON), 1907, p. 30; 1909, p. 12; 1911, p. 16; 1912, p. 147.—SCHILLE, 1906, p. 8 —BARTHOLIN, 1916, p 169— FOLSOM, 1919b, p. 279.—STACH, 1922a, p 20.—BROWN, 1923, p 262— REMY, 1928, p. 64.—HANDSCHIN, 1929, p. 70.

Description.—Olivaceous-greenish, in alcoholic specimens, as the effect of a blue pigment with a yellowish ground color; or yellowish brown Head and body with many pale spots of the ground color. Legs and furcula pale, or pigmented basally. Antennae pigmented distally, paler proximally. Eyes (pl. 32, fig. 362) eight on each side, subequal. Eye spots somewhat elongate, in length to width as 5:3. Postantennal organ (pl. 32, fig. 362) elliptical, two and one-half times as long as the diameter of an adjacent eye. Antennae longer than the head (maximum, 1.5:1); third segment usually a little shorter than the second; occasionally equal to second or even a little longer. Sense organ of third antennal segment as in plate 32, figure 363. Fourth antennal segment without special olfactory setae; with a terminal papilla. Unguis (pl. 32, fig. 364, 365) curving, with a pair of small lateral teeth; inner margin unidentate near the middle (though the tooth is sometimes minute or absent, especially in small individuals). Unguiculus extending half as far as unguis, broadly sublanceolate, apically acuminate, with or without an angle tooth. Tenent hairs absent; in place of these a single long seta. Abdominal segments without ankylosis. Third abdominal segment slightly longer than the fourth (as 12:11); occasionally equal to fourth. Furcula appended to the fifth abdominal segment and extending to the ventral tube. Manubrium with many dorsal and ventral setae. Dentes more than twice as long as manubrium (as 44:19), slender, gradually tapering, dorsally crenulate, the crenulations disappearing at a distance from the mucro equal to two and one-half times the length of the latter. Mucro three-fourths as long as hind unguiculus, quadridentate (pl 32, figs 366–369). Apical tooth the longest, hooked. Anteapical tooth a little shorter, conical, erect or slightly inclined. Third and fourth teeth subequal, almost opposite each other, oblique or suberect, one of them being lateral in position. Rami of tenaculum (pl. 32, fig. 370) quadridentate; corpus with several (5 to 10) setae. Clothing (pl. 32, fig. 371) of dense stiff simple setae, rather short, becoming longer posteriorly; with a transverse row of longer suberect simple setae across the middle of most of the body segments. Length, 1.5 mm (2 mm in large European individuals).

The antennal segments vary greatly in relative lengths, which may be expressed approximately, however, as 8:11:10:17 or 7:16:13:21; occasionally there occurs such a formula as 4:7:7:12.

Remarks.—In European specimens that I have seen the unguis had small lateral teeth, the inner tooth of the unguis and the tooth of the unguiculus being present or absent. In specimens from Canada and Greenland all these teeth were strong.

My European material of this species consists of Swedish specimens determined by Dr. Schött and sent to me by Dr. Schaffer; others from Finland, received from Dr. Linnaniemi; and Poland examples from Dr. Stach.

I sent Canadian specimens to Dr. Stach, who agreed with me that they were *olivacea*.

I. olivacea is found on the ground under stones, wood, or dead leaves, under bark, and often in moss. According to Linnaniemi, *olivacea* prefers damp, even wet, situations, and may be found in great abundance in sphagnum moss and on pools of water. Although a typical summer species, it may occur in winter in thawing weather, and has been taken in winter on snow and in puddles of water on the ice.

Distribution.—This species, which has been reported from Norway, Sweden, Denmark, Finland, Russia, Poland, Germany, Austria, Hungary, Bohemia, and England, is in northern Europe one of the most abundant collembolans

New York: Albany, May 7, D. B. Young (New York State Museum). Rochester, March 9, E A. Maynard.

Illinois: Homer, March 31, April 9.

Canada: Arnprior, Ontario, November, April, May 1, C. Macnamara.

Greenland: Umanak, July 22, in moss, W. E. Ekblaw (American Museum of Natural History; University of Illinois).

ISOTOMA (ISOTOMA) OLIVACEA Tullberg variety NEGLECTA Schäffer

PLATE 32, FIGURES 372–375

Isotoma neglecta SCHÄFFER, 1900b, p. 258.
Isotoma affinis AXELSON, 1900, p. 119.
Isotoma grisescens var. *neglecta* LINNANIEMI, 1907, p. 30; 1909, p. 11.
Isotoma olivacea var. *neglecta* LINNANIEMI, 1912, p. 151.—HANDSCHIN, 1929, p. 70.

Description.— The variety *neglecta* differs from typical *olivacea* in the following respects: Color blue to blackish purple. Postantennal organ one and one-half to two times as long as the diameter of an eye. Apical tooth of mucro long and slender. Proximal teeth about equal, slanting backward, situated side by side. Unguis usually with a small inner tooth. Unguiculus broadly rounded basally, with or without a minute tooth. Length, up to 2 mm (Linnaniemi, 1912).

The specimens that I refer to this variety are pale blue, mottled with rounded pale spots; antennae blue; legs white, pigmented with blue basally; manubrium pigmented; dentes white. The dorsal crenulations of the dens stop at a distance from the mucro equal to one and one-half times the length of the latter. Postantennal organ (pl. 32, fig. 372) one and one-half times as long as the diameter of an eye. Unguis (pl. 32, fig. 374) with a strong tooth near the middle of the inner margin. Unguiculus with a weak angle-tooth. Dentes not twice as long as manubrium (as 23:13). Mucrones (pl. 32, fig. 375) longer than hind unguiculi (as 19:11). Length, 1.1 mm. In other respects the specimens agree with typical *olivacea*.

Remarks.—I have followed Linnaniemi regarding this variety *neglecta*, of which I have seen no European examples.

Distribution.—*I. o. neglecta* is known from Germany, Finland, and possibly Sweden.

Canada: Arnprior, Ontario, August, in green moss, C. Macnamara. De Grassi Point, Lake Simcoe, September 1, on the fungus *Clavaria*, E. M. Walker.

ISOTOMA (ISOTOMA) OLIVACEA Tullberg variety GRISEA Lubbock

PLATE 33, FIGURES 376–383

Isotoma grisea LUBBOCK, 1873, p. 172.—COLLINGE and SHOEBOTHAM, 1910, p. 106.—SHOEBOTHAM, 1917, p. 221.
Isotoma grisescens SCHÄFFER, 1896, p. 188; 1900b, p. 257.—CARPENTER and EVANS, 1899, p. 248.—AXELSON, 1900, p. 119; 1905b, p. 32; 1906, p. 15.— LINNANIEMI (AXELSON), 1907, p. 30; 1909, p. 11.—LIE-PETTERSEN, 1907, p. 62.—EVANS, 1901b, p. 153; 1908, p. 196.—BROWN, 1918, p. 186.
Isotoma olivacea, var. *grisescens* BÖRNER, 1901a, p. 56.—LINNANIEMI, 1912, p. 150.—HANDSCHIN, 1924a, p. 116; 1928c, p. 128; 1929, p. 70.—WOMERSLEY, 1924a, p. 32; 1925, p. 219.
Isotoma olivacea var. *grisea* STACH, 1922a, p. 20.

Description.—This variety differs from typical *olivacea* chiefly in the following respects. Lighter or darker gray. Proximal teeth of mucro mostly directed backward, sometimes spinelike and turned inward, in size variable; apical tooth usually long and slender. Post-antennal organ up to three times as long as the diameter of an eye. Unguis usually with a small inner tooth. Length, 2 mm (Linnaniemi).

The specimens that I refer to this variety are pale yellow, in alcohol, pigmented dorsally with a fine black network, the hypodermal nuclei being indicated by pale spots. Mesonotum, metanotum, and abdominal segments narrowly bordered posteriorly with black. Antennae white; legs unpigmented, except coxae; manubrium pigmented, dentes white. Head in large individuals with a dorsal interocular network of pigment. Postantennal organ (pl. 33, figs. 376, 377) narrowly elliptical, three to four times as long as the diameter of an eye, with or without an anterior notch. Unguis (pl. 33, fig. 379) with a pair of lateral teeth and an inner tooth. Unguiculus with a conspicuous tooth. Maximum length, 1.8 mm.

My specimens differ in coloration from *grisescens*, of which I have European examples from Linnaniemi. Structurally they agree in detail with *olivacea*, except for a constant and puzzling variation in the form of the mucrones. In large, heavily pigmented individuals the mucro is quadridentate (pl. 33, figs. 380, 381) but the apical tooth is short—unlike that of typical *grisescens*. In small, lightly pigmented individuals, however, the mucro has usually a long apical tooth, as in *grisescens*, but the mucro is only tridentate (pl. 33, fig. 382), the lateral (fourth) tooth being present but the third tooth being absent or else being present in the form of a minute rounded lobe (pl. 33, fig. 383).

Discussions of the synonymy are given by Linnaniemi (1912) and Stach (1922a). I have adopted Stach's opinion in regard to the priority of the name *grisea* Lubbock.

Distribution.—This variety occurs in damp humus under dead leaves or wood; also under manure, in moss, and sometimes on fungi. It is known from Finland, Russia, Germany, Switzerland, Hungary, England, and Scotland.

Illinois: Urbana, May, in humus in woods (thousands collected with a Berlese apparatus).

ISOTOMA (ISOTOMA) VIOLACEA Tullberg

PLATE 33, FIGURES 384–388

Isotoma violacea TULLBERG, 1876, p 36 —SCHÖTT, 1894, p. 69; 1902, p. 24; 1923, p 12.—REUTER, 1895, p 27.—LIE-PETTERSEN, 1896, p. 17.—SCHAFFER, 1896, p 187; 1900a, p. 246; 1900b, p 258.—POPPE and SCHAFFER, 1897, p 268.—SCHERBAKOV, 1898b, p 9.—SKORIKOW, 1900, p 206.—BÖRNER, 1901a, p. 57.—BECKER, 1902, p. 28.—ÅGREN, 1903, p. 136; 1904, p. 15.—AXELSON, 1904, p. 72; 1905b, p 33; 1906, p. 15.—SCHILLE, 1906, p. 8.—WAHLGREN, 1906a, p. 224; 1906b, p. 257; 1919, p. 746.—LINNANIEMI (AXELSON), 1909, p. 12; 1911, p. 17; 1912, p. 157.—SHOEBOTHAM, 1911, p. 34.—BARTHOLIN, 1916, p. 169.—FOLSOM, 1919b, p. 280.—REMY, 1928, p. 64.—HANDSCHIN, 1928c, p. 128; 1929, p. 69.

Description.—Clear purple, blackish purple, or dark blue. Legs and furcula white or yellowish throughout, or pigmented basally; antennae purple. Body with many pale spots; head frequently pale laterally. Postantennal organ (pl. 33, fig. 384) situated close to the eyes, elliptical; equal to, or slightly longer than, the diameter of an adjacent eye (as 7:6 or 10:9), with a thick wall. Eyes (pl. 33, fig. 384) eight on each side, subequal (sometimes the two inner proximal eyes of each side smaller than the others). Antennae longer than the head, with segments in relative lengths about as 11:15:18:30 or 9:14:15:29. Sense organ of third antennal as in plate 33, figure 385. Fourth antennal segment without special olfactory setae; with three large unequal apical tubercles and a subapical depression with a papilla. Unguis (pl. 33, fig. 386) curving, with a pair of lateral teeth, and typically with a strong inner tooth (sometimes absent). Unguiculus extending a little more than half as far as the unguis, broadly sublanceolate, acuminate, with an inner angle-tooth, which is usually evident but occasionally obscure. Tenent hairs absent; instead, a long simple hair is present. Abdominal segments without ankylosis. Third and fourth abdominal segments subequal, or third slightly shorter than the fourth (as 6:7). Furcula appended to the fifth abdominal segment, extending to the ventral tube. Dens two and one-half times as long as the manubrium, slender, gradually tapering, crenulate dorsally, the crenulations becoming gradually smaller distally and disappearing far in advance of the mucro (at a distance from the mucro equal to three times the length of the latter). Mucro slightly shorter than hind unguiculus, quadridentate (pl. 33, fig. 387); apical tooth usually the longest. Anteapical tooth suberect, occasionally as large as the apical tooth. Third and fourth teeth proximal, almost opposite each other; one of them being lateral in position. A subapical ventral bristle on the dens extends beyond the middle of the mucro in some individuals; in others it is short. Rami of tenaculum quadridentate; corpus with several (7 to 11) stout ventral setae (as many as 16 in large European examples). General clothing (pl. 33, fig. 388) of numerous strong, stiff or curving setae, moderately long; with long stout outstanding setae, numerous and bowed on the last two abdominal segments. Length, 2 mm.

Remarks.—In European specimens the body color is sometimes more or less brownish (Schäffer, Skorikow). In some of my material from Canada the postantennal organ is twice as long as the diameter of an eye—a variation that Linnaniemi also has found in Europe. In some individuals from Canada, typical in other respects, the two inner proximal eyes of each group are smaller than the others. This variation occurs also in various other species of *Isotoma*.

My material of this species from Canada and Greenland agrees in all essentials with European descriptions of the species and with specimens from Germany received from Dr. Schäffer.

COLLEMBOLA OF THE FAMILY ISOTOMIDAE

I. violacea is found under loose bark, on the ground under dead leaves, logs, and stones, and in moss. It is one of the species that occur in winter on the snow.

Distribution.—The species has been recorded from Norway, Sweden, Denmark, Finland, Russia, Spitsbergen, Siberia, Poland, Germany, Switzerland, England, and Greenland.

Canada: Arnprior, Ontario, November, January, C. Macnamara.
Greenland: Umanak, July 22, in moss, W. E. Ekblaw (American Museum of Natural History, University of Illinois).

ISOTOMA (ISOTOMA) VIOLACEA Tullberg variety MUCRONATA Axelson

PLATE 33, FIGURE 389, PLATE 34, FIGURES 390–396

Isotoma violacea var. *mucronata* AXELSON, 1900, p. 118.—WAHLGREN, 1906b, p. 257.—LINNANIEMI (AXELSON), 1912, p. 158.—FOLSOM, 1919b, p 281.— HANDSCHIN, 1924a, p. 116; 1924b, p. 85.—REMY, 1928, p 64.
Isotoma mucronata AXELSON, 1904, p. 72; 1905b, p. 33; 1906, p. 15.—LINNANIEMI (AXELSON), 1907, p. 30; 1909, p. 12; 1911, p 17.—ÅGREN, 1904, p. 15.

Description.—Clear blue to blackish violet; legs and furcula blue, usually paler than the body. Anterior borders of body segments often unpigmented, giving the effect of narrow pale bands. Apical tooth of mucro the largest. Body setae exceptionally long and outstanding; the largest setae sparsely feathered (pl. 33, fig. 389). Maximum length, 3.1 mm.

According to Axelson, the two inner proximal eyes on each side are smaller than the others; the postantennal organ is small, elliptical, and scarcely as long as the diameter of one of the large eyes; the lateral teeth and inner tooth of the unguis, and the angle-tooth of the unguiculus, are strong (pl. 34, fig. 391).

In specimens from Greenland that I studied (Folsom, 1919b) the inner tooth of the unguis was absent (pl. 34, fig. 392). In a few of these specimens the mucrones were abnormal in having only three teeth (pl. 34, fig. 393). In some instances the subapical seta of the dens extended beyond the middle of the mucro. Length, 1.3 mm.

In specimens from Alaska all the teeth of the claws were well developed; the subapical seta of the dens extended often beyond the mucro; the tenaculum had 14 setae; and the ratio between the length of the postantennal organ and the diameter of a large eye was as 11:12. Length, 2.6 mm. These Alaska specimens were more nearly typical than those from Greenland.

Remarks.—Variety *mucronata* occurs in the same situations as typical *violacea*. My Greenland examples were taken in moss The Alaska specimens, five in number, were found in the nest of the Aleutian rosy finch (*Leucosticte griseonucha*).

Distribution.—This variety has already been recorded from Norway, Sweden, Finland, Switzerland, and Greenland.

Alaska: St. George Island, August 2 (Bureau of Biological Survey).
Greenland: Umanak, July 22, W. E. Ekblaw (American Museum of Natural History; University of Illinois).

ISOTOMA (ISOTOMA) VIOLACEA Tullberg variety CAERULEATRA Guthrie

PLATE 34, FIGURES 397–401; PLATE 35, FIGURES 402, 403

Isotoma caeruleatra GUTHRIE, 1903, p. 70.

Description.—This form agrees exactly with typical *violacea* except in the following respects:

Postantennal organ (pl. 34, fig. 397) narrowly elliptical, almost parallel-sided, three to four times as long as broad, and one and two thirds to three times as long as the diameter of an adjacent eye. Second and third antennal segments subequal. Apical tooth of mucro (pl. 34, figs. 398, 399) a little smaller than, or subequal to, the anteapical; hooked. Teeth of unguis strong.

The types of *caeruleatra* are clear dark blue, almost black; the head marked dorsally with yellow; antennae blue, the first segment paler than the others; legs blue basally, otherwise yellow; manubrium blue dorsally, paler ventrally; dentes yellow except basally.

Canadian specimens that I have studied are less heavily pigmented than the types, being clear blue or purplish with numerous small unpigmented spots; with the body segments narrowly bordered posteriorly with dark blue; with white in place of yellow on head, legs, and furcula; antennae purplish, the segments paler basally.

The lateral teeth and inner tooth of the unguis are strongly developed (pl. 34, fig. 400). The subapical ventral seta of the dens (pl. 34, fig. 398) is short, extending only as far as the base of the mucro. All the setae of the body are simple (pl. 34, fig. 401). Length, 2 mm.

Remarks.—This variety varies into the typical form of *violacea*. Thus, in one individual the postantennal organ was only one-fourth longer than the diameter of an adjacent eye; and in several individuals the wall of the postantennal organ was exceptionally thick.

As a variation, the apical tooth of the mucro may be considerably smaller than the anteapical (pl. 35, fig. 402).

This form approaches closely the European variety *divergens* Axelson.

I received, for study, four cotypes of *caeruleatra*, through the courtesy of Professor H. F. Nachtrieb, of the University of Minnesota.

Distribution.—Recorded as follows:

Wisconsin: Beloit, October, V. G. Davidson.
Minnesota: Near Minneapolis, April 16, O. W. Oestlund (University of Minnesota.
Idaho: Craters of the Moon, August 21, V. G. Davidson.
Canada: Arnprior, Ontario, in siftings, C. Macnamara.

ISOTOMA (ISOTOMA) NIGRIFRONS, new species

PLATE 35, FIGURES 404–411

Description.—Pigment purple. In moderately pigmented individuals the front is covered with a large blackish patch that includes the antennal bases, connects the eye spots anteriorly, and extends backward between the eyes as a triangular mark, at the apex of which there is a median transverse irregular black mark, or two such marks, one in front of the other. Occiput whitish. Usually the first four body segments are pigmented throughout, and the second, third, and fourth abdominal segments have each a broad white posterior band. Often the thorax is heavily pigmented with purple, while the posterior part of the abdomen is paler in color. Antennae purplish throughout, or with the first three segments whitish except apically. Legs purple basally; beyond the coxae, whitish tinged with brownish or greenish; apices of tibiotarsi purple. Furcula white. Eyes (pl. 35, fig. 404) eight on each side, the two inner proximal eyes smaller than the others. Postantennal organ (pl 35, figs. 404, 405) elliptical, from one-fourth longer to twice as long as the diameter of the adjacent eye. Antennal bases well developed. Antennae longer than the head (as 7:5), with segments in relative lengths about as 12:25:23:36. Sense organ of third antennal segment (pl. 35, fig. 406) with a pair of linear curving rods and a chitinous ridge. Fourth antennal segment without special olfactory setae. Third abdominal segment slightly longer than the fourth. Genital and anal segments not clearly ankylosed, though the dorsal suture is sometimes faint. Unguis (pl. 35, fig 407) with a pair of lateral teeth and an evident tooth at the middle of the inner margin. Unguiculus lanceolate, acuminate, strongly unidentate, extending about half as far as the unguis on the second and third pairs of feet, and less than half as far on the first pair. Tenent hairs absent. Furcula extending not quite to the ventral tube. Manubrium with many stiff setae dorsally and ventrally. Dens twice as long as manubrium, slender, tapering, with many stiff setae laterally and ventrally, crenulate dorsally, the crenulations ending distally before the apex, leaving a smooth surface three times as long as the mucro. Mucro (pl. 35, figs. 408–411) half as long as hind unguiculus, quadridentate; apical tooth large, hooked; anteapical tooth large, subconical, erect; third and fourth teeth small, subequal, erect or oblique, almost opposite each other; fourth tooth lateral. Rami of tenaculum quadridentate; corpus with about 12 setae (11–13). Clothing of dense simple setae of moderate length, longer posteriorly; sensory setae long, outstanding, simple. Maximum length, 2.1 mm.

Remarks —*I. nigrifrons* is close to *olivacea* Tullberg, from which, however, it differs strikingly in coloration. Structurally this species differs from *olivacea* chiefly in having unequal eyes and relatively shorter postantennal organs.

This new species occurred in large numbers in moss on rock bluffs, and in some of the individuals the mid-intestine was full of moss spores.

Cotypes —U.S.N M. no. 42969.

Distribution.—Recorded as follows:

Illinois: Alto Pass, March 4, T. H. Frison and H. H. Ross (Illinois State Natural History Survey). Makanda, March 5, T. H. Frison and H H. Ross (Illinois State Natural History Survey).

ISOTOMA (ISOTOMA) GELIDA, new species

PLATE 35, FIGURES 412–417

Description —General color olive-green to purple, densely flecked with minute unpigmented spots; with wide whitish intersegmental bands. Front with a transverse purple mark including the antennal bases, and extending back between the eyes as a median dorsal mark. Antennae purple; first segment paler; second and third often pale proximally. Legs greenish or purplish basally, whitish beyond coxae; tibiotarsi white or pale purplish. Furcula white. Eyes eight on each side, the two inner proximal smaller than the others. Postantennal organ (pl. 35, figs. 412, 413) elliptical, one-third to three-fifths longer than the diameter of an adjacent eye. Antennae one-half to two-thirds longer than the head, with segments in relative lengths about as 9:15:16 18; second and third segments subclavate; fourth elliptical. Sense organ of third antennal segment (pl. 35, fig. 414) with a pair of rods and two guard setae; the integument in the region of the organ being roughly and irregularly tuberculate. Fourth antennal segment without special olfactory setae. Third and fourth abdominal segments equal, or third slightly longer than the fourth (as 23:20). Genital and anal segments ankylosed, with a trace of a dorsal suture. Unguis (pl 35, fig. 415) slender, with a pair of large lateral teeth and a small tooth at the middle of the inner margin. Unguiculus broadly lanceolate, acuminate, untoothed, extending five-sevenths as far as the unguis on the hind feet, and about one-half as far on the other feet. Tenent hairs absent. Furcula extending to the ventral tube. Manubrium with dense short setae dorsally and ventrally. Dens about twice as long as manubrium, slender, dorsally rather coarsely crenulate, the folds merging into coarse tubercles near the mucro; with numerous erect dorsal setae and many short appressed ventral setae. Mucro (pl. 35, figs. 416, 417) four-fifths as long as hind unguiculus, quadridentate; apical tooth hooked; anteapical tooth the largest, with a pair of lamellae extending from its apex to the base of the mucro; third tooth much smaller than the second, erect or slightly oblique, with a small lamella; fourth tooth lateral, almost opposite the third, oblique and acute or erect and blunt. Rami of tenaculum quadridentate; corpus with 25 or more setae of different sizes. General clothing of dense stiff simple setae of various lengths; outstanding sensory setae long, simple. Maximum length, 2.4 mm.

Cotypes.—U.S.N.M. no. 42974. All the cotypes were taken in March; some near a stream, others on ice.

Distribution.—Recorded as follows:

Illinois: Carbondale, March 4, T. H. Frison and H. H. Ross (Illinois State Natural History Survey). Oakwood, March 3, 11, 17, T. H. Frison (Illinois State Natural History Survey).

ISOTOMA (ISOTOMA) SUBAEQUALIS, new species

PLATE 36, FIGURES 418–421

Description.—General color olive-green to purple, darker dorsally, thickly mottled with pale spots of various forms and sizes, with narrow whitish intersegmental bands. Head with a dorsomedian wide irregular mark and a frontal Λ-shaped mark connecting the eye spots. Antennae dull purplish throughout, or with the first segment and the base of the second greenish. Legs and furcula pale green or pale purplish. Eyes eight on each side, the two inner proximal eyes smaller than the others. Postantennal organ (pl. 36, fig. 418) elliptical, one and one-half times as long as the diameter of an adjacent eye. Antennae one and one-half times as long as the head, with segments in relative lengths about as 11:22:22:23. Sense organ of third antennal segment with a pair of minute linear exposed rods. Third abdominal segment from one-ninth to one-sixth longer than the fourth. Genital and anal segments not ankylosed. Anal valves conspicuous, triangular. Unguis (pl. 36, fig. 419) rather slender, not strongly curving, weakly unidentate near the middle of the inner margin, and with strongly developed lateral teeth, which are dentate or fringed distally. Unguiculus extending three-fourths as far as the unguis on the hind feet (shorter on the other feet), broadly lanceolate, untoothed, with an inner basal lobe. Tenent hairs absent. Furcula attaining the ventral tube. Manubrium about one-half as long as dentes, with many short setae on all sides. Dentes crenulate dorsally, setigerous on all sides. Mucrones (pl. 36, figs. 420, 421) almost as long as hind unguiculi, with a basolateral seta, quadridentate; apical tooth strong, hooked; anteapical usually larger, erect; third tooth lateral, oblique, acute; fourth conical, erect, in line with the first two teeth; an outer and an inner lamella extend from the second tooth to the base of the mucro, and a third lamella extends from the lateral tooth to the base. Rami of tenaculum quadridentate; corpus with many anterior setae. General clothing of abundant stiff setae of irregular lengths. Length, 2.3 mm.

The most distinctive characters of *subaequalis* are the subequality of the last three antennal segments and the large size and fringed condition of the lateral teeth of the ungues.

Remarks.—The cotypes of this species were taken on snow by R. McCain, who wrote regarding them: "On a walk a mile or two east of the city I saw some tree sparrows feeding quite extensively on the snow. I was very puzzled as to the nature of this food that they were finding so plentifully, but after repeated examinations of the snow on which I saw them feeding, I found the rather wet snow to be quite alive with snow fleas."

Cotypes.—U S.N.M. no. 42973, taken at Ann Arbor, Mich., February 24, by R. McCain.

ISOTOMA (ISOTOMA) GRANDICEPS Reuter

PLATE 36, FIGURES 422–427

Isotoma grandiceps REUTER, 1891, p. 229.—SCHÖTT, 1894, p. 71.—SCHAFFER, 1896, p 179, 1900a, p. 247.—SCHERBAKOV, 1898b, p. 9.—CARL, 1899, p 302.—AXELSON, 1903b, p. 7.
Isotoma macnamarai FOLSOM, 1918, p. 291.

Description.—Olive-green usually, sometimes blue. Antennae, legs, and furcula pale green. Body segments bordered narrowly with black (North American specimens). Head conspicuously large in proportion to the body, almost as wide as the broadest part of the abdomen, and as long as the thorax. Eyes (pl. 36, fig. 422) eight on each side, on black patches. Postantennal organ (pl. 36, fig. 423) lateral in position, close to the antennal base, elliptical, with very thick wall, and a little longer than the diameter of one of the adjacent eyes. Antennal base well developed. Antennae four-fifths as long as the head, often arcuate, with segments variable in relative lengths but about as 10:12.12:18–24. Sense organ of third antennal segment (pl. 36, fig. 424) with two geniculate sense clubs. Fourth antennal segment elliptical, without special olfactory setae. Third and fourth abdominal segments subequal in length. Genital and anal segments not clearly ankylosed. Tibiotarsus without a distal subsegment. Unguis (pl. 36, fig. 425) exceptionally stout, with a pair of large lateral teeth, and a conspicuous inner tooth one-third from the base. Unguiculus more than half as long as the unguis, broadly lanceolate, unidentate at the middle of the inner margin Tenent hairs absent, represented by a long simple hair. Furcula appended to the fifth abdominal segment, gradually tapering and rather short, extending a little beyond the posterior margin of the second abdominal segment. Manubrium shorter than dentes, with many dorsal and ventral setae. Dentes crenulate dorsally, with about five pairs of long stiff dorsal setae and many stiff ventral setae. Mucrones (pl. 36, fig. 426) two-fifths as long as hind ungues, quadridentate; apical tooth short, almost straight; second and third teeth large, subequal; fourth small, lateral, at base of third Rami of tenaculum quadridentate; corpus with about eight setae. Clothing (pl. 36, fig. 427) of abundant strong curving simple setae of moderate length, with long, outstanding, simple sensory setae. There are usually 4 long setae on the fourth and on the fifth abdominal segment, and 8 or 10 on the sixth; 1 or 2 long lateral setae on the mesothorax and metathorax, respectively, and one such seta on each of the first three abdominal segments. Length, 1.8 mm (3 mm, Reuter).

Remarks.—At the time of making the original description of *macnamarai* I had not found the postantennal organs, owing to their unusual position.

For a full figure of this species see Folsom, 1918.

In view of Axelson's revision of the description of *grandiceps* Reuter, I regard *macnamarai* Folsom as synonymous with that species.

According to Charles Macnamara, "This species seems to be confined to wooded swamps; I have never seen it elsewhere, and it sometimes comes out on the snow in small numbers. This is the only pugnacious springtail I have ever observed. It almost always attacks an *Achorutes* put in the same vial with it and sometimes kills it." The specimens from Illinois were taken in the frozen leaf stratum, under snow.

Distribution.—European writers have recorded this species from Russia, Siberia, and Alaska.

Massachusetts. Framingham, C. A. Frost (according to Mr. Macnamara).
Illinois: Urbana, February 2, I. H. Blake.
Alaska: St. Lawrence Island, Vega Expedition.
Canada: Arnprior, Ontario, December 5, 7, 21, January 8, 15, 26, February, March 21, April, C. Macnamara.

ISOTOMA (ISOTOMA) VIRIDIS Bourlet

PLATE 37, FIGURES 428–433; PLATE 38, FIGURES 437–441

Isotoma viridis BOURLET, 1839, p. 401.—GERVAIS, 1844, p. 433.—NICOLET, 1847, p. 373.—LUBBOCK, 1873, p. 169.—PARONA, 1879, p. 600; 1882, p. 463.—SCHOTT, 1891b, p. 22; 1894, p. 59; 1902, p. 22, 1923, p. 12.—VON DALLA TORRE, 1895, p. 10.—REUTER, 1895, p. 25.—LIE-PETTERSEN, 1896, p. 17; 1898, p. 12; 1907, p. 63.—MACGILLIVRAY, 1896, p. 58.—MEINERT, 1896, p. 169.—SCHÄFFER, 1896, p. 184; 1900a, p. 245; 1900b, p. 256.—POPPE and SCHÄFFER, 1897, p. 268.—SCHERBAKOV, 1898a, p. 58; 1898b, p. 7; 1899a, p. 47.—CARL, 1899, p. 311; 1901, p. 261.—CARPENTER and EVANS, 1899, p. 246.—WAHLGREN, 1899a, p. 186; 1899b, p. 335; 1900a, p. 366; 1900b, p. 4; 1906a, p. 223; 1906b, p. 255; 1907a, p. 5; 1907b, p. 87; 1909, p. 180; 1919, p. 747; 1920, p. 6.—ABSOLON, 1900a, p. 29.—SKORIKOW, 1900, p. 204.—WILLEM, 1900, p. 39.—BÖRNER, 1901a, p. 47; 1903, p. 171; 1906, p. 171.—EVANS, 1901a, p. 156; 1901b, p. 153.—BECKER, 1902, p. 26.—FOLSOM, 1902a, p. 93; 1919a, p. 9.—KRAUSBAUER, 1902, p. 39.—VOIGTS, 1902, p. 523.—ÅGREN, 1903, p. 134; 1904, p. 17.—AXELSON, 1903b, p. 5; 1904, p. 71; 1905b, p. 34; 1906, p. 14.—LINNANIEMI (AXELSON), 1907, p. 21; 1909, p. 10, 1911, p. 18; 1912, p. 162.—GUTHRIE, 1903, p. 68.—PHILIPTSCHENKO, 1905, p. 3.—CARPENTER, 1907, p. 54.—COLLINGE, 1910, p. 9.—COLLINGE and SHOEBOTHAM, 1910, p. 106.—BACON, 1914, p. 150.—SHOEBOTHAM, 1914, p. 61; 1917, p. 221.—BARTHOLIN, 1916, p. 169.—BROWN, 1918, p. 186; 1926, p. 205.—DENIS, 1921, p. 125; 1922a, p. 111; 1924b, p. 230.—STACH, 1921, p. 162, 1922a, p. 22.—CARPENTER and PHILLIPS, 1922, p. 15.—HANDSCHIN, 1924a,

p 116; 1924b, p. 74; 1925a, p. 232; 1928a, p 542; 1928c p. 128; 1929, p. 67.—
Womersley, 1924a, p 32; 1924b, p. 169; 1927, p. 376; 1928, p. 62 —Remy,
1928, p 64.

Isotoma caerulea Bourlet, 1839, p. 401.—Gervais, 1844, p 433.
Desoria virescens Nicolet, 1841, p. 59.—Gervais, 1844, p 428.
Desoria cylindrica Nicolet, 1841, p 60 —Gervais, 1844, p. 429
Desoria viatica Nicolet, 1841, p. 61.—Gervais, 1844, p. 429
Desoria pallida Nicolet, 1841, p. 61.—Gervais, 1844, p 430
Desoria ebriosa Nicolet, 1841, p. 61 —Gervais, 1844, p 430.
Desoria annulata Nicolet, 1841, p 61 —Gervais, 1844, p 430.
Podura viridis Bourlet, 1841-2, p 114
Podura annulata Bourlet, 1841-2, p. 117.
Heterotoma chlorata Gervais, 1844, p. 421.
Isotoma desmaresti Gervais, 1844, p. 436.
Isotoma virescens Nicolet, 1847, p. 372
Isotoma cylindrica Nicolet, 1847, p. 372.
Isotoma viatica Nicolet, 1847, p. 373
Isotoma ebriosa Nicolet, 1847, p. 373
Isotoma annulata Nicolet, 1847, p. 373 —Lubbock, 1873, p 175.—Parona
1882, p. 463.
Isotoma anglicana Lubbock 1873, p. 171.
Isotoma palustris Tullberg, 1871, p. 151, 1872, p. 45; 1876, p 34 —Uzel, 1890,
p. 62
Isotoma belfragei Packard, 1873, p 33.—MacGillivray, 1891, p. 273
Isotoma tricolor Packard, 1873, p. 34 (part).—MacGillivray, 1891, p 274
(part).
Isotoma purpurascens Packard, 1873, p. 34 —MacGillivray, 1891, p. 274.
Isotoma plumbea Packard, 1873, p 35 —MacGillivray, 1891, p 274
Isotoma capitola MacGillivray, 1896, p 56.
Isotoma glauca MacGillivray, 1896, p. 57.

Description—Color very variable: dark green, greenish yellow, dull yellow, lilac, blackish blue, reddish purple, leaden purple or dark brown; usually with small pale dorsal spots (pl. 37, fig. 428). Body segments often banded posteriorly with dark pigment. Without strong longitudinal lines in the typical form. Eyes (pl. 37, fig. 429) eight on each side, subequal. Postantennal organ (pl. 37, fig. 429) broadly elliptical, oval or round; shorter, to a little longer, than the diameter of an eye. Antennae one and one-half to two times as long as the head, with segments in relative lengths about as 4·7:7·8. Sense organ of third antennal segment (pl. 37, fig. 430) consisting of a pair of slender rods, freely exposed. Abdominal segments without ankylosis (pl. 38, fig. 441). Fourth abdominal segment slightly shorter than the third. Unguis (pl. 37, figs. 431–433) long, slender, slightly curving, with a pair of large lateral teeth, with inner margin bidentate, and with parallel basal folds. Unguiculus extending two-fifths to two-thirds as far as the unguis, lanceolate, unidentate near the middle of the inner margin. Tenent hairs absent. Furcula appended to the fifth abdominal segment, strongly developed, attaining the ventral tube. Dentes more than twice as long as the manubrium, slender, gradually tapering, crenulate dorsally, with a distal bristle extending beyond the mucro. Mucro (pl. 38, fig. 437) falcately and subequally tridentate; second and third teeth opposite each other. Rami of tenaculum quadridentate (pl. 38, fig. 438); corpus with numerous ventral setae. Clothing (pl. 38, fig. 439) of dense simple or feebly serrate setae; with long outstanding unilaterally fringed sensory setae. Maximum length, 6 mm.

Remarks.—North American specimens of this well-known species agree with the European examples that I have received.

Having examined Packard's types in the Museum of Comparative Zoology, Cambridge, Mass., I agree with MacGillivray (1896) that *Isotoma belfragei, purpurascens, plumbea,* and the Massachusetts specimens of *tricolor,* all belong to *viridis* Bourlet. The Texas specimens, for which MacGillivray retained the name of *tricolor,* are *palustris* Muller.

Isotoma capitola MacGillivray is synonymous with *viridis* Bourlet, as I have found from a cotype given to me by MacGillivray.

The form referred by MacGillivray to *glauca* Packard is also *viridis* Bourlet, and is specifically distinct from Packard's *glauca.*

Isotoma viridis is one of the most abundant collembolans, is the largest known species of its genus in North America and Europe, and may easily be recognized with the naked eye. It belongs primarily to the fauna of the humus, and occurs in almost any soil that is not too dry—in grass lands, woods, swamps, or cultivated fields—congregating under stones, pieces of wood, dead leaves, or other protection, and in piles of garbage or manure. It occurs in moss, on pools of water, on the seashore under driftwood or seaweed, and in winter on the snow.

In the vicinity of Boston, Mass., I found full-grown specimens of this species practically throughout the year. One individual laid eggs on April 2. Minute specimens, recently hatched, were collected on January 16, March 2, 10, 11, June 8, and October 2.

Distribution.—The typical form of *Isotoma viridis* ranges throughout Europe and North America and is known from Mesopotamia and Mexico also. It has been reported from the following Arctic localities: Northern Siberia, Nova Zembla, Spitsbergen, Bear Island, Jan Mayen, Iceland, Greenland, Northwest Territories, and Alaska.

Maine. Orono, April 20, F. L. Harvey.

New Hampshire: Mount Washington, Mrs. A. T. Slosson (Cornell University).

Massachusetts: Arlington, January 16, March 1, 2, 4, 10, 11, 15, 18, 28, April 2, 8, 12, May 1, 10, 5, July 30. Beverly, A. P. Morse (Cornell University). Cambridge, February 25, 28, March 2, 11, 15, 18, 28, April 22, May 7, June 1, 8, 10, 16, 17, July 7, 16, October 2, 9. Chelsea, C. A. Walker (Museum of Comparative Zoology). Salem, November 10–24, A. S. Packard (Museum of Comparative Zoology). Waltham, July 29.

New York: Albany, June 4, 5, 6, D. B. Young (New York State Museum). Ithaca, September, A. D. MacGillivray (Cornell University). Long Island, N. Banks (Cornell University)　Macedon, April 20, J. D. Hood　Potsdam, May 26, 29, D. B. Young (New York State Museum). Reserve, April 24, C. R. Crosby (Cornell University). Williamson, May 5, H. Glasgow.

District of Columbia: Washington, N. Banks (Cornell University).

Ohio. Salem, April 3, A. D. MacGillivray　Yellow Springs, February 9, March 4, April 3

Illinois: Carbondale, March 4, T. H. Frison and H. H. Ross (Illinois State Natural History Survey). Harrisburg, March 6, T. H. Frison and H. H. Ross (Illinois State Natural History Survey). Homer, February 5, 29, March 14, 21, 25, April 2, 3, 7, 8, 9, 11, 12, 15, 16, 17, 24, May 5, 13, 16, October 15. Metropolis, March 8, T. H. Frison and H. H. Ross (Illinois State Natural History Survey). Urbana, January 1, March 11, 20, April 5, 11, 12, 25, 26, 30, October 4, November 28, December 21, 28.

Iowa: Ames, March 31, May 13, J. E. Guthrie, September 3, H. E. Ewing, September 22, G. Hendrickson. Sioux City, January 17, 29, December 19, C. N. Ainslie.

Minnesota: May, J. E. Guthrie (University of Minnesota).

Tennessee. Knoxville, March 15 (from MacGillivray)

Mississippi: Agricultural College, H. E. Weed (Cornell University).

Louisiana: Alexandria, February 27, E. S. Tucker　Tallulah, April 7, 9.

Texas. Brazos County, N. Banks (Cornell University). College Station, December 22, C. A. Hart　Denison, February 13, C. R. Jones. Waco, G. W. Belfrage (Museum of Comparative Zoology)

California: Claremont, December, C. F. Baker

Washington: Olympia, T. Kincaid. Seattle, May 23, A. G. Webb.

Alaska: Demarcation Point, May 16; Collinson Point, September 27, F. Johansen (National Collection, Ottawa). St. Paul Island, Popof Island, T. Kincaid (U. S. National Museum).

Canada: Bernard Harbour, Northwest Territories, May, F. Johansen (National Collection, Ottawa). East Wentworth, Nova Scotia, March, R. M. Munro.

ISOTOMA (ISOTOMA) VIRIDIS Bourlet variety CATENA Guthrie

Isotoma catena GUTHRIE, 1903, p. 69.—BACON, 1914, p. 152

Description.—This variety is distinguished by the presence on each mucro of a minute additional tooth, situated ventrally at the base of the terminal tooth, as in *palustris*. In every other respect Guthrie's type and two paratypes, which I have studied, agree with typical *viridis*.

Remarks.—This quadridentate variation of *viridis* is not limited to typical *viridis*, however, for it occurred in one specimen from California and in another from Oregon, both of which were yellow, heavily marked with black, resembling the variety *pomona*. In such cases *catena* would become a subvarietal name.

Distribution.—Recorded as follows:

New York: Reserve, April 24, C. R. Crosby (Cornell University).

Indiana: Lafayette, J. J. Davis.

Illinois: Champaign, July 19, M. W. Shackleford.

Minnesota. Lake Vermilion, May 21, J. E. Guthrie (University of Minnesota). Le Sueur, May 26, J. E. Guthrie (University of Minnesota). Minneapolis, O. W. Oestlund (University of Minnesota)

California: Claremont-Laguna region, G. A. Bacon. Palo Alto, V. L Kellogg and L M. Bremner (Stanford University).
Oregon: Corvallis, March 22, H. E. Ewing.

ISOTOMA (ISOTOMA) VIRIDIS Bourlet variety RIPARIA (Nicolet)

PLATE 37, FIGURE 434

Desoria riparia NICOLET, 1841, p. 62.—GERVAIS, 1844, p. 430.
Isotoma riparia NICOLET, 1847, p. 373.
Isotoma palustris var. *riparia* TULLBERG, 1871, p. 151.
Isotoma belfragei PACKARD, 1873, p. 33 (part).
Isotoma viridis var. *aquatilis* SCHÖTT, 1891b, p 22.
Isotoma viridis var *riparia* SCHOTT, 1894, p 61.—VON DALLA TORRE, 1895, p. 10.—REUTER, 1895, p. 26.—SCHAFFER, 1896, p. 185; 1900a, p 245.—POPPE and SCHAFFER, 1897, p. 268.—LIE-PETTERSEN, 1898, p. 12.—SCHERBAKOV, 1898a, p 58; 1898b, p 7.—CARL, 1899, p. 311.—WAHLGREN, 1899a, p 186; 1906a, p 223; 1906b, p. 255.—ABSOLON, 1900a, p 29.—BORNER, 1901a, p. 49.—BECKER, 1902, p 26.—VOIGTS, 1902, p. 523.—ÅGREN, 1903, p. 134; 1904, p 17.—AXELSON, 1903b, p 5; 1905b, p. 34; 1906, p 14.—LINNANIEMI (AXELSON), 1907, p. 30; 1909, p. 11; 1911, p 18; 1912, p. 163.—BROWN, 1918, p. 186; 1926, p 205.—FOLSOM, 1919a, p 11.

Description.—Ground color yellowish, greenish, or brownish. The principal characteristic of this variety is a dark blue or blackish median dorsal stripe (pl. 37, fig. 434). Dark spots on the sides of the body may or may not be present. Maximum length, 5 mm.

Remarks.—This variety prefers humid situations, and is found under damp wood, in moss, on the surface of fresh water, along the shores of ponds or streams and on the seashore under seaweed, driftwood, or stones.

Distribution.—Variety *riparia* ranges over northern and middle Europe and has been recorded from Arctic Siberia and Mesopotamia.

New Hampshire: White Mountains, Mrs. A. T. Slosson (Cornell University)
New York: Ithaca, February 27, March 20, A. D. MacGillivray (Cornell University). Long Island, December 25, N. Banks (Cornell University). Mount McIntyre, July 1, M. D. Leonard (New York State Museum).
Virginia: W. D. Richardson (Cornell University)
Illinois: Champaign, November 29, M. W. Shackleford.
Iowa: Ames, March 31, J. E Guthrie.
Texas: Waco, G. W. Belfrage (Museum of Comparative Zoology).
Canada: Arnprior, Ontario, March 21, April 2, 9, C. Macnamara Bernard Harbour, Northwest Territories, May, F. Johansen (National Collection, Ottawa).

ISOTOMA (ISOTOMA) VIRIDIS Bourlet variety CINCTA Tullberg

Isotoma palustris var. *cincta* TULLBERG, 1876, p. 35
Isotoma viridis var *cincta* SCHÖTT, 1894, p 62.—SCHÄFFER, 1896, p 185; 1900a, p 246.—LINNANIEMI, 1912, p. 164.
Isotoma glauca var *montana* MACGILLIVRAY, 1896, p 57.

Description.—Ground color yellowish green, yellow, or white, with a wide dark blue or blackish transverse band, mottled with the ground color, on each segment. The intersegmental regions, being mostly unpigmented, appear as pale bands. Length, 4 mm.

Remarks.—Schött (1894) gives a figure of this variety, which Tullberg described from Nova Zembla.

Dr. MacGillivray gave me two cotypes of his variety *montana*. One of them agrees with *cincta* in the position of its broad blue bands. The other disagrees; having narrow blue bands along the posterior margins of the segments, such as often occur in the typical form of *viridis*.

Distribution.—Recorded as follows:

New Hampshire: Franconia, Mrs. A. T. Slosson (Museum of Comparative Zoology).

ISOTOMA (ISOTOMA) VIRIDIS Bourlet variety ARCTICA Schött

Isotoma viridis var. *arctica* SCHÖTT, 1894, p. 61.—VON DALLA TORRE, 1895, p. 10.—MACGILLIVRAY, 1896, p. 58.—SCHÄFFER, 1896, p. 185; 1900a, p. 245.—FOLSOM, 1902a, p. 96.

Description.—Ground color yellow', sometimes shading into purplish. Dorsum with dark blue or blackish markings, particularly a deltoid marking on each of the last seven segments, by which the variety may be recognized. The region of the median dorsal line is for the most part unpigmented. Maximum length, 7 mm.

For a figure of this variety see Folsom, 1902a.

Remarks.—This variety has seldom been reported. Schött's two types were taken by the Vega Expedition at Port Clarence, on the American side of Bering Strait. Schäffer gave southern Russia as a second locality. Three specimens (U. S. National Museum) were collected on Popof Island by Prof. T. Kincaid, of the Harriman Expedition.

ISOTOMA (ISOTOMA) VIRIDIS Bourlet variety DELTA MacGillivray

PLATE 37, FIGURE 435

Isotoma viridis var. *delta* MACGILLIVRAY, 1896, p. 58.

Description.—Yellowish, marked with black. This variety was characterized simply as having "each segment marked with three closed and united deltoid-shaped marks."

Remarks.—In the cotype from which plate 37, figure 435, was made, the only marks that are evidently deltoid are the median dorsal marks on the mesonotum to the second abdominal segment, inclusive. Two Texas specimens in my collection are less heavily marked than the cotype, but are nevertheless recognizable.

Type.—U.S.N.M. no. 42970.

Distribution.—Recorded as follows:

Mississippi: Agricultural College, H. E. Weed.
Texas: College Station, December 22, C. A. Hart; March 28, under trash, W. L. Owen, Jr.

ISOTOMA (ISOTOMA) VIRIDIS Bourlet POMONA, new variety

PLATE 37, FIGURE 436

Description.—Yellow marked with black (in alcohol). The color pattern is essentially as in plate 37, figure 436, which represents a heavily pigmented individual. In this figure the insect is slightly flattened dorsoventrally. Antennal bases black; between and behind them is a triangular yellow spot. Vertex with a large roughly U-shaped spot. A median dorsal interrupted yellow stripe may or may not extend for the length of the body, but is constant on the mesonotum and metanotum. The lateral black spots on the segments fall into a wide irregular stripe on each side. Most of the body segments are each bordered posteriorly with a black band. First antennal segment with a dorsal black spot. Coxa with a black band. Furcula unpigmented or nearly so. Length, 4 mm.

Half-grown individuals are mostly yellow, with the dorsal black markings separated into pairs by a continuous yellow median dorsal line. The mesonotum and metanotum are bordered laterally with black, forming a stripe which may continue back along the abdomen for a variable distance. Coxa with a black band; legs otherwise unpigmented.

Cotypes.—U.S.N.M. no. 42972.

Distribution.—Recorded as follows:

California: Claremont, H. Jones, S. Tyler. Indian Hill (Claremont region), February, A. R. Payne.

ISOTOMA (ISOTOMA) SUBVIRIDIS, new species

PLATE 38, FIGURES 442–449

Description.—Violet, mottled with pale spots. Antennae violet throughout, or first segment pale basally. Legs pale violet. Furcula white, with more or less pigment basally. Ocular spots elongate. Eyes (pl. 38, fig. 442) eight on each side, the two inner proximal eyes much smaller than the others. Postantennal organ (pl. 38, fig. 442) oval, very thick-walled, as long as the diameter of an adjacent eye. Antennae about twice as long as the head, with segments in relative lengths about as 11:20:21:27. Sense organ of third antennal segment (pl. 38, fig. 443) with a pair of curving rods subtended by a chitinous ridge. Fourth antennal segment with curving olfactory setae, in form much like the other setae. Third abdominal segment longer than the fourth (as 11:9). Genital and anal segments not ankylosed. Unguis (pl. 38, fig. 444) stout, almost straight, with a pair of lateral teeth, two inner teeth, and numerous basal folds. Unguiculus extending about one-half as far as the unguis, broadly lanceolate, acute, strongly unidentate at the middle of the inner margin. Tenent hairs absent; in their place, a strong simple seta. Furcula attaining the ventral tube. Manubrium short and stout, with a few stiff setae dorsally and ventrally. Dentes almost three times as long as the manubrium (as 11:4), slender and tapering, dorsally multicrenulate, ventrally with many stiff setae and a strong subapical seta extending almost to the end of the mucro. Mucrones (pl. 38, figs. 445–448) shorter than hind unguiculi, tridentate. The teeth of the mucro are quite variable in form and size. Apical tooth slender to stout, acute to obtuse, directed dorsally or subdorsally; anteapical tooth stout, erect; third tooth lateral, large or small. Rami of tenaculum quadridentate. General clothing (pl. 38, fig. 449) of curving simple setae, moderately long; outstanding sensory setae strong, unilaterally fringed. Length, 1 9 mm.

In a partly grown individual, 1.4 mm in length, the body segments are bordered with dark violet and have a fine median dorsal line. Front with a transverse mark connecting the eye spots and antennal bases. Occiput with a Λ-shaped mark connecting the eye spots. Antennae one and one-half times as long as the head, with segments as 6:8:10:15. Third and fourth abdominal segments equal in length. Corpus of tenaculum with five setae: a strong median seta and two pairs of small setae.

Remarks —Plate 38, figures 445 to 448, inclusive, are all from the same individual. The latter was about to molt, and the new mucrones (pl. 38, figs. 446, 448) could be seen inside the dentes.

This species closely resembles *viridis*, from which it differs chiefly as regards mucrones, eyes, and postantennal organs.

Cotypes.—U.S.N.M. no 42971.

Distribution.—Recorded as follows:

Washington: Friday Harbor, June 27, on moss-covered rocks, M. W. Shackleford.

Canada: Arnprior, Ontario, October, C. Macnamara.

UNIDENTIFIED SPECIES

ISOTOMA GLAUCA Packard

PLATE 39, FIGURE 450

Isotoma glauca PACKARD, 1873, p. 33.—MACGILLIVRAY, 1891, p. 273.—VON DALLA TORRE, 1895, p. 10.

Description.—Packard's original description of this species is as follows:

Isotoma glauca, n. sp. A bluish gray species, very slender, intermediate in form between *I. albella* and the stouter species, *I. tricolor*, etc Head shorter than in *I. albella*, eye patches black, conspicuous, broader, less linear than in *I. albella*. Antennae much shorter and stouter than in *I. albella*, basal joint one-half shorter than in that species, second and third joints much more dilated distally. Body a little more hairy than in *I. albella*; spring of much the same size and proportions; the lower edge finely serrulate, with rounded teeth, and the terminal joint, as in *I. albella*, ending in a curved hook, with a supplementary one near it, much as in that species. The spring is slightly more hairy. The feet and tarsal claws are much as in *I. albella*, but the tibiae have stouter spinules. Sucker as long as the thoracic segments are thick.

In two specimens I have observed the tenaculum. When retracted its side is indicated by a flattened, conical swelling, with two stout hairs arising from each side. When extended it has the same general structure as in the tenaculum of *Achorutes*, but is much longer and slenderer; the basal portion or valve is about twice as long as broad, square at the end; the second joint or valve is very narrow, half as long as first joint is wide, with about four rounded teeth along the inner edge.

Length, .05 inch.

Found very abundantly under bark in excrement of boring beetles Salem, Mass. (Packard).

This species differs from *I. albella*, its nearest ally, in its stouter, shorter body and antennae, and broader eye patches, and its bluish gray color.

Remarks.—Plate 39, figure 450, is a copy of a pencil drawing made by Packard during his study of this species.

Among Packard's types in the Museum of Comparative Zoology, I found two tubes labeled *glauca* ("under bark, Salem, May 22"), neither of which contained any specimens.

MacGillivray's specimens of *glauca* in that museum, as well as those in the Cornell collection, proved to be *viridis*.

Packard's *glauca* is evidently not *viridis*, at any rate.

ISOTOMA TRIDENTATA MacGillivray

PLATE 39, FIGURES 451–454

Isotoma tridentata MacGILLIVRAY, 1896, p 51

Description.—Yellowish; body segments narrowly edged behind with purplish; antennae yellowish, with first and second segments purplish apically, and third and fourth purplish except basally; legs white, furcula white. Eye spots black, elongate. Eyes eight on each side. Postantennal organs not studied. Antennae one and one-half times as long as the head, with segments in relative lengths about as 3·5:6 8. Third abdominal segment a little longer than the fourth (as 6·5). Genital and anal segments not ankylosed. Unguis (pl. 39, fig 451) with a pair of lateral teeth and with inner margin unidentate one-third from the apex; outer surface with a rounded protuberance about one-third from the base. Unguiculus broadly lanceolate, acuminate, unidentate. Tenent hairs absent. Furcula appended to the fifth abdominal segment, extending as far as the ventral tube. Manubrium cylindrical. Dentes more than twice as long as the manubrium, slender, tapering, crenulate dorsally. Both manubrium and dentes have numerous dorsal setae and dense stiff ventral setae. Mucro (pl. 39, figs. 452–454) subequally tridentate, the teeth subfalcate; third tooth lateral. Clothing of dense setae of various lengths. Abdomen with dense stiff ventral setae. Strong outstanding unilaterally serrate setae occur in clusters on the anterior region of the mesonotum and of the metanotum and the posterior regions of the abdominal segments, becoming longest and most numerous near the posterior end of the abdomen. Serrate setae occur also on the coxae and the furcula. Length, 1.8 mm.

Remarks.—This redescription of *tridentata*, still incomplete, is from two cotypes: A poor specimen in the Museum of Comparative Zoology, Cambridge, Mass., and one lacking legs and furcula that was given to me by Dr. MacGillivray.

Distribution.—Recorded as follows:

Virginia: Fredericksburg, W. D. Richardson (Museum of Comparative Zoology).

ISOTOMA ASPERA Bacon

PLATE 39, FIGURES 455, 456

Isotoma aspera BACON, 1914, p. 149

Description: Length—1.5 mm. Color—Great variation, dirty white with no markings to mottled gray. Antennae—Longer than head, IV longest and thickest, II and III subequal, I little shorter than II and III. Ocelli—Widely separated, sixteen. Postantennal organ—Elliptical with a rim Claws—Two; superior armed with two teeth on the inner margin, and two teeth on the outer margin; inferior, wide and stout, curved on the inner margin. Furcula—Does not reach ventral tube; dentes nearly three times manubrium; mucrones short and curving, tridenticulate, second and third teeth opposite. Integument—Very hairy

Variation: The color varies a great deal.

Habitat: Camp Baldy, altitude 4700 feet, March. Lytle Creek, April; San Dimas, left fork.

Remarks.—Not having seen this species, I have simply copied the original description and figures. The species evidently resembles *viridis* Bourlet very closely.

Distribution.—Recorded as follows:

California: Claremont-Laguna region, G. A. Bacon.

PROISOTOMA LAGUNA, new name

PLATE 39, FIGURES 457–461

Isotoma bidenticula BACON, 1912, p 842; 1914, p 147.

Description.—Dark, dull brown, mottled; intersegmental bands narrow, pale; sternum dark; legs and furcula pale. Eyes (pl. 39, fig. 457) eight on each side, the two inner proximal eyes much smaller than the others. Postantennal organ (pl. 39, fig. 458) subelliptical. Antennae one-fourth longer than the head, with segments in relative lengths about as 3:4:4:5. Third and fourth urotergites subequal in length, or third slightly shorter (as 10:11). Genital and anal segments not ankylosed. Unguis (pl. 39, fig. 459) strongly curving, untoothed. Unguiculus relatively large, sublanceolate, acute, extending as far as the unguis. Furcula short, not attaining the ventral tube. Manubrium longer than dentes (as 6:5). Dentes subcylindrical, rounded apically, finely crenulate dorsally.   Mucro (pl. 39, fig. 461) bidentate; apical tooth slender, almost straight; second tooth dorsal, slightly hooked.   General clothing of sparse short setae.   Length, 1 mm.

Remarks.—This is not Guthrie's *bidenticula*, which is synonymous with *elongata* MacGillivray.   The present incomplete description is based on that given by Miss Bacon, and the figures have been copied from her original article.   There should be no great difficulty in recognizing this species, with its peculiar claws and mucrones and its littoral habitat.

Distribution.—Recorded as follows:

California: Laguna Beach, in great numbers under stones between tide marks, G A. Bacon.

LITERATURE CITED

ABSOLON, KARL.
1900a Studie o jeskynních šupinuškách. Věstník Klubu Přírodov. Prostě-
jově, vol. 3, pp. 1–39, illus.
1900b. Vorlaufige Mittheilung über die Aphoruriden aus den Hohlen des
mahrischen Karstes Zool. Anz., vol. 23, pp. 406–414, illus
1901. Ueber *Uzelia setifera*, eine neue Collembolen-Gattung aus den
Hohlen des mahrischen Karstes, nebst einer Uebersicht der Anuro-
phorus-Arten. Zool. Anz., vol 24, pp. 209–216, illus.

AGASSIZ, LOUIS JEAN RODOLPHE.
1841. Note sur le *Desoria saltans*. Bibl. Univ. Genève, vol 32, p. 384.

ÅGREN, HUGO.
1903 Zur Kenntniss der Apterygoten-Fauna Sud-Schwedens. Stett. Ent.
Zeit vol. 64, pp. 113–176, illus
1904 Lappländische Collembola Arkiv Zool. Svenska Vetensk., vol.
2, pp 1–30, illus.

AXELSON, WALTER MIKAEL.
1900. Vorlaufige Mittheilung über einige neue Collembolen-Formen aus
Finnland. Medd. Soc. Fauna Flora Fennica, vol. 26, pp. 105–123.
1902. Diagnosen neuer Collembolen aus Finland und angrenzenden Teilen
des nordwestlichen Russlands. Medd Soc. Fauna Flora Fennica,
vol. 28, pp. 101–111.
1903a. Weitere Diagnosen über neue Collembolen-Formen aus Finnland.
Acta Soc. Fauna Flora Fennica, vol. 25, pp. 1–13
1903b Beitrage zur Kenntniss der Collembolen-Fauna Sibiriens. Öfv.
Finska Vet.-Soc. Forh , vol. 45, pp. 1–113.
1904. Verzeichniss einiger bei Golaa im sudostlichen norwegen eingesam-
melten Collembolen. Ent. Tidskr., vol. 25, pp. 65–84.
1905a Einige neue Collembolen aus Finland. Zool. Anz., vol. 28, pp.
788–794.
1905b. Zur Kenntnis der Apterygotenfauna von Tvarminne. Fests.
Palmén, vol. 15, pp. 1–46.
1906 Beitrag zur Kenntnis der Collembolenfauna in der Umgebung Revals.
Acta Soc. Fauna Flora Fennica, vol. 28, no. 2, pp 1–22
(See also under Linnaniemi.)

BACON, GERTRUDE AULD.
1912. Some Collembola of Laguna Beach. Journ. Ent. Zool., Pomona
College, vol. 4, pp 841–845, illus.
1914. The distribution of Collembola in the Claremont–Laguna region of
California. Journ. Ent. Zool , Pomona College, vol. 6, pp. 137–184.

BAGNALL, RICHARD S.
1909. Short notes on some new and rare British Collembola. Trans. Nat.
Hist. Soc Newcastle, vol. 3, pp. 495–509
1914 The British species of the genus *Tetracanthella* (Collembola). Journ.
Econ. Biol , vol 9, pp 5–8, illus.

BARTHOLIN, THOMAS
1916 Forelobig Fortegnelse over danske Apterygoter Vid Medd. Naturh.
Foren. Kjobenhavn, vol. 67, pp. 155–209, illus.

BECKER, ERNST.
1902. Collembolan fauna of the government of Moskow. Mem. Soc. Sci.
Nat. Anthr. Ethnog Univ. Moskow, vol. 98 (Zool. vol 13: Journ.
3, no. 4), pp. 19–30, illus. [In Russian.]

BÖRNER, CARL.
  1901a. Zur Kenntnis der Apterygoten-Fauna von Bremen. Abh. Naturw.
    Ver. Bremen, vol. 17, pp. 1–141, illus.
  1901b. Vorläufige Mittheilung über einige neue Aphorurinen und zur
    Systematik der Collembolen Zool. Anz., vol. 23, pp. 1–15.
  1901c. Ueber einige Theilweise neue Collembolen aus den Hohlen der
    Gegend von Letmathe in Westfalen. Zool Anz., vol. 24, pp.
    332–345.
  1902a. Ueber das Antennalorgan III der Collembolen und die systematische
    Stellung der Gattungen *Tetracanthella* Schott und *Actaletes* Giard.
    Zool Anz., vol. 25, pp. 92–116.
  1902b. Wieder ein neues Anurophorinen-Genus. Zool Anz., vol. 25, pp.
    605–607, illus
  1903. Neue altweltliche Collembolen nebst Bemerkungen zur Systematik
    der Isotominen und Entomobryinen. Sitz. Ges Naturf. Freunde
    Berlin, 1903, pp. 129–182, illus
  1906. Das System der Collembolen Mitt. naturh. Mus. Hamburg, vol.
    23, pp 147–188.
  1907. Collembolen aus Ostafrika, Madagaskar und Sudamerica. Sep:
    Voeltzkow Reise in Ostafrika in den Jahren 1903–1905, vol. 2,
    pp 147–178, illus.
  1913a. Die Familien der Collembolen. Zool. Anz., vol. 41, pp. 315–322.
  1913b. Zur Collembolenfauna Javas Das Trochanteralorgan der Ento-
    mobryiden. Tijdschr. Ent., vol 56, pp. 44–61, illus.
BOURLET, ABBÉ.
  1839. Mémoire sur les podures. Mém. Soc. Sci. Agr. Lille, part 1, pp. 377–
    417, illus.
  1841-2 Mémoire sur les podurelles Mém. Soc. Agr., ... Nord Sept
    1843, Douai, pp. 89–128, illus.
BROWN, JAMES MEIKLE.
  1918. Apterygota from Yorkshire and Derbyshire. The Naturalist, 1918,
    pp. 185–187, June.
  1919. The Apterygota of Yorkshire and Derbyshire. The Naturalist, 1919,
    pp. 63–66, Feb.
  1923 Additional notes on the Apterygota of Yorkshire and Derbyshire.
    The Naturalist, 1923, pp. 261–264, Aug.
  1925 On a new shore-dwelling collembolan, with remarks on the British
    littoral species of Collembola Ann. Mag. Nat. Hist, ser. 9, vol.
    16, pp. 155–160, illus.
  1926. On some Collembola from Mesopotamia. Journ. Linn. Soc. Zool., vol
    36, pp. 201–218, illus.
CARL, JOHANN.
  1899. Ueber schweizerische Collembola. Rev. Suisse Zool., vol. 6, pt. 2, pp.
    273–362, illus.
  1901. Zweiter Beitrag zur Kenntnis der Collembolafauna der Schweiz. Rev.
    Suisse Zool., vol. 9, pp. 243–278.
CARPENTER, GEORGE HERBERT.
  1900. Collembola from Franz-Josef Land. Sci. Proc. Roy. Dublin Soc., vol.
    9 (new ser.), pt. 3, pp. 271–278, illus.
  1907. Aptera. Irish Nat., vol. 16, pp. 54–56, illus.
  1908. On two Collembola new to the Britannic fauna. Irish Nat., vol. 17,
    pp. 174–179, illus.
  1916. The Apterygota of the Seychelles. Proc. Roy. Irish Acad., vol. 33,
    sec. B, no. 1, pp. 11–70, illus.

CARPENTER, GEORGE HERBERT, and EVANS, WILLIAM.
>   1899. The Collembola and Thysanura of the Edinburgh district. Proc.
>   Roy. Phys. Soc. Edinburgh, vol. 14, pp. 221–266, illus.
>   1904 Some spring-tails new to the British fauna, with description of a new
>   species. Proc Roy. Phys Soc Edinburgh, vol 25, pp 215–220, illus
CARPENTER, GEORGE HERBERT, and PHILLIPS, JOYCE K C
>   1922 The Collembola of Spitsbergen and Bear Island. Proc. Roy. Irish
>   Acad., vol. 36, sec. B, no. 2, pp. 11–21, illus.
COLLINGE, WALTER EDWARD.
>   1910. The fauna of the Midland Plateau. A preliminary list of the Thysa-
>   nura and Collembola. Birmingham Nat. Hist. Soc., sep. 14 pp.
COLLINGE, WALTER EDWARD, and SHOEBOTHAM, JOHN W.
>   1909. Notes on some Collembola new to Great Britain. Journ Econ. Biol ,
>   vol 4, pp. 87–90
>   1910. The Apterygota of Hertfordshire. Journ. Econ. Biol , vol. 5, pp.
>   95–132, illus.
DALLA TORRE, KARL WILHELM VON.
>   1888. Die Thysanuren Tirols. Ferd Zeitschr., ser 3, vol. 32, pp. 147–160
>   1895. Die Gattungen und Arten der Apterygogenea (Brauer). Sep. 46 Prog
>   St.-Gym. Innsbruck. 23 pp.
DAVENPORT, CHARLES BENEDICT.
>   1903 The Collembola of Cold Spring Beach, with special reference to the
>   movements of the Poduridae. Cold Spring Harbor Monogr. no
>   2, pp 1–32
DENIS, JEAN ROBERT.
>   1921. Sur les Aptérygotes de France. Bull Soc Zool France, vol. 46, pp.
>   122–134, illus
>   1922a. Sur la faune française des Aptérygotes. II. Collemboles de l'Île
>   d'Yeu. Bull. Soc. Zool. France, vol 47, pp. 108–116, illus.
>   1922b Sur les Aptérygotes de France. III Description d'un collembole
>   nouveau. Bull. Soc. Ent. France, 1922, pp. 135–138, illus.
>   1923 Notes sur les Aptérygotes. Ann. Soc. Ent. France, vol. 92, pp.
>   209–246, illus.
>   1924a Sur la faune française des Aptérygotes (IV note). Arch. Zool. Exp.
>   Gen , vol. 62, pp. 253–297.
>   1924b Sur les collemboles du Muséum de Paris. Ann. Soc. Ent. France,
>   vol. 93, pp. 211–260, illus.
>   1924c. Sur la faune française des Aptérygotes (V note). Bull Soc. Zool.
>   France, vol 49, pp 554–586, illus.
>   1924d. Sur la faune italienne des collemboles. Mem Soc Ent. Ital , vol.
>   3, pp. 201–214, illus.
>   1925. Sur la faune française des Aptérygotes (VII note). Bull Soc Ent.
>   France, 1925, pp. 145, 146.
>   1926 Notes sur les Aptérygotes Le dimorphisme sexuel d'*Archisotoma*
>   *besselsi* (Pack) Bull Soc. Zool. France, vol. 51, pp. 16–19, illus.
>   1927 Sur la funae italienne des Aptérygotes. Ann Sci Nat Zool , ser. 10,
>   vol. 10, pp. 169–208, illus.
EVANS, WILLIAM
>   1901a Some records of Collembola and Thysanura from the "Clyde" area.
>   Scottish Nat , 1901, 154–157.
>   1901b A preliminary list of Perthshire Collembola and Thysanura. Trans.
>   Perthshire Soc Nat Sci , vol 3, pt. 3, pp. 150–154.
>   1908 Some further records of Collembola and Thysanura from the Forth
>   area Proc. Roy. Phys. Soc. Edinburgh, sess. 1907–1908, pp.
>   195–200.

FOLSOM, JUSTUS WATSON.

1901. The distribution of Holarctic Collembola Psyche, vol 9, pp. 159–162.

1902a Papers from the Harriman Alaska Expedition. XXVII. Proc. Washington Acad Sci , vol. 4, pp. 87–116, illus.

1902b Collembola of the grave. Psyche, vol. 9, pp. 363–367, illus.

1916. North American collembolous insects of the subfamilies Achorutinae, Neanurinae, and Podurinae. Proc. U. S. Nat Mus , vol. 50, pp 477–525, illus.

1918. A new *Isotoma* of the snow fauna. Can Ent., vol. 50, pp. 291, 292, illus

1919a Collembola of the Canadian Arctic Expedition, 1913–18 Rept. Can. Arctic Exp. 1913–18, vol. 3, pt. A, pp. 1–29, illus

1919b. Collembola from the Crocker Land Expedition Bull. Amer. Mus Nat. Hist , vol 41, pp 271–303, illus.

1924. New species of Collembola from New York State. Amer. Mus. Nov , no. 108, pp 1–12, illus

1927. Insects of the subclass Apterygota from Central America and the West Indies. Proc. U. S. Nat Mus., vol 72, art. 6, pp. 1–16, illus.

GERVAIS, PAUL

1844 Thysanoures. Walckenaer Histoire naturelle des insects Aptères 3, pp 377–456, illus.

GIARD, ALFRED.

1889. Sur un nouveau genre de collembole marin et sur l'espèce type de ce genre. *Actaletes neptuni* Le Naturaliste, vol. 11, p. 123.

GMELIN, JOHANN FRIEDRICH

1788–93. *In* Linnaeus, Systema naturae, ed. 13, vol. 1. Lipsiae.

GUTHRIE, JOSEPH EDWARD.

1903. The Collembola of Minnesota Rep. Geol. Nat Hist Surv. Minnesota, zool. ser. no. 4, pp. 1–110, illus.

HALLER, GOTTFRIED

1880. Mittheilungen über Poduriden. Mitt. Schweiz Ent. Ges., vol. 6, no 1, pp 1–6

HANDSCHIN, EDUARD

1919. Ueber die Collembolenfauna der Nivalstufe Rev. Suisse Zool , vol 27, pp 65–98, illus

1924a. Die Collembolenfauna des schweizerischen Nationalparkes. Denkschr Schweiz. Naturf Ges , vol 60, no 2, pp. 89–174, illus.

1924b. Ökologische und biologische Beobachtungen an der Collembolenfauna des schweizerischen Nationalparkes. Verh. Naturf. Ges Basel, vol. 35, pt 2, pp 71–101.

1925a. Beiträge zur Kenntnis der Tierwelt Norddeutscher Quellgebiete. Collembola. Deutsche Ent Zeitschr., 1925, pp 227–234.

1925b. Contributions a l'étude de la faune du Maroc. Bull Soc. Sci. Nat. Maroc, vol. 5, pp. 160–177.

1926. Subterrane Collembolengesellschaften. Archiv Naturg , vol. 91, pt A, no 1, pp. 119–138, illus

1927. Collembolen aus Costa Rica. Ent Mitteil., vol. 16, pp. 110–118, illus.

1928a. Collembola from Mexico. Journ. Linn. Soc. Zool , vol 36, pp. 533–552, illus.

1928b. Über die von H Gauthier in den Sümpfen Algeriens gesammelten Collembolen. Archiv Naturg., vol. 92 (1926), pt. A, no 7, pp. 1–18, 1 fig

1928c. Die Collembolen des Zehlaubruches Schrift Phys -Ökon Ges. Königsberg, vol. 65, no. 3/4, pp. 124–154, illus.

1929. Urinsekten oder Apterygota Die Tierwelt Deutschlands Vol. 16, pp. 7–125, illus.

IMMS, AUGUSTUS DANIEL.
1912. On some Collembola from India, Burma, and Ceylon; with a catalogue of the oriental species of the order. Proc. Zool. Soc. London, 1912, pp. 80–125.

KRAUSBAUER, THEODOR.
1898. Neue Collembola aus der Umgebung von Weilburg a./Lahn. Zool. Anz., vol 21, pp. 495–499; 501–504.
1902. Beiträge zur Kenntnis der Collembola in der Umgegend von Weilburg a. Lahn. Sond. 34, Ber. Oberhess. Ges. Nat. Heilk. Giessen, pp. 29–104, illus.

LATZEL, ROBERT.
1917. Neue Kollembolen aus den Ostalpen und dem Karstgebiete. Verh. Zool.-Bot. Ges. Wien, 1917, pp. 232–252.

LIE-PETTERSEN, O. J.
1896. Norges Collembola. Bergens Mus. Aarb. No. 8, 24 pp., illus.
1898. Apterygogenea in Sogn und Nordfjord 1897 u. 1898 Eingesammelt. Bergens Mus. Aarb. No. 6, 18 pp., illus.
1907. Zur Kenntnis der Apterygotenfauna des nordlichen Norwegens. Tromsø Mus. Aarshefter, vol. 28, pp. 51–76, illus.

LINNANIEMI (AXELSON), WALTER MIKAEL.
1907. Die Apterygotenfauna Finlands. I. Allgemeiner Teil, 146 pp. Helsingfors.
1909. Zur Kenntnis der Collembolenfauna der Halbinsel Kanin und benachbarter Gebiete. Acta Soc. Fauna Flora Fennica, vol. 33, no. 2, pp. 1–17.
1911. Zur Kenntnis der Apterygotenfauna Norwegens. Bergens Mus. Aarb. No. 1, pp. 1–28
1912. Die Apterygotenfauna Finlands. II. Spezieller Teil. Acta Soc. Sci. Fennicae, vol. 40, no. 5, pp. 1–361, illus.
(See also under Axelson.)

LINNAEUS, CAROLUS.
1758. Systema naturae, ed. 10, vol. 1. Holmiae.

LUBBOCK, JOHN.
1873. Monograph of the Collembola and Thysanura. 255 pp., illus. London.
1898. On some Spitzbergen Collembola. Journ. Linn Soc. London, vol 26, pp. 616–619, illus.

MACGILLIVRAY, ALEXANDER DYER
1891. A catalogue of the Thysanoura of North America. Can. Ent., vol. 23, pp. 267–276.
1893. North American Thysanura IV. Can. Ent., vol. 25, pp. 313–318.
1896. The American species of Isotoma. Can. Ent., vol. 28, pp. 47–58.

MEINERT, FREDRIK.
1896. Neuroptera, Pseudoneuroptera, Thysanopoda, Mallophaga, Collembola, Suctoria, Siphunculata, Groenlandica. Vidensk. Medd. Dansk. Naturh. Foren. Kjøbenhavn, 1896, pp. 167–173.

MONIEZ, ROMAIN.
1889. Notes sur les Thysanoures. I. Espèces qui vivent aux Açores. Rev. Biol. Nord France, vol. 2, pp. 24–31.
1890. Notes sur les Thysanoures. III. Sur quelques espèces nouvelles ou peu connues, récoltées au croisic. Rev. Biol. Nord France, vol. 2, pp. 429–433, illus.
1891. Notes sur les Thysanoures. V. Espèces nouvelles pour la faune française. Rev. Biol. Nord France, vol. 3, pp. 68–71.

MÜLLER, OTTO FREDERIK.
　　1776. Zoologiae Danicae prodromus, pp. 183, 184 Havniae.
NICOLET, HERCULE.
　　1841. Recherches pour servir à l'histoire des podurelles. Nouv. Mém.
　　　　Soc Helv. Sci. Nat., vol. 6, pp. 1–88, illus.
　　1847. Essai sur une classification des insectes aptères de l'ordre des Thysa-
　　　　noures. Ann Soc Ent. France, ser. 2, vol. 5, pp 335–395.
OUDEMANS, JOHANNES THEODORUS.
　　1888. Beitrage zur Kenntniss der Thysanura und Collembola. Bijdr.
　　　　Dierkunde, Zool. Genootsch., Natura Artis Magistra, pp. 147–226,
　　　　illus. Amsterdam.
PACKARD, ALPHEUS SPRING, Jr.
　　1871. Embryological studies on *Diplax*, *Perithemis*, and the thysanurous
　　　　genus *Isotoma* Mem Peabody Acad. Sci., vol. 1, no. 2, 21 pp.,
　　　　illus.
　　1873. Synopsis of the Thysanura of Essex County, Mass, with descrip-
　　　　tions of a few extralimital forms. 5th Ann. Rept. Trust. Peabody
　　　　Acad. Sci., pp 23–51.
　　1887. Explorations of the Polaris Expedition to the North Pole. Amer.
　　　　Nat., vol. 11, pp. 51–53.
PARFITT, EDWARD.
　　1891. Devon Collembola and Thysanura. Trans Devonshire Assoc. Adv.
　　　　Sci. Lit. Art, vol 23, pp. 322–352.
PARONA, CORRADO.
　　1879. Collembola. Saggio di un catalogo delle Poduridi Italiane. Atti
　　　　Soc Ital Sci Nat., vol 21, pp. 559–611.
　　1882. Di alcune Collembola e Thysanura raccolte dal Professore P. M.
　　　　Ferrari, con cenno corologico delle Collembola e Thysanura Italiane.
　　　　Ann. Mus. Civ. St. Nat Genova, vol. 18, pp. 453–464.
　　1885. Collembola e Thysanura di Sardegna Atti Soc. Ital. Sci. Nat,
　　　　vol 28, pp 32–53.
　　1895. Elenco di alcune collembole dell'Argentina. Ann. Mus. Civ. St.
　　　　Nat. Genova, ser. 2, vol. 14, pp. 696–700.
PHILIPTSCHENKO, Y. A.
　　1905. Apterygota of the Province of Bologoi. Biol. Works, Imp. Soc. Nat.
　　　　St Petersburg, vol. 2, pp. 1–11. [In Russian.]
POPPE, S. ALBRECHT, and SCHÄFFER, CAESAR.
　　1897. Die Collembola der Umgegend von Bremen. Abh. Naturw. Ver.
　　　　Bremen, vol 14, pp. 265–272.
REMY, PAUL.
　　1928. Les collemboles du Groenland. Sep. Meddelelser om Grønland,
　　　　vol 74, pp. 57–70.
REUTER, LINA and ODO MORANNAL.
　　1880. Collembola and Thysanura, found in Scotland in the summer of
　　　　1876 Scottish Nat., vol. 5, pp. 204–208.
REUTER, ODO MORANNAL
　　1876. Catalogus praecursorius poduridarum Fenniae. Medd Soc. Fauna
　　　　Flora Fennica, vol 1, pp 78–86.
　　1890. Collembola in caldariis enumeravit novasque species descripsit.
　　　　Medd. Soc. Fauna Flora Fennica, vol. 17, pp. 17–28, illus.
　　1891. Podurider från nordvestra Sibirien, samlade af J R. Sahlberg. Öfv.
　　　　Finsk. Vet Soc Förh, vol 33, pp. 226–229
　　1895. Apterygogenea Fennica. Acta Soc. Fauna Flora Fennica, vol. 11,
　　　　no. 4, pp 1–35, illus.

SCHÄFFER, CAESAR.

1894. Verzeichniss der von den Herren Prof. Dr. Kukenthal und Dr. Walter auf Spitzbergen gesammelten Collembolen. Zool. Jahrb. (Abt. Syst. Geogr. u. Biol. Tiere), vol. 8, pp. 128–130.

1896 Die Collembola der Umgebung von Hamburg und benachbarter Gebiete. Mitt. Naturh. Mus. Hamburg, vol 13, pp. 147–216, illus.

1898. Die Collembola des Bismarck-Archipel nach der Ausbeute von Prof. F. Dahl. Archiv Naturg., vol. 64, pt. 1, no. 3, pp. 393–425, illus.

1900a. Die arktischen und subarktischen Collembola. Fauna Arctica, vol. 1, no 2, pp 237–258.

1900b. Ueber württembergische Collembola. Jahresb. Ver vaterl. Naturk. Württenberg, vol. 56, pp. 245–280, illus.

SCHERBAKOV, A. M.

1898a Einige Bemerkungen uber Apterygogenea, die Bei Kiew 1896–1897 Gefunden Wurden. Zool Anz., vol. 21, pp. 57–65, illus.

1898b. Materials for the Apterygogenea-Fauna of the vicinity of Kief, pp. 1–31, Kief. [In Russian.]

1899a. Zur Collembolen-Fauna Spitzbergens. Zool. Anz., vol 22, p 47.

1899b. Collembola of Spitsbergen, pp. 1–6. Kief. [In Russian.]

1899c. Vier neue Collembolen-Formen aus dem südwestlichen Russland. Zool. Anz., vol. 22, pp 79–81, illus.

SCHILLE, FRYDERYK.

1906 Przyczynek do Fauny Szczeciogonek (Apterygogenea) Galicyi. Spraw. kom fizyogr. Akad. umiej. Krakowie, vol. 41, pp. 1–17, illus.

SCHÖTT, HARALD.

1891a. Nya Nordiska Collembola Beskrifna. Ent. Tidskr., vol 12, pp. 191–192

1891b. Beiträge zur Kenntniss kalifornischer Collembola. Bih. K. Svenska Vet.-Akad. Handl. 17, afd. 4, no. 8, pp. 1–25, illus.

1894. Zur Systematik und Verbreitung palaerctischer Collembola. K. Svenska Vet.-Akad. Handl., vol. 25 (1893), no. 11, pp. 1–100, illus.

1896a. North American Apterygogenea. Proc. California Acad. Sci., ser. 2, vol. 6; pp. 169–196, illus.

1896b. Collembola på snö och is. Ent. Tidskr., vol 17, pp. 113–128.

1902 Études sur les colemboles du Nord. Bih. Svenska Vet.-Akad. Handl., vol 28, pt. 4, no 2, pp 1–48, illus.

1923 Collembola. Rep. Sci Res. Norwegian Exp. Novaya Zemlya 1921: No 12, pp 3–14. Kristiania.

SHOEBOTHAM, JOHN W.

1911. Some records of Collembola new to England, with description of a new species of Oncopodura. Ann. Mag. Nat. Hist., ser. 8, vol. 8, pp. 32–39, illus.

1914. Notes on Collembola: Part 2. Some Irish Collembola and notes on the genus Orchesella. Ann Mag Nat. Hist., ser. 8, vol 13, pp 59–68, illus

1917. Notes on Collembola Part 5. Some Lancashire and Cheshire Collembola. Lancashire and Cheshire Nat, pp. 219–223

SKORIKOW, ALEKSANDR STEPANOVIČ

1900. Zoologische Ergebnisse der russischen Expedition nach Spitzbergen im Jahre 1899. Collembola Ann. Mus. Zool. Acad. Imp. Sci. St. Pétersbourg, vol. 5, pp. 190–209, illus.

STACH, JOHANN
1921. Vorarbeiten zur Apterygoten-Fauna Polens. Teil II Apterygoten aus den Pieniny. Boll Acad. Polonaise Sci Lett, May–July, 1919 (B), pp. 133–233, illus.
1922a. Apterygoten aus dem nordwestlichen Ungarn Ann. Mus. Nat Hungarici, vol 19, pp. 1–75, illus.
1922b. Explorationes zoologicae ab E. Csiki in Albania peractae IX Collembola. Magyar Tudom. Akad Balkán-kutat tud. ered, vol. 1, pp. 109–139, illus.
1924 Eine alte Reliktenform in der heutigen Apterygoten-Fauna von Malta, zugleich uber einige Collembolen von Dieser Insel und aus Tunis. Ann Mus Nat. Hungarici, vol 21, pp 105–130, illus
1926. Spinisotoma pectinata n. g, n. sp., eine neue interessante Gattung der Familie Isotomidae (Schffr, CB) [Ordo Collembola]. Bull. Acad. Polonaise Sci. Lett. (B), pp. 579–588, illus.
STUXBERG, ANTON.
1887. Faunån på och kring Novaja-Semlja. In Nordenskiold· Vega-Expeditionens Vetenskapliga Jaktagelser, vol. 5
TOMOSVÁRY, ÒDONTOL.
1882. Adatok Hazánk Thysanura-Faunájához. Math. Term Kozlem. Magyar Akad., vol 18, pp 119–130, illus
TULLBERG, TYCHO
1869 Om Skandinaviska Podurider af Underfamiljen Lipurinae. Akad. Afhandl., pp 1–20. Upsala
1871 Forteckning ofver Svenska Podurider Öfv K. Vet.-Akad Forh., vol 28, no. 1, pp 143–155.
1872 Sveriges Podurider K. Svenska Vet.-Akad Handl, vol 10, no. 10, pp. 1–70, illus
1876. Collembola Borealia. Ofv. K. Vet.-Akad Forh, vol 33, no. 5, pp. 23–42, illus.
UZEL, JINDRICH.
1890. Thysanura Bohemiae. Sitzb. Boh. Ges Wiss, vol 2, pp 3–82, illus.
1891. Verzeichniss der auf Helgoland gefundenen Apterygogenea Zool Jahrb (Abt Syst Geogr. U. Biol Tiere), vol. 5, pp 919–920
VOIGTS, HANS
1902 Verzeichnis der im Jahre 1901 um Göttingen gesammelten Collembolen Zool Anz. vol 25, pp. 523–524
WAHLGREN, EINAR
1899a. Beitrag zur Kenntniss der Collembola-Fauna der äusseren Schären Ent Tidsk, vol 20, no. 2–3, pp 183–193
1899b Ueber die von der schwedischen Polarexpedition 1898 gesammelten Collembolen Öfv K Vet.-Akad Forh., vol 56, no. 4, pp 335–340
1899c On some Apterygogenea collected in the Volga-Delta and in Transcaspia by Dr E. Lonnberg Ofv K. Vet.-Akad Forh, vol 56, no 8, pp. 847–850
1900a Collembola, wahrend der schwedischen Gronlandsexpedition 1899 auf Jan Mayen und Ost-Gronland eingesammelt Ofv K Vet.-Akad Forh, vol. 57, no 3, pp 353–375
1900b. Beiträge zur Fauna der Bären-Insel. Collembola Bih K Svenska Vet.-Akad. Handl, vol 26, no. 6, pp 3–8
1906a Collembola från Torne Lappmark och Angransande Trakter Ent. Tidskr, vol. 27, pp. 219–230
1906b Svensk Insektfauna Ent. Tidskr, vol 27, pp. 233–270, illus

1906c. Antarktische und subantarktische Collembolen gesammelt von der schwedischen Südpolarexpedition Wiss Ergebn Schwed. Südpolarexp. 1901–1903, vol. 5, pt 9, pp. 1–22, illus. Stockholm.

1907a. Collembola from the 2nd Fram Expedition, 1898–1902, 6 pp , illus. Kristiania.

1907b. Über die Farbenvariationen von *Isotoma viridis* Bourl. Zool. Studier Prof Tullberg, pp. 87–92

1909 Islandska Collembola   Ent. Tidsk , vol. 30, p. 180.

1919. Über die alpine und subalpine Collembolenfauna Schwedens. Naturw. Unters Sarek. Schw -Lapp , vol. 4, pt. 7, pp. 743–762.

1920. De Europeiska Polaröarnas Insektfauna, dess Sammansättning och Harkomst Ent. Tidsk., vol. 41, no. 1, pp. 1–23.

WILLEM, VICTOR.

1900. Recherches sur les Colemboles et les Thysanoures. Mém Cour. Mem Sav. Étr. Acad Roy Belgique, vol. 58, pp. 1–144, illus.

1902a La position des Anurophoriens dans la classification des collemboles. Ann. Soc. Ent. Belgique, vol 46, pp. 21–23.

1902b Note préliminaire sur les collemboles des Grottes de Han et de Rochefort Ann Soc. Ent. Belgique, vol. 46, pp 275–283.

1902c. Collemboles. Résultats du voyage du S. Y. *Belgica*, pp. 1–19, illus Anvers.

WOMERSLEY, H

1924a. The Apterygota of the south-west of England. Proc. Bristol Nat. Soc., ser 4, vol. 6, pt. 1 (1923), pp 28–37.

1924b. The Apterygota of the south-west of England. Part 2 Proc. Bristol Nat Soc , ser. 4, vol. 6, pt 2, pp 166–172

1925. The Apterygota of the south-west of England Part 3 Proc. Bristol Nat Soc , ser. 4, vol. 6, pt 3, pp 217–221

1927. The Apterygota of the south-west of England. Part 4. Proc. Bristol Nat Soc , ser 4, vol 6, pt 5, pp. 372–379, illus.

1928. Some records of Apterygota from Lundy Island, Devonshire, with the description of a new species of *Entomobrya* (Collembola). Ann. Mag. Nat. Hist , ser. 10, vol 2, pp. 62–65, illus.

EXPLANATION OF PLATES

PLATE 1

Tetracanthella wahlgreni·

1. Specimen, × 42.
2. Eyes and postantennal organ of right side, × 252.
3. Sense organ of third antennal segment of left side, × 825
4. Left hind foot, × 505.
5. Extremity of abdomen, × 185.
6. Dorsal aspect of anal spines, × 250
7. Furcula and tenaculum, × 505.
8. Dorsal aspect of mucrodentes, × 505.
9. Dorsal setae of first abdominal segment, × 295.

PLATE 2

Anurophorus laricis:

10. Specimen, × 65.
11. Eyes and antennal base of left side, × 302.
12. Postantennal organ and adjacent eyes of right side, × 397.
13. Sense organ of third antennal segment of right side, × 847.
14. Right hind foot, × 888.
15. Dorsal setae of first abdominal segment, × 275.

Folsomides parvus:

16. Specimen, × 106.
17. Eye patches, postantennal organ, and first antennal segment of right side, × 535.
18. Right hind foot, × 881.
19. Right aspect of ventral tube, × 307.
20. Right aspect of furcula, × 535.

Folsomides stachi·

21. Eye and postantennal organ of left side, × 926.
22. Right midfoot, × 1,411
23. Right hind foot, × 1,322.

PLATE 3

Folsomides stachi:

24. Right aspect of furcula, × 941.
25. Dorsal aspect of furcula, × 941.
26. Extremity of mucrodens, × 1,991.

Isotomodes tenuis:

27. Specimen, × 93.
28. Left postantennal organ, × 594
29. Sense organ of third antennal segment of left side, × 1,880.
30. Right hind foot, × 847.
31. Right aspect of furcula, × 576; the manubrial hooks are on the left side of the dens
32. Left mucro, × 847.
33. Right aspect of tenaculum, × 576.
34. Dorsal setae of fourth abdominal segment, × 376.

PLATE 4

Folsomia silvestrii:

35. Eyes and postantennal organ of right side, × 594.
36. Outline of eye patch, postantennal organ, and first antennal segment of right side, × 594.
37. Right hind foot, × 929.
38. Right aspect of dens and mucro, × 594.
39. Dorsal setae of first abdominal segment, × 453.

Folsomia elongata·

40. Eyes and postantennal organ of right side, × 937.
41. Sense organ of third antennal segment of right side, × 941.
42. Left hind foot, × 576.
43. Left dens and mucro, × 564.
44 Right mucro, × 970.
45. Abnormal left mucro, × 847.
46. Dorsal setae of first abdominal segment, × 347.

PLATE 5

Folsomia guthriei:

47. Eyes and postantennal organ of right side.   From Guthrie.
48. Right aspect of furcula.   From Guthrie.
49. Mucro.   From Guthrie.

Folsomia sexoculata:

50. Eyes of left side, × 594.
51. Left fore foot, × 594.

Folsomia quadrioculata·

52. Eyes and postantennal organ of left side, × 594.
53. Sense organ of third antennal segment of right side, × 970.
54. Right hind foot, × 594.
55. Portion of furcula, × 347.
56. Left dens and mucro, × 347.
57. Left mucro, × 747
58. Dorsal setae of second abdominal segment, × 347.

PLATE 6

Folsomia diplophthalma:

59. Eye and postantennal organ of right side, × 735.
60. Eye and postantennal organ of right side, × 758.
61. Sense organ of third antennal segment of right side, × 1,260.
62. Right fore foot, × 952.
63. Left hind foot, × 952.
64. Right dens and mucro, with manubrial teeth showing through the dens, × 570.
65. Manubrial teeth, in ventral aspect, × 735.
66. Mucro, × 1,026.
67. Dorsal setae of first abdominal segment, × 570.

PLATE 7

Folsomia fimetaria:

68. Postantennal organ of left side, × 576.
69. Postantennal organ and first antennal segment of left side, × 465.
70. Postantennal organ and base of first antennal segment of right side, × 465   Specimen from New Jersey.
71. Postantennal organ and first antennal segment of left side, × 465. Specimen from Illinois.

72. Sense organ of third antennal segment of right side, $\times$ 988.
73. Right hind foot, $\times$ 467.
74. End of abdomen, showing ankylosis of last three segments, $\times$ 100.
75. Ventral aspect, for comparison with figure 74, $\times$ 100.
76. Left mucro, $\times$ 576 Specimen from Europe.
77. Left mucro, $\times$ 576. Specimen from Massachusetts
78. Left aspect of tenaculum, $\times$ 200.
79. Dorsal setae of first abdominal segment, $\times$ 306.

PLATE 8

Folsomia fimetaria caldaria.
80. Right hind foot, $\times$ 808.
Folsomia nivalis:
81. Left postantennal organ, $\times$ 1,344.
82. Postantennal organ and first antennal segment of right side, $\times$ 560.
83. Sense organ of third antennal segment of left side, $\times$ 1,344.
84. Left fore foot, $\times$ 1,152.
85. Left mucro and end of dens, $\times$ 1,320.
86. Left mucro and end of dens, $\times$ 1,152.
87. Left mucro, $\times$ 1,152.
88. Abnormal left mucro, $\times$ 1,040.

PLATE 9

Guthriella antiqua.
89. Specimen, $\times$ 102.
90. Eyes and postantennal organ of right side, $\times$ 434.
91. Sense organ and third antennal segment of left side, $\times$ 1,043.
92. Left hind foot, $\times$ 788.
93. Right hind unguiculus, $\times$ 987
94. Manubrial hooks, ventral aspect, $\times$ 627
95. Dentes and mucrones, $\times$ 366
96. Left mucro, $\times$ 900
97. Right mucro, $\times$ 900.
98. Dorsal aspect of right mucro, $\times$ 987
99. Dorsal setae of third abdominal segment, $\times$ 627.

PLATE 10

Guthriella vetusta
100. Eyes and postantennal organ of left side, $\times$ 480.
101. Sense organ of third antennal segment of left side, $\times$ 1,185.
102. Left hind foot, $\times$ 757.
103. Left dens and mucro, $\times$ 435
104. Left mucro, $\times$ 1,185
105. Right mucro, oblique-dorsal aspect, $\times$ 1,185
106. Dorsal setae of first abdominal segment, $\times$ 435

PLATE 11

Guthriella muskegis·
107. Female, $\times$ 27
108. Male, $\times$ 28
109. Postantennal organ and adjacent eye of right side, $\times$ 1,053.
110. Left hind foot of female, $\times$ 487.
111. Left mucro of female, $\times$ 507.
112. Right mucro of female, $\times$ 507

PLATE 12

Guthriella muskegis:

113. Dorsal aspect of left mucro of female, × 493.
114. Dorsal aspect of left mucro of male, × 507.
115. Dorsal setae of first abdominal segment of female, × 300
116. Dorsal aspect of left lateral lobe of fourth abdominal segment of male, × 143.
117. Clavate fringed tubercle of male, × 487.
118. Capitate seta of male, × 773.
119. Dorsal aspect of fourth antennal segment of right side of male, × 247.

Proisotoma (Ballistura) schotti:

120. Right fore foot, × 387.   Specimen from California.
121. Left hind foot, × 407.   Specimen from New York.
122. Left mucro, × 673.   Specimen from California.
123. Left mucro, × 673.   Specimen from California.
124. Left mucro, × 673.   Specimen from New York.
125. Dorsal setae of first abdominal segment, × 230.

PLATE 13

Proisotoma (Ballistura) ewingi:

126. Eyes and postantennal organ of left side, × 673.
127. Left hind foot, × 1,053
128. Left dens and mucro, × 673.
129. Left aspect of tenaculum, × 673.
130. Dorsal setae of first abdominal segment, × 673.

Proisotoma (Ballistura) excavata:

131. Dorsal aspect of head, × 193.
132. Eyes and postantennal organ of right side, × 673.
133. Dorsal aspect of right antenna, × 400.
134. Sense organ of third antennal segment of left side, × 1,067.
135. Left hind foot, × 847.
136. Dorsal aspect of dentes and mucrones, × 673.

PLATE 14

Proisotoma (Ballistura) excavata:

137. Right mucro, × 847.
138. Dorsal setae of first abdominal segment, × 673.

Proisotoma (Ballistura) laticauda:

139. Eyes and postantennal organ of left side, × 667.
140. Sense organ of third antennal segment of left side, × 980.
141. Left hind foot, × 667.
142. Left dens and mucro, × 467.
143. Left mucro, × 653.
144. Right mucro, × 504.
145. Left aspect of tenaculum, × 571.
146. Dorsal setae of first abdominal segment, × 485.

Archisotoma besselsi:

147. Eyes and postantennal organ of left side, × 480.
148. Left hind foot, × 793.
149. Part of left hind femur and tibiotarsus, × 673.

Proisotoma (Proisotoma) longispina:
190. Dorsal aspect of head, × 109.
191. Eyes, postantennal organ, and base of antenna of right side, × 400.

PLATE 19

Proisotoma (Proisotoma) longispina:
192. Right midfoot, × 673.
193. Left mucro and end of dens, × 613
194. Dorsal aspect of left mucro, × 1,060.
195. Right mucro, × 1,060.
196. Dorsal aspect of right mucro, × 1,060.
197. Dorsal setae of second abdominal segment, × 507.
Proisotoma (Proisotoma) minuta:
198. Eyes and postantennal organ of left side, × 653.
199. Sense organ and third antennal segment of left side, × 1,640.
200. Left hind foot, × 1,728
201. Left hind foot, × 1,100
202. Left aspect of furcula, × 527.
203. Right mucro, × 1,728.
204. Left mucro, × 980.
205. Left mucro, × 1,120.
206. Left mucro, × 980.
207. Left aspect of tenaculum, × 960.

PLATE 20

Proisotoma (Proisotoma) sepulcralis:
208. Eyes and postantennal organ of left side, × 757.
209. Sense organ of third antennal segment of left side, × 757.
210. Right hind foot, × 630.
211. Right mucro, typical, × 1,012.
212. Mucro, common variation, × 1,012.
213. Right mucro, rare variation, × 870.
214. Right mucro, very rare variation, × 731.
215 Left aspect of tenaculum, × 735.
Proisotoma (Proisotoma) frisoni:
216. Postantennal organ and base of antenna of right side, × 757.
217. Right postantennal organ, × 952.
218. Sense organ of third antennal segment of left side, × 1,896.
219. Right hind foot, × 952

PLATE 21

Proisotoma (Proisotoma) frisoni:
220. Left aspect of furcula, × 640.
221. Left mucro, × 1,053.
222. Right mucro, from same specimen as figure 221, × 1,053.
Proisotoma (Proisotoma) brevipenna:
223. Left fore foot, × 960.
224. Left mucro and end of dens, × 960.
225. Dorsal setae of metathorax, × 411.

Proisotoma (Proisotoma) obsoleta:
   226. Claws, × 785.
   227. Right mucro, × 850.
   228. Dorsal setae of mesonotum, × 673.
Proisotoma (Proisotoma) vesiculata:
   229. Eyes and postantennal organ of right side, × 400.
   230. Sense organ of third antennal segment of right side, × 1,067.
   231. Left hind foot, × 673.
   232. Left aspect of furcula, × 247.

PLATE 22

Proisotoma (Proisotoma) vesiculata:
   233. Left mucro, × 757.
   234. Right mucro, × 757.
   235. Dorsal setae of first abdominal segment, × 443.
   236. Surface view of reticulate cuticula of an intersegmental membrane, × 2,040. The rows are transverse.
   237. Reticulate cuticula of an intersegmental membrane in transverse section, × 2,040.
Proisotoma (Proisotoma) bulbosa:
   238. Eyes and postantennal organ of right side, × 450.
   239. Eyes and postantennal organ of right side, × 450.
   240. Sense organ of third antennal segment of right side, × 1,200.
   241. Left hind foot, × 757.
   242. Left mucro, × 1,192.
   243. Dorsal aspect of right mucro, × 1,192.
   244. Dorsal setae of second abdominal segment, × 690.
Proisotoma (Proisotoma) aquae:
   245. Eyes and postantennal organ of left side, × 735.
   246. Eyes and postantennal organ of left side, with pigment patches, × 757.

PLATE 23

Proisotoma (Proisotoma) aquae:
   247. Left postantennal organ, × 1,260.
   248. Sense organ of third antennal segment of left side, × 1,260.
   249. Pit and sensory papilla, in a radial section of third antennal segment of right side, × 2,400.
   250. Left hind foot, × 1,237.
   251. Right mucro and end of dens, × 1,102.
   252. Dorsal setae of second abdominal segment, × 375.
Proisotoma (Proisotoma) decemoculata:
   253. Eyes, ocular pigment, and postantennal organ of right side, × 757.
   254. Right hind foot, × 1,190.
   255. Left mucro, × 1,190.
Proisotoma (Proisotoma) simplex:
   256. Left postantennal organ and adjacent eyes, × 757.
   257. Right hind foot, × 757.
   258. Left mucro, × 1,200.
Proisotoma (Proisotoma) tenelloides:
   259. Right postantennal organ and adjacent eyes, × 757.
   260. Left hind foot, × 1,139.
   261. Left mucro and end of dens, × 1,185.

PLATE 24

Proisotoma (Proisotoma) immersa·

262. Dorsal aspect of head, × 230
263. Eyes and postantennal organ of right side, × 673
264. Dorsal aspect of left antenna, × 427.
265. Sense organ of third antennal segment of right side, × 1,640
266. Ventral aspect of anal lobes, × 1,280.
267. Right hind foot, × 960.
268. Left mucro, × 927.

Proisotoma (Proisotoma) constricta:

269. Postantennal organ and adjacent eyes of right side, × 673
270. Sense organ of third antennal segment of right side, × 1,067.
271. Left hind foot, × 673
272. Left mucro, × 1,067.

Proisotoma (Proisotoma) cognata

273. Left postantennal organ and adjacent eyes, × 407.
274. Right hind foot, × 673.
275. Left mucro and end of dens, × 850.

PLATE 25

Isotomurus retardatus:

276. Eyes and postantennal organ of right side, × 347.
277. Left fore foot, × 373
278. Right hind foot, × 373
279. Left mucro, × 640
280. Spinulate seta from abdomen, × 680.

Isotomurus palustris·

281. Typical form, × 40

Isotomurus palustris texensis:

282. Specimen, × 45
283. Specimen, × 46

PLATE 26

Isotomurus palustris·

284. Eyes and postantennal organ of right side, × 340.
285. Right hind foot, × 560.
286. Left hind foot, × 407.
287. Left mucro, × 853
288. Dorsal aspect of left mucro, × 1,120
289. Left aspect of tenaculum, × 333
290. Spinulate seta from fourth abdominal segment, × 673.

Isotomurus palustroides

291. Eyes and postantennal organ of left side, × 173.
292. Postantennal organ and adjacent eyes of left side, × 393.
293. Right hind foot, × 393
294. Left mucro and end of dens, × 673.
295. Dorsal setae of second abdominal segment, × 513.

PLATE 27

Isotoma (Pseudisotoma) sensibilis·

296. Eyes and postantennal organ of right side, × 473.
297. Right hind foot, × 1,120
298. Left mucro, × 1,067
299. Right mucro, × 960.

Isotoma (Vertagopus) cinerea·
  300. Eyes and postantennal organ of left side, × 597.
  301. Sense organ of third antennal segment of left side, × 1,120.
  302. Left hind foot, × 1,120.
  303. Left mucro, × 1,120
  304 Left mucro, × 1,120.
  305 Left mucro, × 1,120.
  306. Dorsal aspect of right mucro, × 1,120
  307 Left mucro, × 1,120.
  308. Left aspect of tenaculum, × 467.

PLATE 28

Isotoma (Vertagopus) arborea:
  309 Eyes and postantennal organ of left side, × 333.
  310 Sense organ of third antennal segment of left side, × 1,120.
  311 Right hind foot, × 1,120
  312. Left mucro, × 720.
  313. Left mucro, × 1,100.
  314. Right mucro, × 1,120.
  315. Left mucro, × 1,100

Isotoma (Vertagopus) arborea nigra·
  316. Right mucro, × 960
  317. Eyes and postantennal organ of right side, × 340.
  318. Sense organ of third antennal segment of left side, × 1,100.
  319. Dorsal aspect of left mucro, × 960.

Isotoma (Isotoma) difficilis·
  320. Eyes and postantennal organ of right side, × 610.
  321 Left hind foot, × 673
  322 Right mucro, × 1,067.
  323 Right mucro, × 1,067.

PLATE 29

Isotoma (Isotoma) marissa·
  324 Eyes and postantennal organ of right side, × 450
  325 Sense organ of third antennal segment of left side, × 1,200
  326 Right hind foot, × 952.
  327 Right mucro, 2,525
  328 Right mucro, × 1,200.
  329 Left mucro, × 1,190.
  330 Dorsal aspect of right mucro, × 1,190.

Isotoma (Isotoma) trispinata·
  331. Eyes and postantennal organ of left side, × 757.
  332 Left hind foot, × 952
  333 Right mucro, × 975.
  334 Right mucro, × 1,249
  335 Left mucro, × 1,185
  336. Left mucro, × 1,080

Isotoma (Isotoma) eunotabilis·
  337. Eyes and postantennal organ of left side, × 757.

Isotoma notabilis Schaffer
  338 Eyes and postantennal organ of left side, × 735. Specimen from
    Finland

Isotoma (Isotoma) eunotabilis
  339 Left hind foot, × 1,158

PLATE 30

Isotoma (Isotoma) eunotabilis
    340. Left mucro and end of dens, $\times$ 2,016.
    341. Left mucro and end of dens, $\times$ 1,920.
    342. Right mucro and end of dens, $\times$ 1,908.
    343. Dorsal aspect of right mucro, $\times$ 2,016.
    344. Dorsal setae of first abdominal segment, $\times$ 757.
Isotoma (Isotoma) finitima
    345. Mucro. From Scherbakov.
Isotoma (Isotoma) minor:
    346. Sense organ of third antennal segment of right side, $\times$ 1,890.
    347. Ventral aspect of right antenna, showing sensory cones and setae, $\times$ 1,200.
    348. Right hind foot, $\times$ 1,200.
    349. Left mucro and end of dens, $\times$ 1,908.
    350. Right mucro and end of dens, $\times$ 1,920.
    351. Right mucro and end of dens, $\times$ 1,920.
    352. Spinulate seta from abdomen, $\times$ 1,200.

PLATE 31

Isotoma (Isotoma) albella:
    353. Left eye patch, $\times$ 280.
    354. Eyes and postantennal organ of left side, $\times$ 512.
    355. Eyes and postantennal organ of left side, $\times$ 512.
    356. Sense organ of third antennal segment of left side, $\times$ 1,344.
    357. Left hind foot, $\times$ 808.
    358. Last four abdominal segments, $\times$ 136.
    359. Left mucro and end of dens, 1,264.
    360. Left mucro, $\times$ 1,016.
    361. Dorsal setae of first abdominal segment, $\times$ 768.

PLATE 32

Isotoma (Isotoma) olivacea:
    362. Typical form, eyes and postantennal organ of left side, $\times$ 360.
    363. Sense organ of third antennal segment of right side, $\times$ 952.
    364. Right hind foot, $\times$ 952.
    365. Left hind foot, $\times$ 757.
    366. Left mucro, $\times$ 1,192.
    367. Left mucro, $\times$ 1,192.
    368. Right mucro, $\times$ 1,249.
    369. Left mucro, $\times$ 1,192.
    370. Left aspect of tenaculum, $\times$ 735.
    371. Dorsal setae of first abdominal segment, $\times$ 360.
Isotoma (Isotoma) olivacea neglecta:
    372. Eyes and postantennal organ of right side, $\times$ 443.
    373. Sense organ of third antennal segment of right side, $\times$ 952.
    374. Left hind foot, $\times$ 952.
    375. Left mucro and end of dens, $\times$ 952.

PLATE 33

Isotoma (Isotoma) olivacea grisca:
    376. Left postantennal organ and adjacent eyes, $\times$ 407.
    377. Eyes and postantennal organ of left side, $\times$ 510.
    378. Sense organ of third antennal segment of left side, $\times$ 653.
    379. Left fore foot, $\times$ 653.
    380. Left mucro and end of dens, $\times$ 1,067.

381. Left mucro, × 1,067.
382. Left mucro, × 653
383. Left mucro, × 1,120.
Isotoma (Isotoma) violacea·
    384. Eyes and postantennal organ of right side, × 393
    385. Sense organ of third antennal segment of right side, × 1,100
    386. Left fore foot, × 1,060.
    387. Right mucro, × 1,060
    388. Dorsal setae of second abdominal segment, × 340
Isotoma (Isotoma) violacea mucronata
    389. Dorsal setae of second abdominal segment, × 653.

PLATE 34

Isotoma (Isotoma) violacea mucronata
    390. Eyes and postantennal organ of left side, × 267
    391. Fore foot, × 350. Specimen from Alaska.
    392. Left hind foot, × 1,060. Specimen from Greenland.
    393. Left mucro, abnormal in having only 3 teeth, × 1,696.
    394. Left mucro, × 1,696
    395. Sense organ of third antennal segment of right side, × 847.
    396. Left aspect of tenaculum, × 673
Isotoma (Isotoma) violacea caeruleatra·
    397. Eyes and postantennal organ of right side, × 653
    398. Left mucro, × 700
    399. Dorsal aspect of right mucro, × 1,060
    400. Right hind foot, × 653
    401. Dorsal aspect of first abdominal segment, × 247.

PLATE 35

Isotoma (Isotoma) violacea caeruleatra:
    402. Left mucro and end of dens, × 1,192
    403. Sense organ of third antennal segment of right side, × 1,200.
Isotoma (Isotoma) nigrifrons·
    404. Eyes and postantennal organ of right side, × 322.
    405. Postantennal organ and adjacent eyes of right side, × 322
    406. Sense organ of third antennal segment of right side, × 960.
    407. Left hind foot, × 457.
    408. Left mucro, × 1,200
    409. Left mucro, × 1,200.
    410. Left mucro, × 1,200
    411. Left mucro, × 1,200
Isotoma (Isotoma) gelida:
    412. Postantennal organ and adjacent eyes of left side, × 375.
    413. Postantennal organ and adjacent eyes of left side, × 375.
    414. Sense organ of third antennal segment of left side, × 1,200.
    415. Right hind foot, × 457.
    416. Left mucro, × 960
    417. Left mucro, × 757.

PLATE 36

Isotoma (Isotoma) subaequalis·
    418. Postantennal organ and adjacent eye of left side, × 333
    419. Left hind foot, × 407.
    420. Left mucro and end of dens, × 673
    421. Left aspect of right mucro and end of dens, × 673

Isotoma (Isotoma) grandiceps::

422. Eyes of left side, $\times$ 347.
423. Base of antenna, postantennal organ, and adjacent eyes of left side, $\times$ 333.
424. Sense organ of third antennal segment of right side, $\times$ 1,120.
425 Right hind foot, $\times$ 653
426 Right mucro and end of dens, $\times$ 653
427. Dorsal setae of third abdominal segment, $\times$ 347.

PLATE 37

Isotoma (Isotoma) viridis:

428. Typical form, $\times$ 20
429. Eyes and postantennal organ of left side, $\times$ 185
430. Sense organ of third antennal segment of left side, $\times$ 490.
431. Left hind foot, $\times$ 395.   Specimen from Massachusetts
432. Left hind foot, $\times$ 295.   Specimen from Greenland.
433. Concave aspect of unguis, $\times$ 395.

Isotoma (Isotoma) viridis riparia:

434 Specimen, $\times$ 25.

Isotoma (Isotoma) viridis delta:

435 Specimen, $\times$ 25.

Isotoma (Isotoma) viridis pomona:

436. Specimen, $\times$ 30.

PLATE 38

Isotoma (Isotoma) viridis:

437. Left mucro and end of dens, $\times$ 576.
438. Left aspect of tenaculum, $\times$ 218
439. Dorsal setae of third abdominal segment, $\times$ 171.
440. Spinulate seta, $\times$ 153
441 Last four abdominal segments, $\times$ 52

Isotoma (Isotoma) subviridis:

442. Eyes and postantennal organ of left side, $\times$ 297
443. Sense organ of third antennal segment of right side, $\times$ 594.
444. Left fore foot, $\times$ 594.
445 Left mucro, $\times$ 935
446. Left mucro, $\times$ 935
447 Right mucro, $\times$ 935
448 Right mucro, $\times$ 935.
449 Dorsal setae of second abdominal segment, $\times$ 153.

PLATE 39

Isotoma glauca

450 Tenaculum   From a pencil drawing by Packard

Isotoma tridentata

451. Right hind foot, $\times$ 520.
452 Lateral aspect of right mucro, $\times$ 1,300.
453 Dorsolateral aspect of right mucro, $\times$ 1,300.
454 Dorsal aspect of right mucro, $\times$ 1,300.

Isotoma aspera

455 Claws.   From Bacon
456 Left mucro.   From Bacon.

Proisotoma laguna:

457. Eyes of right side   From Bacon.
458 Postantennal organ   From Bacon.
459. Claws   From Bacon.
460. Furcula   From Bacon.
461. Mucro.   From Bacon.

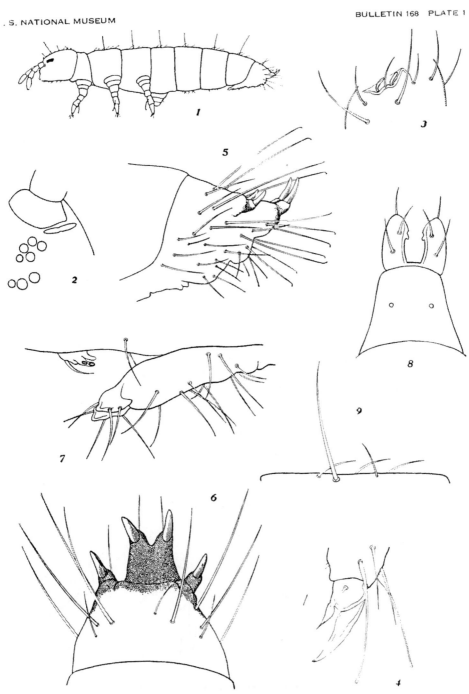

TETRACANTHELLA WAHLGRENI.

FOR EXPLANATION OF PLATE SEE PAGE 109.

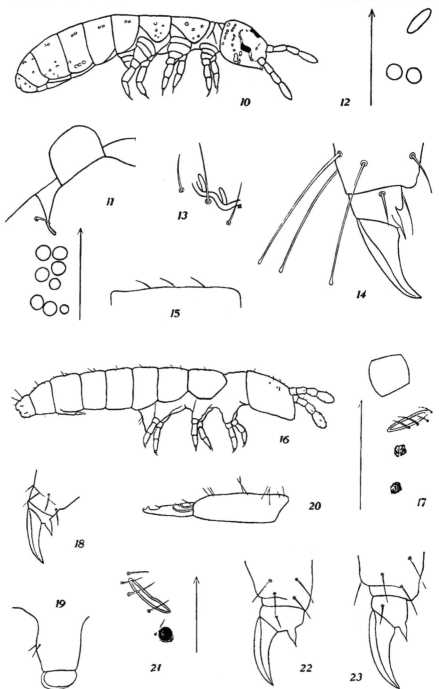

SPECIES OF ANUROPHORUS AND FOLSOMIDES.

FOR EXPLANATION OF PLATE SEE PAGE 129

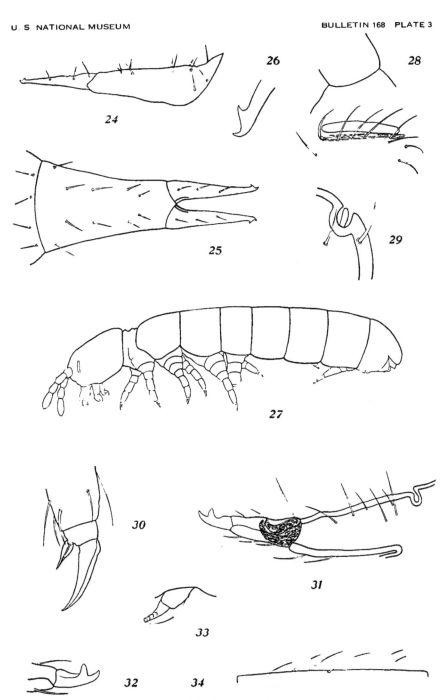

SPECIES OF FOLSOMIDES AND ISOTOMODES.

FOR EXPLANATION OF PLATE SEE PAGE 149

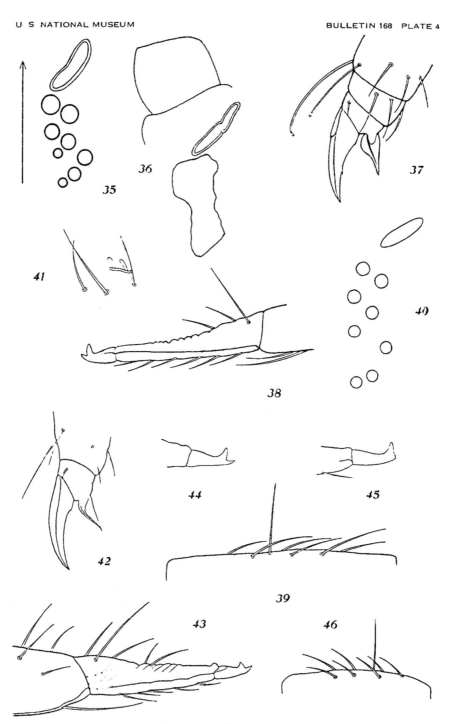

SPECIES OF FOLSOMIA

FOR EXPLANATION OF PLATE SEE PAGE 139

BULLETIN 168   PLATE 5

SPECIES OF FOLSOMIA.

FOR EXPLANATION OF PLATE SEE PAGE 130.

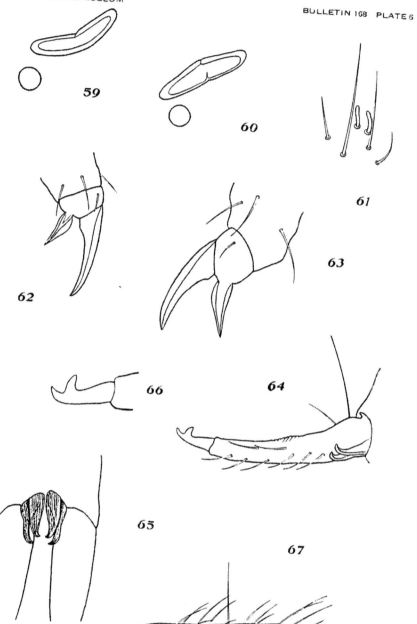

FOLSOMIA DIPLOPHTHALMA.

FOR EXPLANATION OF PLATE SEE PAGE 130.

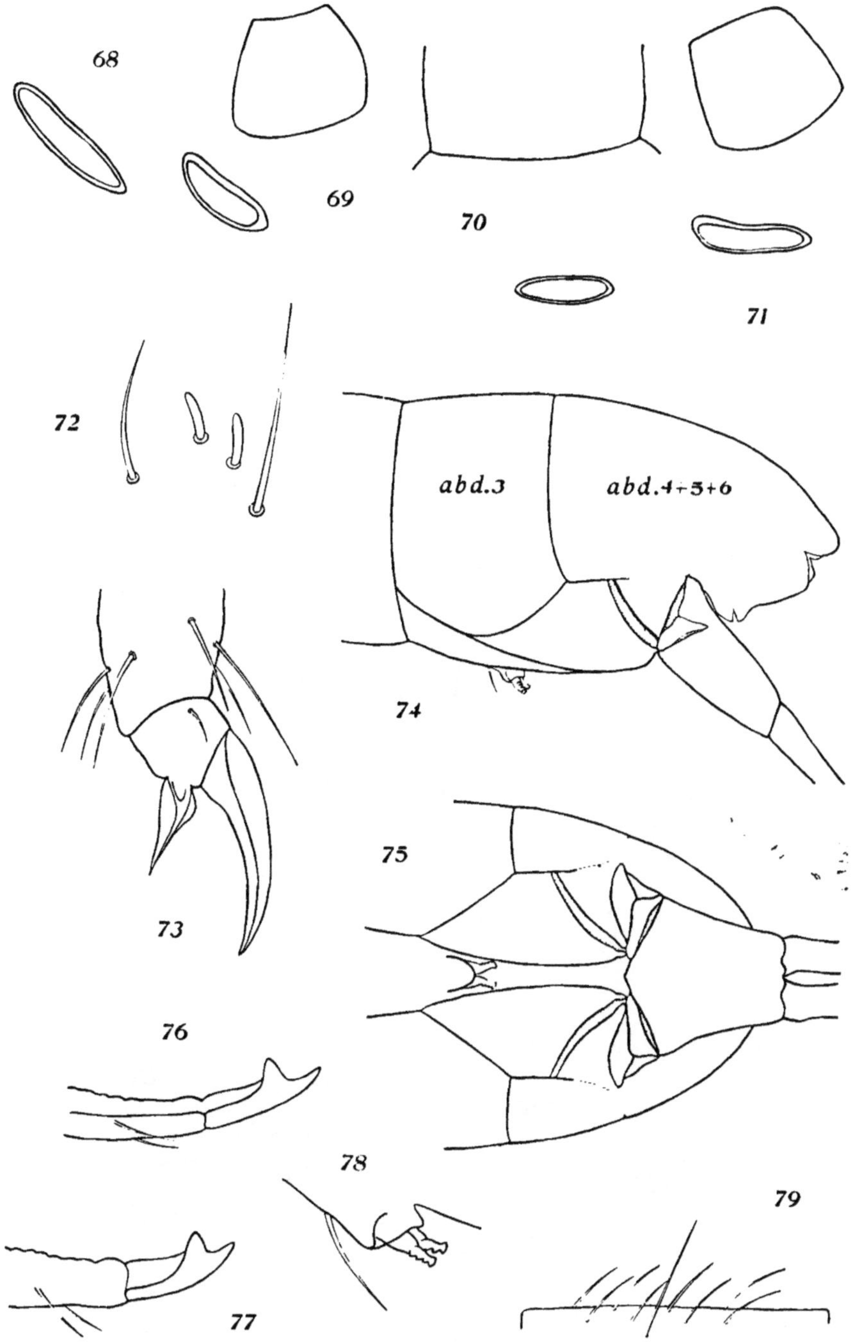

68

69

70

71

72

abd.3   abd.4+5+6

74

73

75

76

78

79

77

FOLSOMIA FIMETARIA

FOR EXPLANATION OF PLATE SEE PAGES 130–13

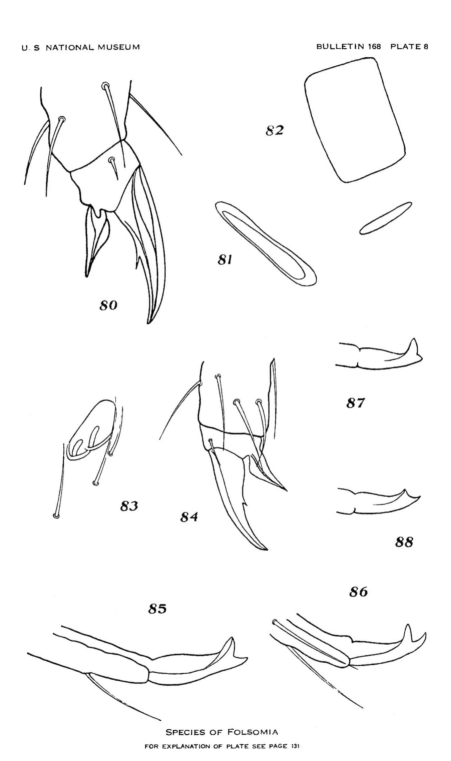

SPECIES OF FOLSOMIA

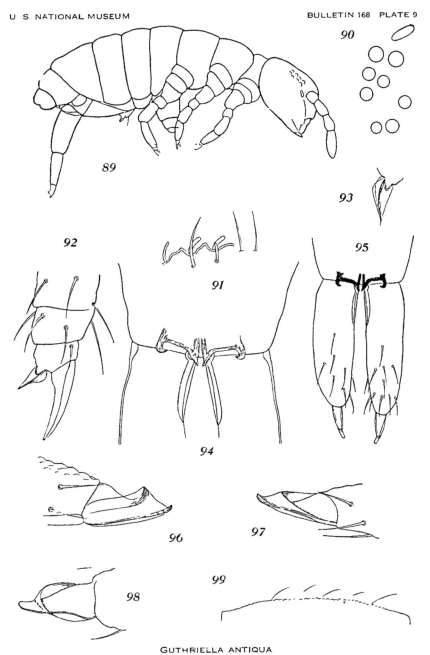

GUTHRIELLA ANTIQUA

FOR EXPLANATION OF PLATE SEE PAGE 131

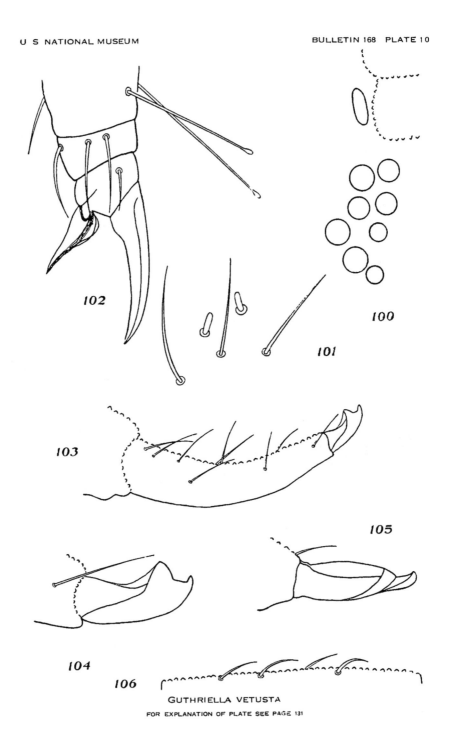

GUTHRIELLA VETUSTA

FOR EXPLANATION OF PLATE SEE PAGE 131

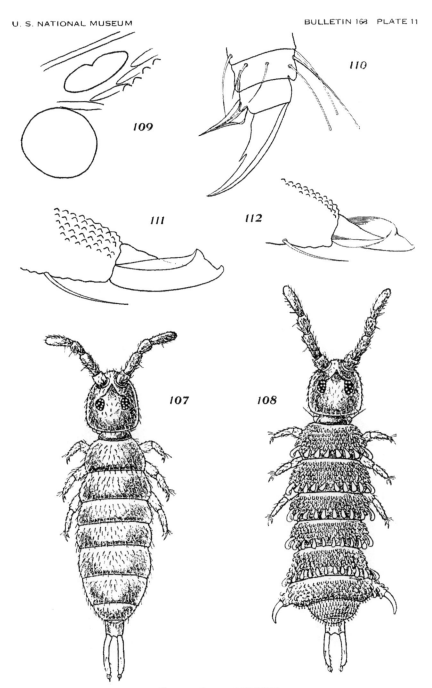

GUTHRIELLA MUSKEGIS.

FOR EXPLANATION OF PLATE SEE PAGE 131.

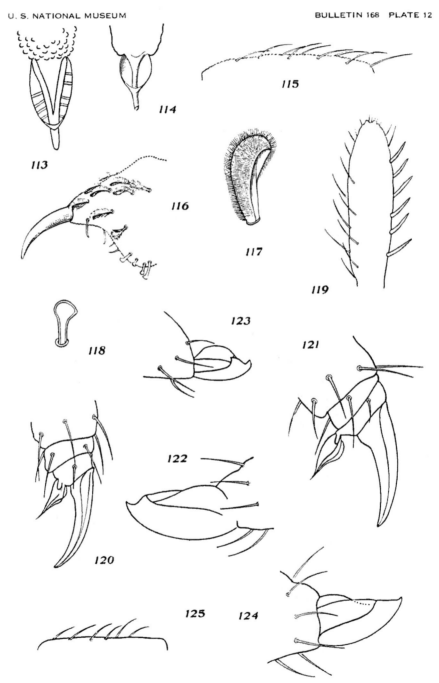

SPECIES OF GUTHRIELLA AND PROISOTOMA.

FOR EXPLANATION OF PLATE SEE PAGE 132.

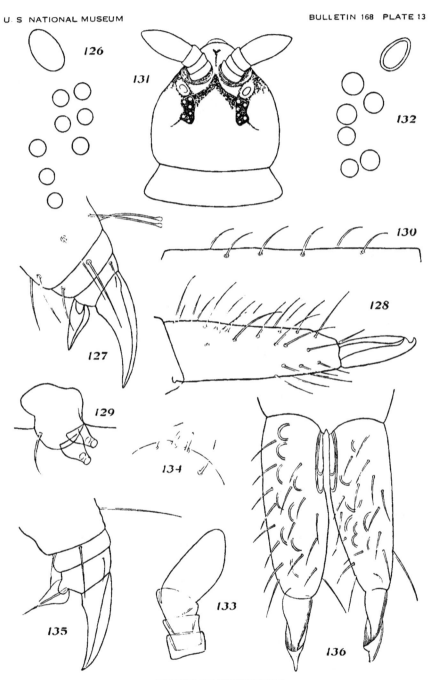

SPECIES OF PROISOTOMA

FOR EXPLANATION OF PLATE SEE PAGE 132

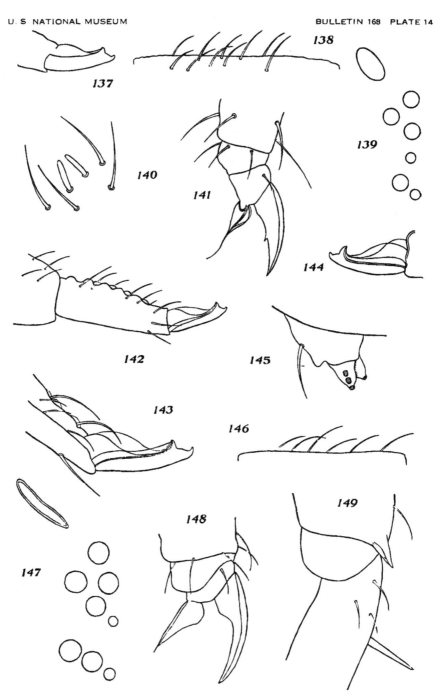

SPECIES OF PROISOTOMA AND ARCHISOTOMA

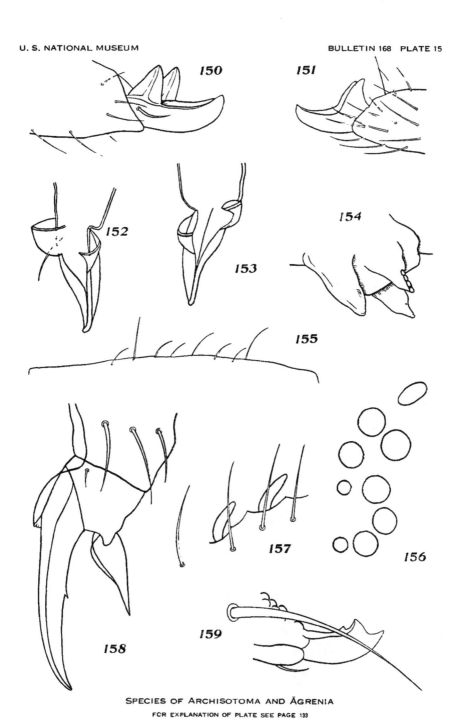

SPECIES OF ARCHISOTOMA AND ÅGRENIA

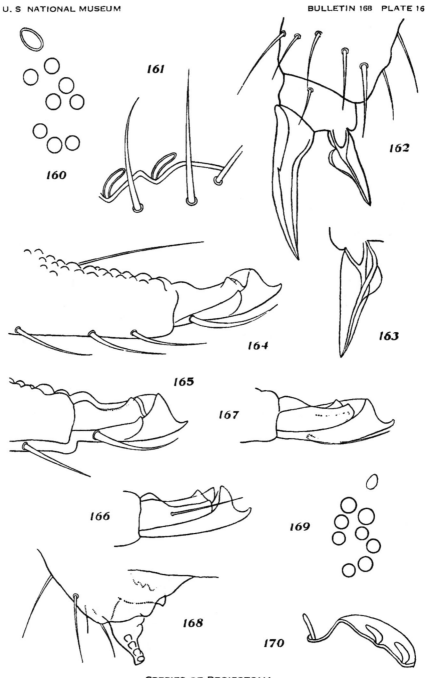

SPECIES OF PROISOTOMA

FOR EXPLANATION OF PLATE SEE PAGE 133

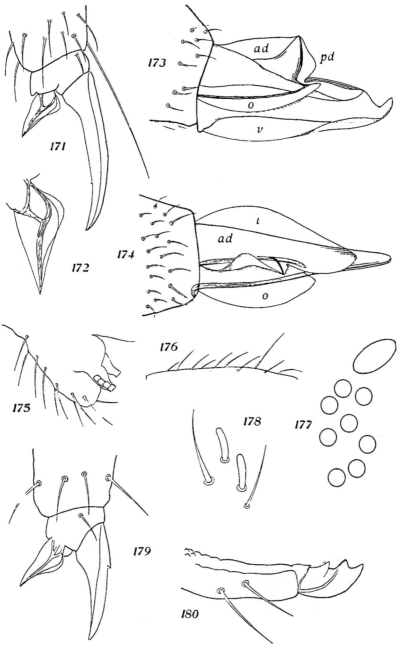

SPECIES OF PROISOTOMA

SPECIES OF PROISOTOMA

FOR EXPLANATION OF PLATE SEE PAGES 133-134.

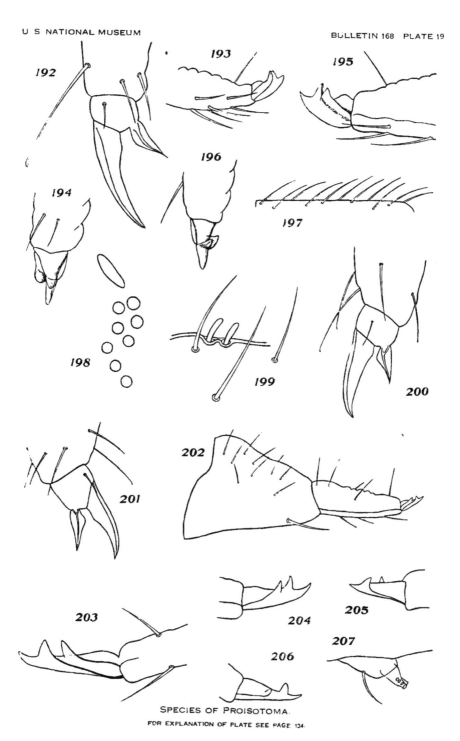

SPECIES OF PROISOTOMA.

FOR EXPLANATION OF PLATE SEE PAGE 134.

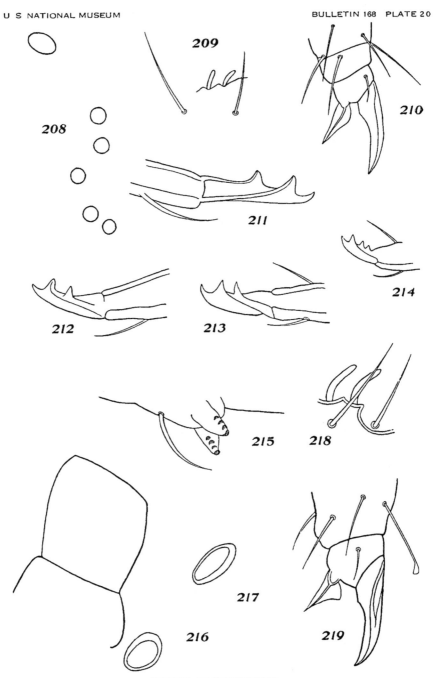

SPECIES OF PROISOTOMA

SPECIES OF PROISOTOMA.

FOR EXPLANATION OF PLATE SEE PAGES 134-135.

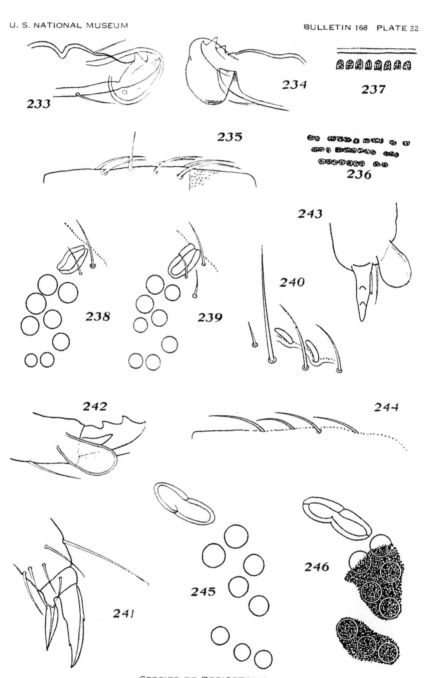

SPECIES OF PROISOTOMA.

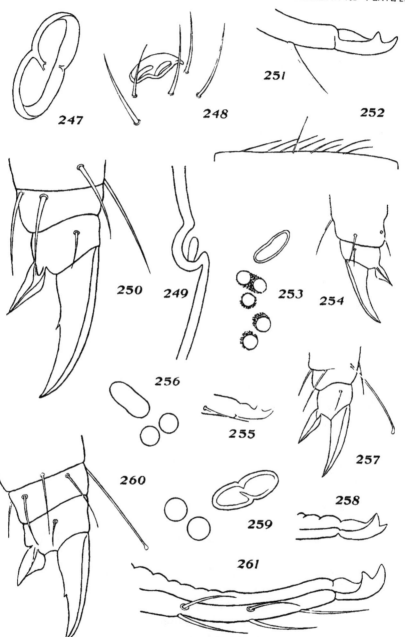

SPECIES OF PROISOTOMA

FOR EXPLANATION OF PLATE SEE PAGE 135

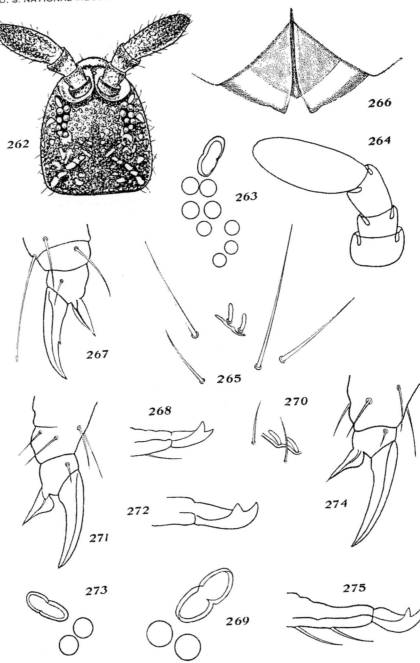

SPECIES OF PROISOTOMA.

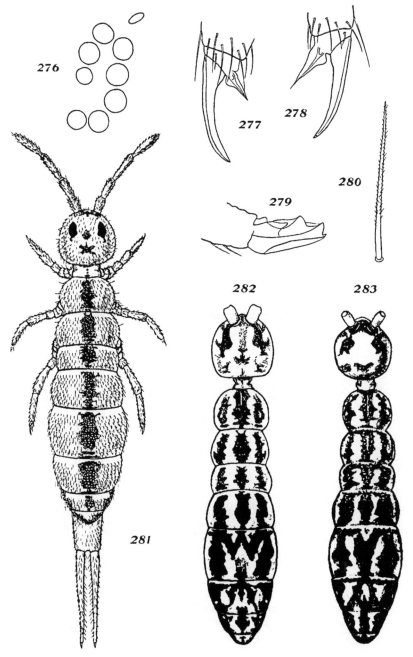

SPECIES OF ISOTOMURUS

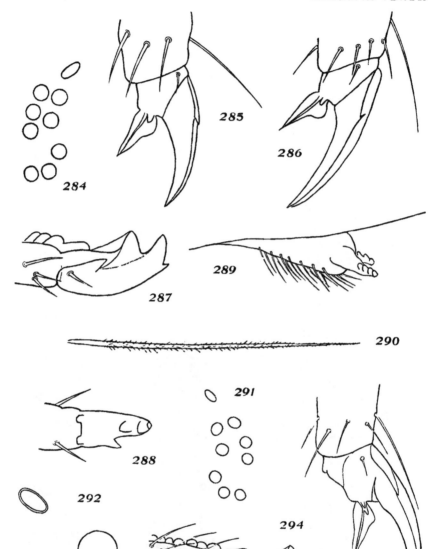

SPECIES OF ISOTOMURUS

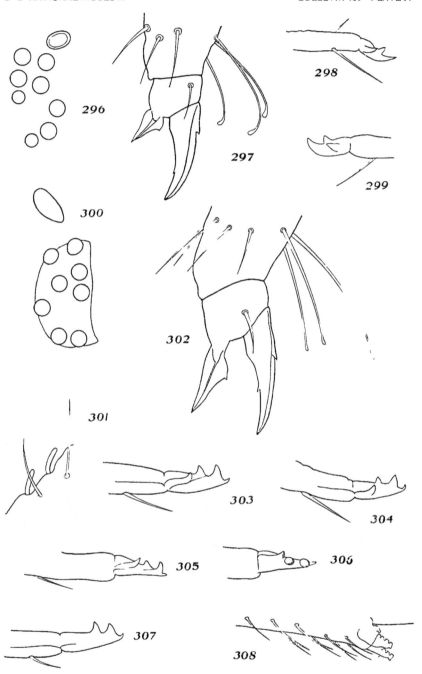

SPECIES OF ISOTOMA

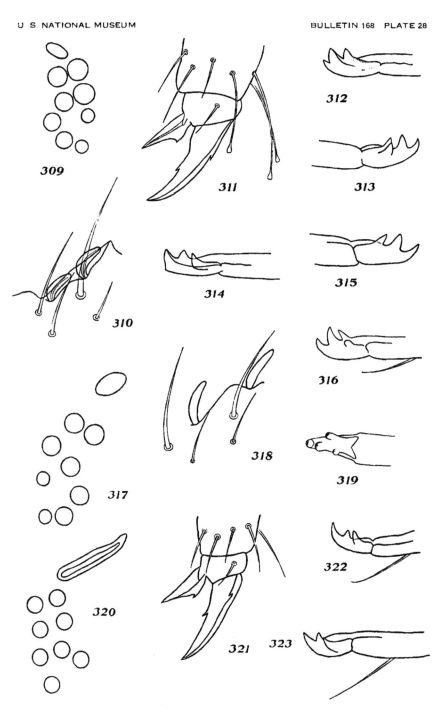

SPECIES OF ISOTOMA

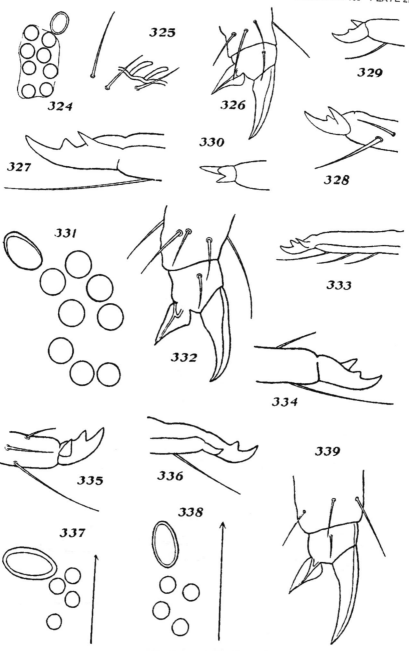

SPECIES OF ISOTOMA

FOR EXPLANATION OF PLATE SEE PAGE 137

SPECIES OF ISOTOMA.

FOR EXPLANATION OF PLATE SEE PAGE 138

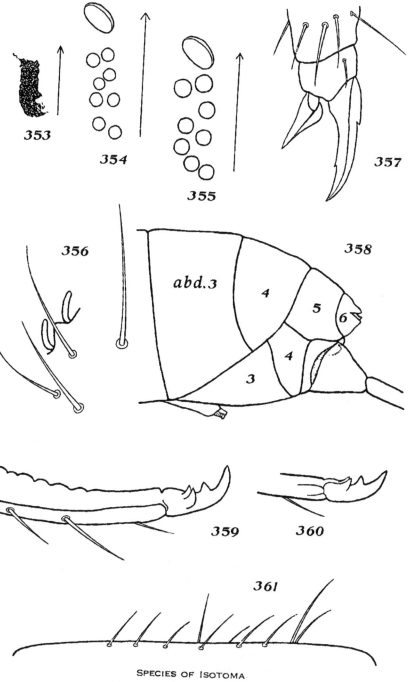

SPECIES OF ISOTOMA

FOR EXPLANATION OF PLATE SEE PAGE 138

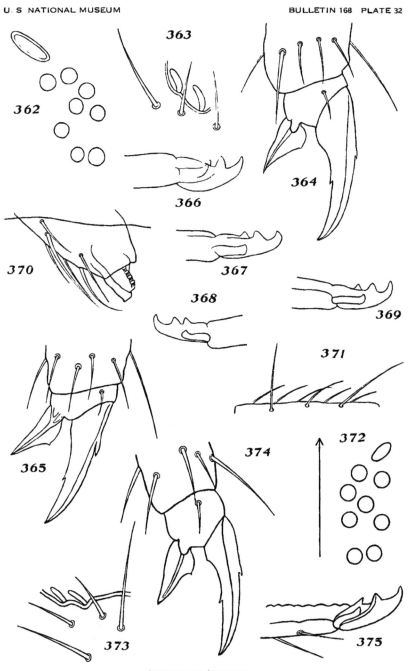

SPECIES OF ISOTOMA

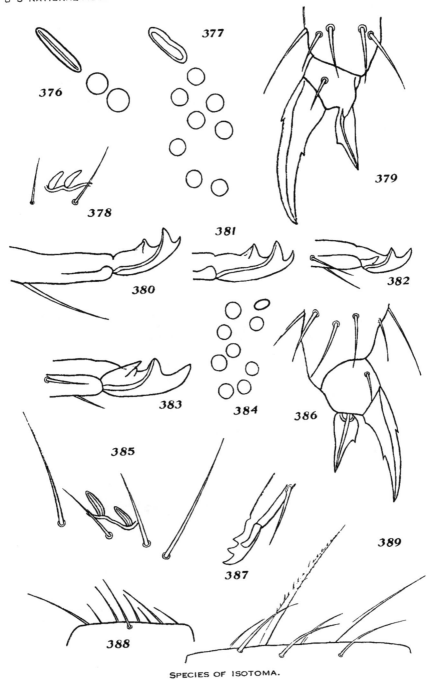

SPECIES OF ISOTOMA.

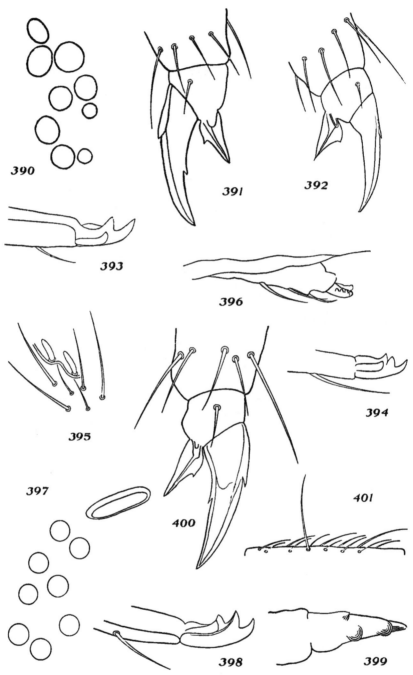

390

391

392

393

396

395

394

397

400

401

398

399

SPECIES OF ISOTOMA

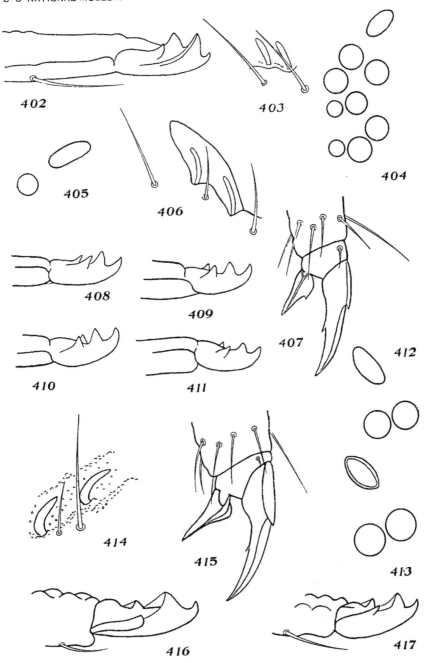

402

403

404

405

406

408

409

407

412

410

411

414

415

413

416

417

SPECIES OF ISOTOMA

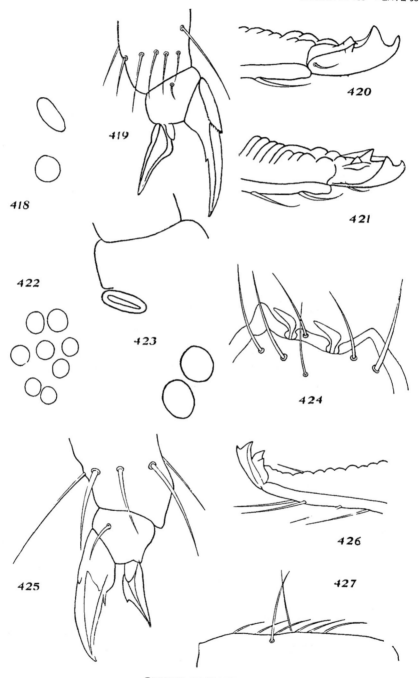

418
419
420
421
422
423
424
425
426
427

SPECIES OF ISOTOMA

FOR EXPLANATION OF PLATE SEE PAGES 139-141

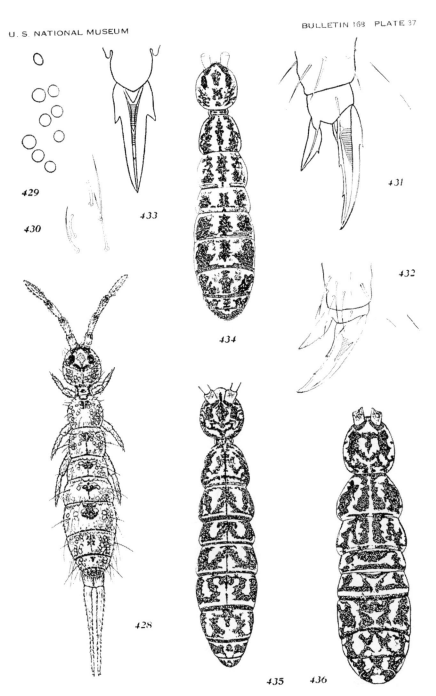

SPECIES OF ISOTOMA.

FOR EXPLANATION OF PLATE SEE PAGE 140.

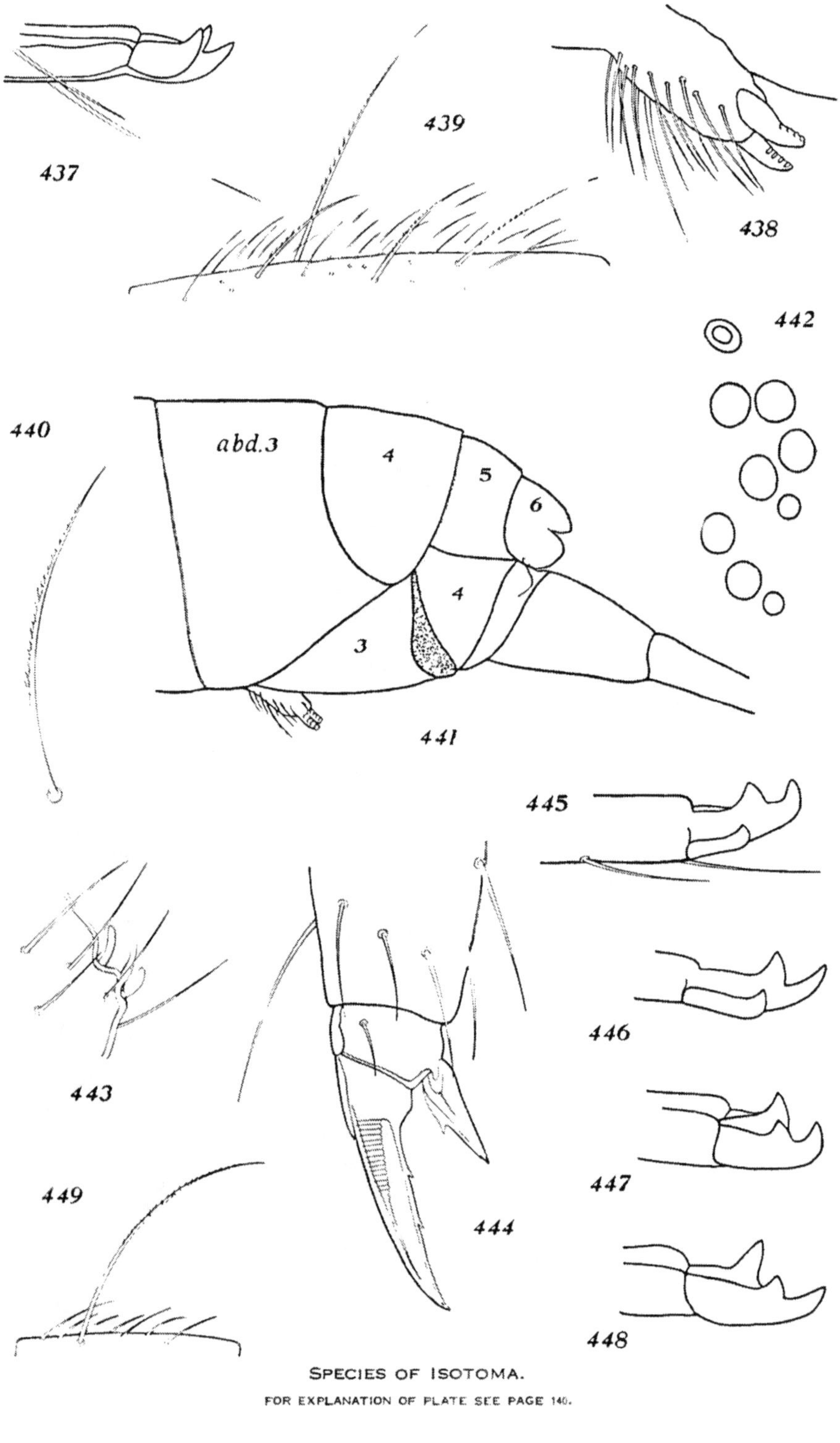

437

439

438

442

440

abd.3

4

5

6

4

3

441

445

446

443

449

444

447

448

SPECIES OF ISOTOMA.

FOR EXPLANATION OF PLATE SEE PAGE 140.

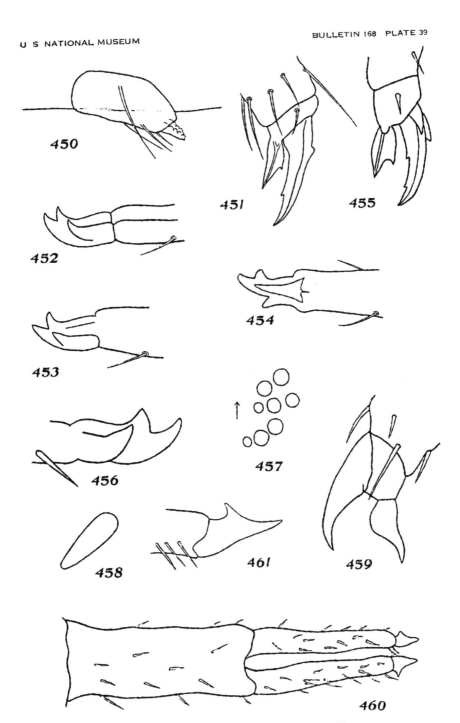

SPECIES OF ISOTOMA AND PROISOTOMA
FOR EXPLANATION OF PLATE SEE PAGE 140

INDEX

(Principal references are printed in **boldface**)

plumbea, Isotoma, 110, 111.
Podura, 4, 47, 70
    annulata, 110
    aquatica, 47.
    arborea, 83
    fimetaria, 28
    palustris, 70, 72.
    viridis, 110
Poduridae, 5.
pomona, Isotoma viridis, 112, 115, 140.
prasina, Isotoma palustris, 75
    Isotoma stuxbergi, 75
prasinus, Isotomurus palustris, 75.
Proctostephanus, 6
productus, Isotomodes, 16, 17.
Proisotoma, 3, 5–7, 10, 14, 17, 23, 38, 43
    aquae, 45, 59, 135
    angularis, 61
    besselsi, 66.
    brevipenna, 44, 56, 134.
    bulbosa, 7, 43, 44, 58, 135.
    cognata, 45, 65, 136
    communa, 3, 43, 48, 133
    constricta, 45, 64, 136.
    decemoculata, 45, 60, 135.
    ewingi, 39, 40, 132
    excavata, 39, 41, 132.
    frisoni, 44, 55, 134.
    guthrici, 22.
    immersa, 44, 63, 136.
    laguna, 118, 140
    laticauda, 39, 42, 132.
    longispina, 44, 50, 134.
    minuta, 23, 44, 51, 134
    obsoleta, 44, 56, 135
    rainieri, 3, 5, 43, 45, 133
    schafferi, 3, 5, 43, 46, 133.
    schotti, 5, 39, 132.
    sepulcralis, 3, 6, 44, 54, 134.
    simplex, 45, 61, 135
    tenella, 63
    tenelloides, 45, 62, 135
    titusi, 3, 4, 7, 44, 49, 133
    vesiculata, 7, 44, 57, 135
Proisotoma, subg , 38, 43
Pseudanurophorus, 6.
Pseudisotoma, subg , 78.
Pseudisotoma sensibilis, 79
pulchella, Isotoma, 66.
purpurascens, Isotoma, 110, 111
quadri-denticulata, Isotoma, 81.
quadrioculata, Folsomia, 20, 24, 28, 130
    Isotoma, 24, 25
rainieri, Proisotoma, 3, 5, 43, 45, 133
retardatus, Isotomurus, 3, 71, 136.
reuteri, Isotoma, 83.
riparia, Desoria, 113
    Isotoma, 113.
    Isotoma palustris, 113
    Isotoma viridis, 113, 140.
schafferi, Isotoma, 46.
    Proisotoma, 3, 5, 43, 46, 133
schotti, Proisotoma, 5, 39, 132.
schotti(i), Isotoma, 39.

sensibilis, Isotoma, 78, 136.
    Pseudisotoma, 79.
sepulcralis, Isotoma, 54
    Proisotoma, 3, 6, 44, 54, 134.
sexoculata, Folsomia, 20, 23, 130
    Isotoma, 23.
silvestrii, Folsomia, 20, 130.
simplex, Proisotoma, 45, 61, 135
Sminthuridae, 70
socialis, Achorutes, 3–5
speciosa, Isotoma, 86.
Spinisotoma, 6
spitzbergenensis, Isotoma, 66.
stachi, Folsomia, 14, 16, 129
Stenus, 76
stuxbergi(i), Isotoma, 72
stuxbergi prasina, Isotoma, 75.
subaequalis, Isotoma, 87, 107, 139.
subviridis, Isotoma, 87, 115, 140
synonymica, Isotoma, 84–86.
tenella, Proisotoma, 63
tenelloides, Proisotoma, 45, 62, 135
tenuis, Isotomodes, 17, 129
terminata, Isotoma, 84–86
Tetracanthella, 4, 7, 8, 10.
    coerulea, 10
    pilosa, 10.
    wahlgreni, 10, 129
texensis, Isotomurus palustris, 76, 136.
thermophila anomala, Isotomina, 63.
titusi, Proisotoma, 3, 4, 7, 44, 49, 133.
tricolor, Isotoma, 72, 73, 110, 111, 116.
tridentata, Isotoma, 117, 140.
trifasciata, Isotoma, 74
trispinata, Isotoma, 4, 87, 91, 137.
tullbergi, Isotoma, 72
Tullbergia, 6
unica, Isotoma, 81
Uzelia, 6, 7.
Vertagopus, subg., 78, 81.
Vertagopus arborea, 84
    cinerea, 81.
vesiculata, Proisotoma, 7, 44, 57, 135.
vetusta, Guthriella, 3, 34, 35, 131.
viatica, Desoria, 110.
    Isotoma, 110.
violacea, Isotoma, 88, 101, 139.
violacea caeruleatra, Isotoma, 88, 104, 139
violacea divergens, Isotoma, 104.
violacea mucronata, Isotoma, 103, 139
virescens, Desoria, 110.
    Isotoma, 110
viridis, Isotoma, 74, 78, 87, 109, 116, 140.
    Podura, 110
viridis aquatilis, Isotoma, 113.
viridis arctica, Isotoma, 114.
viridis catena, Isotoma, 87, 112.
viridis cincta, Isotoma, 113.
viridis delta, Isotoma, 114, 140
viridis pomona, Isotoma, 112, 115, 140.
viridis riparia, Isotoma, 113, 140
walkeri, Isotoma, 97.
wahlgreni, Tetracanthella, 10, 129

Lightning Source UK Ltd.
Milton Keynes UK
UKHW052239180321
380610UK00005B/350